Ten
Notable
Women
of
Latin
America

# Ten
# Notable
# Women
# of
# Latin
# America

## James D. Henderson
## Linda Roddy Henderson

Illustrations and Maps by Edwin Pinkston

nh

Nelson-Hall, Chicago

Library of Congress Cataloging in Publication Data

Henderson, James D 1942-
   Ten notable women of Latin America.

   Bibliography: p.
   Includes index.
   1.  Women—Latin America—Biography.  2.  Latin
America—Biography.  I.  Henderson, Linda Roddy,
1944-    joint author.  II.  Title.
CT3290.H46         920.72'098         78-15253
ISBN 0-88229-426-1 (cloth)
ISBN 0-88229-596-9 (paper)

Reprinted 1989

Manufactured in the United States of America.

10   9   8   7   6   5   4   3   2

The paper used in this book meets the
minimum requirements of American
National Standard for Information
Sciences—Permanence of Paper for
Printed Library Materials, ANSI
Z39.48-1984.

To our *comadre* Lucero and our daughter Elizabeth,
both notable women of Latin America.

# Acknowledgments

We wish to acknowledge the considerable help extended us by personnel of the Biblioteca Nacional and Biblioteca Luis Angel Arango in Bogotá, Colombia; Howard Tilton Memorial Library, Tulane University; and the Latin American Library, University of Texas at Austin.

Thanks are due Gary Le Blanc, Thomas P. Jimison, III, and Kent Reeves of Louisiana Tech University, Ruston, Louisiana, for their able assistance in preparing the illustrative materials for publication; and Joan B. Roddy, whose translations of portions of Leopoldina's correspondence from the German were carried out in a most generous spirit.

# Contents

# Illustrations

# Maps

# Introduction:

# Latin American Women, Old Perspectives and New

FOR MORE THAN six months the little army piloted its brigantines down the swelling river sea. That river, as fabulous in its way as the Land of Cinnamon the Spaniards set out to find over a year before, had grown so wide that from midstream the huge trees on either shore were but narrow, dark bands sandwiched between river and sky. Along the way the army fought pitched battles with Indians who succeeded in killing several of the Spaniards, often pursuing them for miles along the shore in their own canoes. Earlier they had met friendly Indians who bolstered their spirits with stories of rich lands farther downstream and of a great queen called Coñori whose empire was defended by armies of tall, powerful female warriors.

Captain Francisco de Orellana and his followers had no reason to doubt these tales. Many of them had seen the great ruined Aztec city of Tenochtitlán, destroyed just twenty years before by men such as they, and they themselves had helped Pizarro humble the Incas and loot their great empire. Women soldiers had not yet been seen by any modern man, but the ancients wrote extensively about warrior women who cauterized the right breast of female children that they better use the bow—Amazons they were called. And was it not true that just a few years ago the popular writer Garcí-Ordóñez recalled the same legend in his book about the young knight Esplandián and his adventures in a

Overview of
South America
NOT TO SCALE

mythical land called California? Man-eating griffins fought there at the command of an Amazon queen, and Esplandián barely escaped with his life. Could it be that God had chosen them as the first to meet these formidable women?

The warrior queen and her nubile soldiers remained mere phantoms until June 24, 1542, when the rude fleet rounded a bend in the river and, as Friar Gaspar de Carvajal recalled in his famous account, "here we came suddenly upon the excellent land and dominion of the Amazons."* Drawing close to shore the explorers saw houses that shone white in the distance, and at the water's edge Indians taunted the Spaniards, goading them into battle. After an hour the conflict still raged along the river bank and in chest-deep water. "I want it to be known why these Indians defended themselves in this manner," wrote the chronicler of Orellana's expedition. "They are the subjects of, and tributaries to, the Amazons, and . . . we ourselves saw these women, who were there fighting in front of all the Indian men as women captains, and these latter fought so courageously that the Indian men did not dare to turn their backs, and anyone who did turn his back they killed with clubs right there before us. . . ."

The good friar, who almost lost his own life in the contest, described the women as very tall and robust, almost naked, with long hair coiled about their heads. They did as much fighting as ten men and fired so many arrows that the brigantines soon "looked like porcupines." Carvajal marveled that one sent an arrow "a span deep" into one of the vessels.

In his own day skeptics scoffed at Carvajal's description of Amazons along the great river, calling the incident either an outright fabrication or the product of a tropical fever. Francisco López de Gómara, author of the widely read *General and Natural History of the Indies*, wrote: "I do not believe either that any woman cuts off her right breast in order to be able to shoot with the bow, because with it they shoot very well . . ." Modern students are a bit more tactful, reasoning that the Orellana party probably fought with Tapuya Indian women who commonly accompanied their tribe into battle. Whether they were flesh-

---

*This and all subsequent translations from Spanish and Portuguese, both prose and poetry, are by the authors.

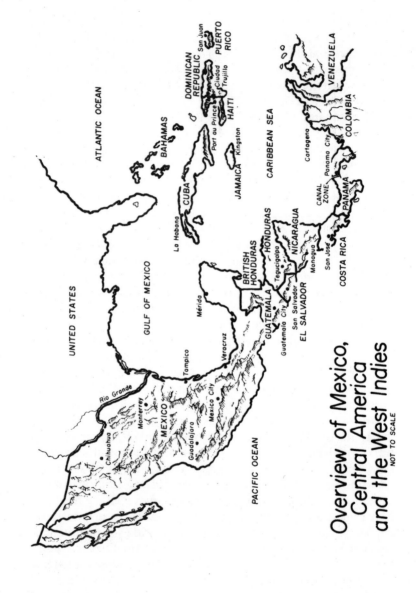

Overview of Mexico,
Central America
and the West Indies
NOT TO SCALE

and-blood women or wondrous creatures that Carvajal perceived in his mind's eye, similar visions drove Spanish, Portuguese, and even English and French explorers to undertake the arduous voyages of discovery that unlocked the secrets of two vast continents. It was a case of Quixotic adventurers whose flights of fancy lured them to strange new lands.

A short step takes us from the misty world of the Amazons into that of real women whose roles in the Latin American drama were as significant as those of their male contemporaries. If the warrior women of Orellana's riverside battle can be dismissed as rather commonplace Indian footsoldiers who happened to be women, the same cannot be said for the twenty-year-old Indian woman named María Candelaria. Some hundred years after the conquest of Central America and the forced conversion of the indigenous people to Christianity, María Candelaria led a general insurrection to restore the old gods and end foreign exploitation. That seventeenth-century Jeanne d'Arc was a genuine menace to Spanish rule in Central America, and though her revolt failed she herself was never captured.

Another heroic and tragic incident of Latin American women's history was the defense of Paraguay by its women during the Paraguayan War of 1864–1870. Over the course of the war, that landlocked South American country was so devastated that it would take a century to recover from the war's effects. When most Paraguayan regular soldiers fell before the relentless advance of largely Brazilian armies, teen-age boys filled the ranks until they too were gone. Then women and children took their places, fighting with outdated weapons, and ultimately sticks and stones. Six hundred Paraguayan women—mostly Indian and *mestiza*—died at Piribebuy in mid-1868, but not before showering the enemy with sand and empty bottles in one of the most sublime yet futile acts of defiance recorded in military history. At the end of the contest even the women were gone, leaving preadolescents to maintain the resistance. A Brazilian officer surveying the dead after the battle of Campo Grande was moved to remark that "there is no pleasure in fighting with so many children."

Not all heroic episodes of Latin American women's history are as somber and violent as those surrounding María Candelaria and the Paraguayan women. The story of ten wives of Spanish soldiers who accompanied the Narváez expedition to settle the Florida country has a much happier conclusion. On April 4, 1528, Pánfilo de Narváez landed three hundred men and forty-two horses at Tampa Bay, leaving one of his officers on board ship to protect the women and to find a harbor farther north where the expedition could reunite. The soldiers and their wives were to settle there, forming the nucleus of a new Spanish outpost. For more than a year the three supply ships sailed up and down the coast looking for Narváez and his luckless followers. Finally, assuming that all had perished, the search was called off and the ships made port in Mexico, then called New Spain. And the women? They married sailors from the ships and settled in New Spain, far from the wild north Florida frontier that was their original destination.

The Spanish and Portuguese in America did their best to re-create the Mediterranean culture they left behind. Except in the old centers of Aztec and Inca civilizations where European and Indian ways formed an uneasy amalgam, they were remarkably successful in bringing customs of late medieval times to their new home. An eight-hundred-year struggle to reconquer Spain and Portugal from the Moslems stamped on them a proud, warlike character tempered by a militant Catholicism that gave them the spiritual strength to carry the long struggle to success. Amazons had little place in such society.

Male-female relations were dominated by the concept of *machismo*, a form of radical individualism among men stressing all that is "manly" and virile. In everyday attitudes *machismo* translated into valor in battle, sensitivity to all insult, unwillingness to compromise, and an aggressive, domineering attitude toward women. The *macho* tried to impose his will on women around him, making love to as many as possible before marriage, fiercely jealous and protective of his own wife, yet willing and eager to continue his own outside love affairs. The institution of *machismo* tolerated the "double standard" and reveled in it. If the ideal male was aggressive and sexually promiscuous, the ideal woman was just the opposite. Custom and law demanded that she be chaste before marriage and a virtuous homebody afterward. Church teachings more than a thousand years old at the time of the Conquest instructed that she was the lesser vessel, obligated to respect her husband's judgment in all things.

Although limited to the confines of her home, the Latin American woman played a pivotal role in her culture. The home whose walls shut her away from the outside world was her bastion and source of strength. Mediterranean social theory singled out the family as society's fundamental building block, and the person around which the family centered was the mother. The father's presence was also important, but his principal field of action was the larger world. He was free to be a model of irresponsible parenthood if he so chose, but no such option was possible for his mate. She had to be a tower of strength through strict adherence to codes laid down by the church. The church provided her a supreme model for feminine conduct in the Virgin Mary. Mary, the greatest of all mothers, was to Latin American women the tearful saint of comfort and forgiveness whose example of divine forbearance gave them courage to persevere in adversity and to forgive and understand the manifold sins of husbands, sons, and brothers. This cult of the Virgin, or *marianismo,* was a necessary antidote to the willful individualism deeply rooted in Latin American culture. *Marianismo* also gave the woman who exemplified its ideals a universally recognized moral superiority. She could be justifiably proud that more than anyone else she bore the burden of preserving and transmitting all the best in Latin Christian culture to her sons and daughters.

The ideal of selflessness and abnegation did more than give Latin American women a sense of identity and self-worth. It also provided a delicate link of sympathy and understanding among women of all races and social conditions who bore equally the burden of *machismo,* motherhood, and certain of the homely tasks. Yet the shared experiences among the women of Latin America in no way made them a cohesive, self-conscious class within their culture. The powerful forces of economics, race, and family connections deeply divided Latin American women, as they did men. Recent applications of sociological analysis to the field of women's studies have given us new and intriguing ways of perceiving the Latin American woman within the context of her group or class.

At the top of Latin American feminine society stood the

woman of pure European descent whose wealth came from her own family or that of her husband. Two complementary views of upper-class women have traditionally held. The first depicts them as living in the lap of luxury, surrounded by slaves or servants, having little to occupy their time except gossip and innocent flirtations; the second reveals them as hopelessly ignorant creatures barely able to read and write or to pursue conversation much beyond questions involving needlework and the care of children.

Stories of upper-class women who were creatures of petty vice and unenlightened leisure come from all over Latin America. For many years the heavily veiled *tapadas* of colonial Lima upset society by wandering the streets at all hours peering furtively and seductively through their veils, secure in the knowledge that not even their husbands could recognize them. The count of Nieva, fourth viceroy of Peru, and many of his successors considered the veils a threat to morality and tried unsuccessfully to prohibit their use. Mexican women of the mid-nineteenth century were described as grossly ignorant of events taking place outside their homes, never reading anything more controversial than a prayerbook. One of their great pleasures, according to a sympathetic but mildly scandalized foreign observer, was the smoking of small, pungent cigars. Well-to-do Brazilian women of the great sugar estates, or *fazendas*, were as poorly educated as those in Spanish America but tended to suffer more from fanatically protective husbands. Even physicians were usually refused permission to examine women. They were outsiders, after all, and had to content themselves with diagnosing from another room after hearing husbands describe the symptoms through an open doorway.

Easy generalizations like these never applied to all women of the elite. Research shows that wives of the wealthy had more freedom of action than was once thought possible and were not wholly slothful and ignorant. The restrictions they suffered are better explained through the technique of class analysis. Wealthy women were part of an all-powerful Latin American ruling group. Consequently they were always under pressure to marry men of good family so that the interlocking network of elite interests might remain unbroken. Through the use of this analytic technique a new view emerges of the upper-class woman as one limited in her actions by group pressure, not indolence, by calculated economic self-interest, not stupidity.

Down the social scale from aristocratic European and Creole women, or *criollas,* were those of the same racial stock but outside the monied class. They were a fortunate group in many ways, on one hand free from the stigma of "mixed blood" and on the other not shackled by the demands imposed on women of the upper class. Their relative poverty gave them leeway in choosing a mate (or not choosing one for that matter), engaging in economic activity outside of the home, and taking up other pursuits not deemed proper for women of status. Excluded from high society they may have been, but nonelite women enjoyed an independence that made their place an enviable one in the Latin American world.

The gap between white women and all others was wide. In Spanish- and in Portuguese-speaking America ancestry was a key factor which could unlock the portals of social ascent or could slam them shut. Indians, *mestizos,* and blacks (the term is used here to include mixed-blood blacks) formed the three largest groups, with Indians predominating in Andean America, *mestizos* in Mexico and mountainous parts of northern South America, and blacks in the Caribbean and extensive portions of Brazil. The first group, the women of Indo-America, occupied a unique place in society. Taken as mistresses, and sometimes as wives, by the first Spanish invaders, considerable numbers of them learned Spanish customs and soon began bearing the conquistadors' children. A few daughters of Aztec and Inca nobles married influential Spaniards, thus making their way into the upper echelons of colonial society. The others had to be content with using their European lovers to gain entry into the Hispanic world. Their sex provided them mobility not possible for males, who were regarded as a potential source of revolt. The Indian woman was also an important economic force in Latin America. She ordinarily ran the village and city markets supplying farm produce and household goods to the townspeople.

Offspring of Indian women and European men made up a

second element of nonwhite population—the *mestizos*. In some parts of Latin America a *mestizo* elite sprang up and after the Independence Period gained enough wealth and influence to challenge Creole dominance. But generally they held an intermediate social position, excluded from white society and both unable and unwilling to take up Indian ways. A few philosophers called the men and women of *mestizo* America a "cosmic race" uniting the best from their mixed ancestry. Many others held that they were "half-breeds" possessing neither Indian nor European heritage in appreciable measure. Whether the *mestiza* is considered one of the chosen or one of the damned, she and her brothers were an ever-growing and significant population group in Latin America.

Stigmatized by the racial prejudice against all nonwhites, the third group, black women, bore the hateful additional burden of slavery. They were transported to Latin America with two, some would say three, strikes against them, and forced into the lowest positions in society. Not until the abolition of slavery during the nineteenth century were the majority of blacks able to seek an improved lifestyle. Like Indian women, black females sometimes used their sex to gain social mobility for themselves and their mixed-blood offspring, and they were also likely to gain positions as domestics, and if free, to engage in small businesses. Black males, whether slave or free, were mistrusted by the members of other groups who feared their tendency to lead slave revolts.

## II

Two kinds of writing have dominated the field of Latin American women's history. The first is biography, usually written to laud heroines of national independence or females notable in the arts. A slightly less common but nonetheless popular biographical form is that treating the unorthodox woman who flew in the face of social convention for romantic or other reasons. In recent years this kind of "great woman history" has been deemphasized in favor of studies dealing with women in groups. The logic is that only mass/class analysis can give valid insights into the day-to-day problems of the people. Biographies, it is argued, tend to glorify the gifted or unique individual while ignoring her less fortunate sisters. Traditionalists counter with the charge that the sociological approach tends to economic and sexual determinism and squeezes the lifeblood from its subject matter.

This study combines both approaches to Latin American women's history. Biographical in nature, it treats flesh-and-blood actresses in a great drama spanning nearly five hundred years even as it draws on subjects representing all major ethnic and economic groups. These ten figures are slaves and aristocrats, blacks, Indians, and *mestizas*, as well as women of purest Spanish lineage. Their fields of action run from Mexico to Argentina, from Peru to Brazil and the Caribbean, and even to Spain and Central Europe.

This diversity makes it possible to deal with a variety of issues important to Latin American women. For example, many people assume that in a male-dominated society women were thoroughly oppressed, enjoying only brief moments of happiness during their lifetimes. In reality this was far from the case. The free black woman Mariana Grajales was forced by circumstance to spend most of her life bearing children in an isolated part of rural Cuba. Yet she held powerful sway over her family, and when the Cuban independence struggle began she willed that her sons play a heroic role in the fighting. The Indian woman Malinche demonstrated similar strength of character during a lifetime of adversity. Sold into slavery as a child and given in concubinage to conquistadores at an early age, she effectively aided in the destruction of a great empire.

Another groundless assumption is that noble lineage or special intellectual gifts were sufficient to free elite women of the disabilities imposed by role and custom. Archduchess Leopoldina of Hapsburg, later empress of Brazil, had the bluest blood of Latin American royalty. But her ordained function was to have children, which she did admirably but with dire consequences to herself. The poet Juana Inés de la Cruz, endowed as no other with intellectual gifts, gave up her beloved studies after decades of struggle against religious rules that forbade them. Her personal religious convictions were a potent force causing her to bend before the champions of conformity.

Neither is it true that unorthodox feminine behavior was absolutely forbidden by a *machista* society. Two notable examples of middle-class Spanish women who broke every custom yet lived to enjoy approval and even respect were Inés de Suárez and Catalina de Erauzo. The former became a pillar of colonial society after living many years as the mistress of a conquistador, and the latter, an outlaw and transvestite, was ultimately absolved of all sin by the Pope himself!

The actions of the women described here provide vivid examples of race and class as motive forces in Latin American history. One wonders, for example, if it was not in part dislike of her own dark skin and *mestizo* ancestry that moved Nobel Laureate Gabriela Mistral to write her bittersweet poems of youth and of the land she loved but rarely visited. Creole patriot Policarpa Salavarrieta made no secret of her hatred for the peninsular Spaniards or *peninsulares* who oppressed her class. She went to her death heaping verbal abuse upon her executioners and immortalizing herself as a leader of the New Granadan independence movement.

Finally, we examine women who used a talent for leadership to place themselves at the head of movements for social reform. Eva Perón, the populist, and Tania Bunke, the communist guerrilla, were important figures in two political movements aimed at vindicating the dispossessed of Latin America. Men as well as women followed these strong personalities.

All the figures examined here illustrate the truth that biography extends to ideas, attitudes, and groups, and that social and intellectual history can be fruitfully explored through the unfolding of a human life. Their lives underline the humanistic view that individuals have the power to rise above circumstance and impersonal forces of history through sheer force of intelligence, perseverance, and character. These facts as well as the fascination inherent in the colorful personalities themselves inspired this study of women who played significant roles in Latin American history.

# I

# Malinche, 1504?-1528?

T HE FINEST MOMENT in the European Age of Exploration came long before dawn on an April morning in 1492. A lookout on Columbus's ship *Pinta* sighted white cliffs shining in the moonlight and cried out that land had at last been discovered. That event and the later explorations of Columbus marked the first effective European penetration of America.

Columbus and the men and women who quickly followed him into the Caribbean region did so as agents of the Spanish Queen Isabella of Castile. With the notable exception of Columbus, the great majority of them were Spanish. They brought with them the customs and language of Spain, and within a generation they firmly fixed their Iberian culture upon the society that developed in Hispañola, Cuba, and the other Caribbean islands.

Those Europeans who spoke wonderingly of America as a "New World" were not the first human beings to set foot on the land. For many thousand years people of Asian descent had made the Americas their home and had developed their own unique civilizations. When the intruders arrived late in the 1400s, several of those "Indian" cultures rivaled anything that Europe could offer at the time. One of them was the great Aztec empire, lying west of the small Spanish island settlements.

In the early 1500s the Spaniards launched a series of probing expeditions along the seemingly endless coast to the west, each

time bringing back rumors of fabulous wealth somewhere on the mysterious land mass. Early in 1519 the fateful expedition of Fernando Cortés departed Cuba, and in a matter of months the dazzling Aztec civilization was revealed to European eyes.

The story of the conquest is one of the most incredible in American history. Cortés the conquistador and Montezuma the emperor soon confronted each other at the gates of the Aztec capital. The date was November 8, 1519. Their encounter was the first act of a drama that would soon destroy one of them and immortalize them both. And standing at the side of the Spaniard was a third figure—that of the Indian woman Malinche.

History has played a cruel trick on the consort of Cortés. It has largely overlooked her as a striking personality in her own right—someone without whom Cortés surely would have failed to defeat Montezuma and the Aztecs by 1521. Yet irony surrounds La Malinche, or Doña Marina as the Spaniards called her, for instead of being remembered for her human qualities of intelligence, loyalty, and courage, or even for her strength and beauty, the slave girl who helped conquer an empire is despised by her own descendants. Today her name is used as a synonym for one who betrays his own people, and in art she is depicted as the Mexican Eve who led her people into enslavement by foreigners.

Such is the controversy surrounding the first significant female figure of American history. That *Malinche* has become a word of contempt and a symbol of treason in Mexico cannot be denied. But let history judge Malinche the person.

Montezuma's reign as emperor of the Aztec empire was barely a decade old when frightening things began to happen. The lake around his island city of Tenochtitlán rose in sudden waves without apparent reason. Comets appeared in the sky and could be seen even by day. A temple burned to the ground, struck by lightning, and mournful voices were heard everywhere, yet seemed to come from no living person. In 1515 Montezuma, the proud warrior-prince, consulted his great ally Nezahuapilli, chief of the Texcocans and famed reader of astrological signs. His verdict: the powerful Aztec empire would soon fall. Montezuma, always aloof and stern, became increasingly withdrawn as he pondered the disturbing signs from the gods.

Some two hundred miles to the east of Montezuma's gleaming city, in the hot lowlands near the Gulf of Mexico, lived a small girl who would soon play a vital role in fulfilling those omens. Malinali, as she may have been called then, was born a princess, daughter of the *cacique* of a town of Coatzacoalcos province. As a *cacique's* daughter she enjoyed a degree of education not available to daughters of less powerful parents and looked forward to a life of comfort and power. This pleasant future was never to be. While she was still a child, Malinali's father died and her mother remarried, soon bearing a son. In order to clear the boy's path to power, Malinali's mother plotted to rid herself of the little girl, and under cover of darkness gave Malinali to another tribe, the Xicalangos. Later she was given to yet another tribe, the Tabascans, who lived farther to the south.

Malinali's life as a slave of the Tabascans was one of daily toil and drudgery. There was corn to grind and bread to make. The many religious festivals called for the cooking of special dishes and the sewing of elaborate clothing decorated with feathers and embroidery. And in addition to these endless chores there were always children to be cared for. While she lived with the Tabascans, however, Malinali faced a further task. Her native language, Nahuatl, spoken by the Aztecs and other subject peoples, was not the language of the Tabascans. Nevertheless she soon learned to speak their Mayan dialect as fluently as her own.

During 1517 and 1518, the Tabascans and other Mexican tribes were troubled by rumors and stories that spread from town to town, even reaching the shining palaces of Montezuma. It was reported that strange canoes of immense size had appeared and moved ominously up and down Mexico's coast. The men who traveled in those ships were bearded and fair-skinned, clothed in steel. They carried arms far different from the arrows, darts, and two-bladed clubs of the Indians, and their language could not be understood even by those who knew several Indian tongues.

Stories linking these intruders to the benign Aztec god Quetzalcoatl sprang up among the people of Mexico. Tall, fair-skinned, and bearded, Quetzalcoatl was the great civilizing god who had led his followers to a period of abundance many years before. According to legend, the gentle god was forced to leave Mexico and sailed away into the rising sun promising to return someday to reestablish his kindly rule. When he heard these reports, Montezuma pondered the similarities between Quetzalcoatl's legend and the sudden appearance of strangers along Mexico's coast.

In spite of dreadful omens and news of the strange visitors from the east, Montezuma's reign had never seemed more secure. His huge empire stretched in all directions from the mountain-locked Valley of Mexico—over high passes and down into the hot, tropical lands to the south and east, and westward to the Pacific Ocean. From all the towns and cities in this vast region came caravans of slaves loaded with goods produced throughout the empire. They bore cotton cloth richly embroidered with feathers and gems, gold and silver ornaments of every size and design, jadeite and precious stones. Traveling with them were people of all ages who were to be sold in the huge marketplace of Tenochtitlán. This great flood of riches was the tribute Montezuma exacted from subject towns.

To guarantee his continued good fortune, Montezuma dedicated much of his time and wealth to satisfying the Aztec gods. Large pyramid-shaped temples towered over the one- and two-story houses of Tenochtitlán, and somber temple drums beat to the rhythm of the gods' demands for more and more human lives. Once rare in Aztec religion, the sacrifice of slaves and captive warriors had become part of almost every ceremony. Only recently the pious Montezuma had sacrificed ten thousand people during the dedication of Tenochtitlán's principal temple.

That great structure was a monument to the Aztec architectural genius. Around the temple's entryway were immaculate courtyards swept clean by black-robed priests whose lives were closely governed by penance and self-denial. At the top were dark, blood-spattered rooms where sacrifices were performed. There the person to be sacrificed was bent backward over a stone altar and his chest laid open with a sharp flint knife. A priest then twisted out his still-beating heart, raising it high as a dripping tribute to his god. Only the most important priests were permitted to perform this rite, and their long, black hair, tangled and matted with dried human blood, easily set them apart from others.

After sacrifice, the victim's body was cut up and disposed of according to strictly regulated religious practice. The head was displayed outside the temple, strung with many others on long poles; the torso was fed to wild animals that Montezuma kept on his palace grounds; and the arms and thighs were sometimes cooked and eaten by worshippers. Great numbers of sacrifices were needed to insure the favor of the many Aztec gods. Hence, Montezuma ordered his warriors to capture rather than kill enemies during battle, and he often demanded tribute in the form of slaves from the towns within his empire. Almost no one, even the most valiant of warriors, was entirely safe from the possibility of being sacrificed. And a simple slave girl like Malinali knew that repeated disobedience or other such offense could result in that very fate.

Malinali was about fifteen years old in March 1519 when word came that the strange canoes had again been sighted along the coast to the south. The Tabascans quickly assembled twelve thousand warriors to defend their towns from the strangers. But they soon discovered that the intruders, Castilians as they called themselves, were unlike any enemy force they had ever before faced. Armed with powerful arrows, swords, and long metal rods that shot fire from one end, the new enemy was able to beat back the Indians even though they were outnumbered by three hundred to one. Their most awesome weapon was the horse, a frightening creature never before seen on Mexican soil. Even the bravest Indian warrior turned and ran from the animal that seemed half man and half monster and stood far taller than the strongest fighter.

Faced with defeat, the Tabascans decided that the Castilians were not ordinary men but rather gods—*Teules,* as they came to be called throughout Mexico. Hoping to placate them and regain peace, the Tabascan *caciques* assembled gifts to offer their conquerors. A large party of chieftains from Tabasco and neighboring towns arrived at the Castilian camp with slaves carrying maize cakes and every kind of fish and fruit known to that region. Among the gifts they brought were rolls of quilted cotton material used as armor by Indian warriors, presents of gold ornaments shaped like lizards, little dogs and ducks, several masks, and gold-soled sandals. And last among the gifts were twenty slave women to do the back-breaking work of grinding corn and making bread for the Spanish *Teules*. Among them was Malinali, the only one of the twenty who is remembered by history.

The prospect of being given to these fearsome, godlike men must have been frightening for Malinali. Yet in spite of her fears, the chance to see them and their weapons, dogs, and horses excited her interest, and she was able to keep her poise when brought before them. In spite of her years of subjugation, Malinali was gifted with grace and a quick intelligence that set her apart from the other slave women. Her long, black hair and regular features gave her a sweet but dignified look that attracted attention wherever she went.

Through Aguilar, a Spaniard who learned the Mayan language when shipwrecked earlier on the Mexican coast, the slave women learned that their new master was named Cortés and that he had given one of them to each of his most important captains. Malinali was given to Cortés's friend, Captain Alonso Hernández de Puertocarrero, and she was told to do as he commanded.

The next day Cortés called all the Indian women together and, through Aguilar the interpreter, introduced them to Father Olmedo. This man, he said, was a priest of the Catholic faith who would teach them about the religion of their Castilian masters. Malinali was amazed to see a man so unlike the Indian priests she knew. Gone were the black robe, the blood-matted hair, the ears disfigured by self-inflicted cuts and cheeks pierced by cactus thorns. Instead, Malinali saw a barefoot man, simply dressed, whose words told of a kindly father-god, his baby son, and the virgin mother. Instead of human sacrifice, this god asked only that believers be baptized, and on that day, shortly before Palm Sunday, 1519, Malinali was herself baptized. From that time forth she was known as Doña Marina to the Castilian soldiers, who never failed to call her *"doña,"* a title of respect given to the Christian daughters and wives of Indian *caciques*.

Six days later, on the Monday after Palm Sunday, the Castilians boarded their eleven ships and sailed northward along the coast. Marina was impressed by the size and swiftness of these "canoes" and more than astonished that in a short time they passed the Coatzacoalcos River, the same river that flowed through her native province.

On the Thursday before Easter the ships had hardly dropped anchor at San Juan de Ulúa when two large canoes approached Cortés's flagship. As soon as the Indians spoke, Doña Marina recognized their language, for it was her own Nahuatl. She pointed it out to Cortés and suddenly found herself interpreting for the mighty Cortés himself, translating from Nahuatl to Mayan so that Aguilar could then translate their words into Castilian. Immediately after an exchange of formalities with the Indians, Cortés called Marina aside. If she would serve him faithfully, he said, and translate as honestly as she could, he would protect her and treat her well. Marina pledged that she would indeed serve him as interpreter, and from that time on she found herself always at Cortés's side.

Montezuma knew about Cortés's victory at Tabasco the day after it happened. In less than twenty-four hours an elaborate system of runners carried the news from the coast to Tenochtitlán, a distance of two hundred miles. The events of the previous day gave Montezuma ample cause for worry. Unlike the members of the short Spanish expeditions of 1517 and 1518, Cortés and his soldiers were successful in battle and had won the allegiance of a whole province formerly counted among the Aztec prince's subjects. Montezuma suspected that these foreigners might indeed be representatives of the god Quetzalcoatl, and, concerned about the proper course of action, he called together his allies and priests. Some of his counselors urged him to assemble a great army of warriors that could capture all the Castilians for sacrifice. Others advised him that the strangers were *Teules* and should be treated carefully, like gods. Montezuma, himself afraid of angering the gods, decided to send messengers to Cortés with word that the Spanish should accept gifts from the Mexican prince but should not try to come to Tenochtitlán to see him. Hoping to intimidate the Spanish with his wealth and power, he sent his best diplomat, Tendile, to San Juan de Ulúa to meet with Cortés.

Tendile and his caravan arrived at the Spanish settlement on Easter, 1519. Marina and Aguilar were called to Cortés and between them translated words of welcome from Castilian to Mayan to Nahuatl and back again. Gifts were exchanged and Cortés ordered his cavalry to demonstrate their horsemanship on the firm sand of the beach. Aztec artists carefully painted everything they saw—ships, horses, cannon, the Castilians' bearded faces and clothing, even Marina and Aguilar—so that Montezuma could see these things as if with his own eyes.

Some time after this meeting, Tendile returned to the Castilian camp with a caravan of one hundred slaves carrying gifts of immense value from Montezuma. Many of the ornaments were taken from the temple of Quetzalcoatl: a large, wheel-sized disk of gold, a larger one made of burnished silver, many ornaments of precious metals, and enough gold dust to convince the Spanish that a visit to Montezuma would be well worth the effort. Tendile, however, cautioned them against traveling to Tenochtitlán and urged them instead to be content with their gifts and to stay on the coast.

During the long conversations between Tendile and the Castilians, Cortés told of his allegiance to Carlos V of Spain, the great king in whose name he had come to Mexico, and of the Catholic religion that he hoped all Mexico would embrace. Father Olmedo and Cortés's four hundred soldiers paraded with great reverence before the large wooden cross they had raised in their camp. Tendile asked many questions about the new religion and after a great show of friendship withdrew and quickly carried news of all these things to his prince.

One morning several days later the Spaniards awoke to find themselves alone. Indians no longer came to their camp bringing food or seeking to trade. Soon supplies ran low and the Castilians, cut off from local sources of food, were reduced to a scant diet of fish. From his distant palace Montezuma had received news of the Spanish religion with alarm. If these intruders were messengers from Quetzalcoatl, how could they not worship Mexico's traditional gods? Beset by doubt, Montezuma ordered the Spanish cut off from local towns, hoping that starvation would force them to leave his empire.

It had been days since any Indians had come to Cortés's camp when sentries reported the approach of five brightly dressed chieftains, *caciques* of the Totonac tribe. Cortés called Marina and Aguilar and through them learned that the Totonacs were dissatisfied with Montezuma's taxes and constant demands for more tribute and more slaves. In this way Cortés learned that Montezuma's rule was not absolute, and, much encouraged, he decided to move his camp inland to Cempoala, the largest Totonac city. Along the way, the Castilians passed many towns that were deserted as they approached. Everywhere they reacted with dismay to the blood-stained temples that offered clear evidence of the Indians' practice of human sacrifice. Marina explained the use of sacrifice to Cortés and told him that slaves, captive warriors, and even infants were used. She was surprised that the Spanish, so brave in battle, were horrified by what had seemed a normal religious ritual to her.

The Cempoalans, led by their wise and overweight cheiftain, the "fat *cacique*," met with Cortés and his soldiers in the broad central plaza of their city. Marina was by now accustomed to translating from her permanent spot at Cortés's side. She talked easily with the Cempoalans and translated their long list of complaints against Montezuma so that Cortés would understand their bitterness. At that moment, as if to illustrate their complaints, five men strode into the plaza. They were clad in brilliantly colored cloaks; their long, black hair was tied at the crown of their heads; and each carried a sheaf of roses in one hand, a crooked staff in the other. The Totonacs fell back from them trembling with fear as the men, Montezuma's tax collectors, scolded them for aiding the Spaniards. As punishment they demanded twenty Totonac men and women for sacrifice.

Cortés was amazed at this spectacle and asked Marina what had happened. She explained that Montezuma wished to enslave the Castilians and had forbidden his subject tribes to aid them. Cortés rose to his feet and in the name of Carlos V of Spain ordered the Totonacs to seize the tax collectors and imprison them. No longer would his friends the Totonacs pay tribute to Monte·

zuma, he said, for the great emperor Carlos V prohibited his people from robbing and sacrificing human beings to Montezuma's false gods. The Totonacs did as Cortés commanded and, frightened by their own act of rebellion, allied themselves more closely with the Castilians, hoping for protection from Montezuma's certain anger.

That same night Cortés secretly freed two of the five tax collectors and with a great show of regret and friendliness claimed that the Totonacs alone were responsible for their imprisonment. He then urged them to go quickly to Montezuma with the warmest expressions of friendship from Cortés. By the time the two escapees reached Tenochtitlán, however, Montezuma had learned of the Totonac rebellion. Preparations were already underway to wage war on the Totonacs and their Castilian allies, but the soothing messages from Cortés aborted these plans. Instead of war, Montezuma sent greetings to Cortés and maintained an attitude of watchfulness. The Indians of the coast were astonished at this mild response, and Cortés's reputation improved rapidly, attracting many more allies among the towns and cities of the Totonacs and neighboring tribes.

So many gifts of gold and silver, precious gems, and embroidered cloth had been given to the Spanish forces that Cortés decided to send a ship to Spain laden with an impressive array of gifts for Carlos V. Alonso Hernández de Puertocarrero was chosen to be Cortés's representative on this mission, and he embarked for Spain during the summer of 1519. Cortés refused to send Marina on the voyage. She had become far too valuable to him in her role as interpreter. By this time, too, she had learned Castilian so well that she could talk easily with the Spanish in their own tongue. No one among Cortés's troops understood the Indians as well as she; no one else could grasp the subtleties of their speech and make them instantly clear. Without her he would have been like a deaf-mute, unable to communicate or understand anything but the grossest gestures and expressions.

So Marina remained with the Spanish in Mexico, where her own special position did not go unnoticed by her countrymen. Was she not the *Teules's* tongue? Did she not speak for the great Cortés himself? Her prestige was so great that the two of them—

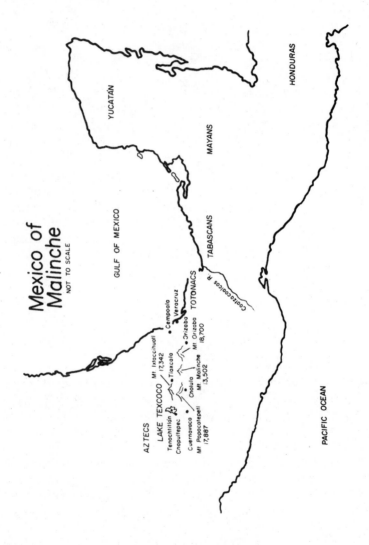

Mexico of
Malinche
NOT TO SCALE

GULF OF MEXICO

YUCATÁN

MAYANS

HONDURAS

TABASCANS

Coatzacoalcos R.

TOTONACS

Cempoala
Veracruz

Orizaba
Mt Orizaba
18,700

AZTECS
LAKE TEXCOCO    Mt Ixtaccihuatl
Tenochtitlán      17,342
Chapultepec    Tlaxcala
Cuernavaca    Cholula
Mt Popocatepetl    Mt Malinche
17,887              13,502

PACIFIC OCEAN

Cortés and Marina—came to be called by the same name, "Malintzin." A corruption of her own Christian name with the respectful title -*tzin* added, *Malintzin* or *Malinche* was what the Indians called both the man Cortés and the woman who spoke for him. In the eyes of the Indians, they functioned as one person.

Yet Cortés must have had some doubts about Marina. He knew from sad experience that a disloyal interpreter could cause disaster and even death. Would the allegiance Marina once felt for Montezuma be stronger than her seeming obedience to the Castilians? Would she be able to resist a call to return to her own people? As yet he had no cause to doubt her loyalty, but he still could not trust her totally. Marina herself probably never wondered about these things. Life with her people had been hard and disillusioning. She had been denied her inheritance and passed from one tribe to another, finally to be given to these strange invaders. If anything, she felt fortunate that the Castilians treated her so well. Had they not promoted her from slave girl to Cortés's own translator? Was she not a vital part of this quest for wealth and power, always there when decisions were made and when great *caciques* came to confer with Cortés? Indeed, there was nothing in her past that could compete with the excitement of life with the Castilians. Very soon, any question Cortés might have had about her loyalty vanished.

The Castilians left Cempoala in August 1519 and began the tortuous journey over the mountains to Tenochtitlán. In battle after battle they subdued each town along the way. Montezuma watched with mounting anxiety as Cortés's few soldiers defeated huge armies of defenders, using tactics undreamed of by even the best Indian warriors. First Cingapacinga, then Zocotlán, finally Tlaxcala fell under Cortés's rule. How could these *Teules* be stopped and by whom?

Montezuma decided that Cholula would be the place to defeat the Castilians. To that end he sent twenty thousand warriors to the rocky ravines west of the city where an ambush could most effectively be executed. At the same time the *caciques* of Cholula were ordered to receive the Castilians with every sign of friendship. Within three days of Cortés's arrival, however, signs of the plot began to surface. Two high priests secretly told Marina of the barricades and trenches dug in the city streets in preparation for battle. The Cholulans, at first lavish with food and supplies, soon relaxed their two-faced efforts and mockingly carried only water to the Spanish soldiers. Then one evening an old woman, the wife of a Cholulan chieftain, came clandestinely to Marina to warn her of the danger she was in as long as she stayed with the Spanish *Teules*. She had taken pity on Marina, so young and pretty, and offered her a safe place in her own home as her son's wife. Marina thanked her warmly and, pretending to accept the offer, arranged to meet her later that night after packing her clothes and gold jewels. But instead of escaping, Marina ran to Cortés and told him the details of Montezuma's plot just as she had learned them from the old woman.

The next day Cortés summoned all the Cholulan *caciques*, chieftains, and several thousand of their warriors to the courtyard where the Spanish were camped. Mounted on horseback, with Marina at his side, he told them of the bad treatment he had received from them and described the plot against his life and the lives of his men. Marina translated his words in a loud, clear voice, adding color to his anger by the force of her own. Malinche knew, she said, that priests were already prepared to sacrifice the Castilians, that pots with peppers and tomatoes stood ready to cook them for the postbattle feast. But such treason against the great emperor Carlos V could not go unpunished. At that moment a musket was fired as a signal to Cortés's soldiers, who, armed with broadswords and some mounted on horseback, fell on the Indians trapped in the courtyard. The slaughter of their best warriors was a blow the Cholulans could not withstand. Soon *caciques* from towns throughout the province came to pledge their allegiance to Cortés and his Spanish king, and Montezuma's warriors hastily withdrew to Tenochtitlán with word of the disastrous defeat suffered at Cholula.

If Cortés had ever doubted Marina's loyalty, such suspicions never again crossed his mind. Given the chance to escape from the Castilians and to marry the son of a wealthy *cacique*, she chose instead to remain with Cortés. No further proof of her trustworthiness was required. Cortés and Marina, firmest collaborators in public, soon extended that partnership to their private lives as well. Their union was informal, sanctioned neither by law nor religion, yet common enough in an age when a woman, slave or princess, could be given away as a mere gift to a wealthy or powerful man. From that time until the end of the conquest three years later, Cortés and Marina were inseparable companions, in war as well as peace, in triumph as well as defeat.

After the massacre of his Cholulan subjects, Montezuma realized to his dismay that he could no longer avoid meeting Cortés at his own gates. For two anguished days he consulted with his priestly advisers and finally decided to welcome the Spanish to Tenochtitlán. There, enclosed and surrounded, they could at last be defeated in one giant bloodletting. Confident that this desperate plot would succeed, he ordered all the *caciques* of the cities of Mexico to prepare for Cortés's arrival.

On the evening of November 7, 1519, his heart heavy with foreboding, Montezuma left his palace and crossed the broad flagstone courtyard to the great temple. He climbed the 114 steps slowly and, as he reached the top, paused to contemplate his beautiful city. What had once been a mud island in the middle of a lake was now a metropolis of sixty thousand families. Flat-roofed, whitewashed houses stretched out around the central plaza with its towering temples and palaces. A system of canals and portable bridges crisscrossed the island, and Montezuma could see hundreds of his people poling their canoes through the canal network, carrying food and merchandise to market. Floating gardens ringed the island and supplied Tenochtitlán with an abundance of flowers of every kind. Farther out Montezuma could see the aqueduct that brought fresh water from Chapúltepec to his capital, and stretched out in front of him were the three long causeways that crossed the shallow lake and connected Tenochtitlán with the shore. The causeways, some twenty feet wide, were broken here and there by canals crossed by portable wooden bridges. The hills rising from the lake shore were almost barren. Montezuma knew that little food could be grown there, but turning southward he caught a glimpse of the fertile lands of Cuernavaca where corn and other foods were cultivated. To the south he could see a long caravan of slaves, each carrying fifty pounds of grain on his back, laboring along the road toward the city.

Reluctantly, Montezuma turned toward the east. Far away

on the crest of a hill he saw the glint of metal weapons and the movement of many figures. So these were the invincible Castilians, he thought, the much-feared *Teules*. Tomorrow they would finally meet.

Cortés's soldiers and thousands of his Indian allies were assembled on the shore when Montezuma, accompanied by a huge escort of *caciques* and warriors, crossed the causeway to receive them. The Aztec prince was carried under a canopy of green feathers embroidered with gold and silver, pearls, and jadeite. On his feet were gold-soled sandals, their tops encrusted with precious gems of every color; his cloak and loincloth were likewise richly adorned. His subjects, forbidden to raise their eyes before his power, wealth, and magnificence, fell back as he passed.

By contrast, the Castilians looked plain and worn. Cortés's red velvet cap provided one spot of color, but his captains and men were dressed as simple soldiers whose weapons were more valuable to them than all the pearls of the sea. Faced with the prospect of entering that glistening city, the more fainthearted of the Spaniards longed for escape. Cortés fully understood the danger, yet he was determined to lead his men even into the enemy's stronghold. When he spoke with Montezuma, no sign of hesitation or fear could be heard in his voice, and Marina, inspired by his composure, calmly translated for the two great leaders.

After the welcoming ceremonies were over, Montezuma arranged for the Castilians to stay in large houses built by his own father during a long and fruitful reign. Inside the central palace was a section of wall that had been freshly plastered. Cortés ordered it secretly opened and on the other side discovered a breathtaking hoard of gold and jewels. The wall was again closed, carefully so as to escape notice.

Soon after Cortés was established in Tenochtitlán, an Indian messenger arrived from the coast with news that Indian allies in Cempoala and in the mountains to the east were in revolt against the Spanish. Only Montezuma could have encouraged so widespread a rebellion. Cortés and his captains decided that for their own protection Montezuma had to be taken hostage and forced to live under the watchful eyes of the Castilians to prevent further treachery.

Cortés, his captains, and Marina went directly to Montezuma's palace. Courteously, Cortés complained to Montezuma about his double-dealing and ordered him to move to the *Teules* quarters. Montezuma was astonished at such a request and refused even to consider it. For more than half an hour the two men argued, until one of Cortés's captains lost his temper and began shouting threats at Montezuma. Startled by the outburst, the Aztec prince turned to Marina for an explanation. She quickly replied that Cortes's soldiers were angry and would try to kill him if he didn't go with them at once. Under Cortés's protection, she added, he would be quite safe. Marina's words convinced Montezuma, and from that time on he was Cortés's royal hostage—the Castilians' guarantee of safe passage while in Tenochtitlán.

While he lived with the Spanish, Montezuma continued to govern his great empire, receiving tribute and visits from his priests and allied *caciques*. Many Mexican leaders urged him to declare war on the Spanish *Teules*, but Montezuma realized that an attack on them would cause his own death, and for that reason he betrayed each plot to Cortés. The silent but constant threat against Montezuma's life was balanced by the outward respect and constant flattery he received from Cortés and his men. In this way the prince, formerly a fearless warrior, was robbed of his will and became a pawn of the Spanish.

Early in May 1520, Cortés, Marina, and most of the soldiers left Tenochtitlán for the coast, leaving Captain Alvarado and a band of soldiers to guard Spanish interests in the capital. Soon after Cortés's departure, Alvarado mistook a religious celebration in a nearby temple for the prelude to an attack on his small force. Frightened by the sound of drums and dancing, Alvarado and his men attacked the unarmed revelers and brutally killed or mutilated many of Tenochtitlán's young noblemen. This cruel error of judgment was more than the Aztecs could bear; had Montezuma not calmed them, massacre of the Castilians would surely have followed. On receiving news of the disaster, Cortés returned at once, and with an army of thirteen hundred soldiers, swollen by his victories on the coast, he arrived to find the streets of Tenochtitlán deserted and his quarters in a state of siege.

There followed two weeks of constant fighting. Sometime

during that period, Montezuma was led to the roof to implore his people to cease their attack. A stone from an Indian's sling struck his head, and after three days the great Montezuma died, betrayed by his own gods, ruined and alone among his enemies. Cortés ordered the regal body to be laid in the street outside his quarters; it was never again seen by the Spanish.

After Montezuma's death, the Aztecs attacked with renewed energy. Food and water were almost gone. Since neither salt nor oil was left to treat the many wounded, Cortés's soldiers heated the fat of slain Aztecs until it liquefied and applied it to their open wounds. Their situation had become so desperate that early in July the Spaniards decided to leave the city by night in a daring attempt to save their lives. First to depart were four hundred Indian warriors allied with the Castilians and one hundred and fifty soldiers who were to guard the all-important causeway bridge. Then came Indian carriers laden with treasure and guarded by Cortés himself, his captains, and a large number of soldiers. At the rear were two captains, thirty soldiers, and three hundred Indians who were to guard Cortés's Mexican prisoners and the few women, including Marina, who traveled with that desperate army.

Almost as soon as the Castilians and their Indian allies left the center of Tenochtitlán, the attack began. By the time they reached the causeway, Aztec warriors had already surrounded it and, filling the air with their screams and taunts, soon succeeded in destroying the bridge, the vital link to safety. So many soldiers and horses were killed or drowned at that spot that some of the rear guard escaped by walking over bodies that filled the shallow lake. Among them was Marina, who, with another Indian woman, managed to get away unharmed and was soon reunited with Cortés and the few fortunate survivors of the *Noche Triste*, the Sad Night of Cortés's defeat.

When he saw what was left of his army, Cortés sat under a tree on the shore and wept. His trained force that had grown to thirteen hundred Spaniards was reduced to four hundred, all of them wounded. Not one horse had escaped unhurt, and some of Cortés's most trusted captains had lost their lives in the terrible confusion of that night.

Rather than give up his dream of conquering the Aztecs, Cortés regrouped his small army. Within a year he had recruited many thousand new Indian allies and again stood at the gates of Tenochtitlán. By that time the city was already much weaker than it had been on the *Noche Triste*. Late in May 1521, the aqueduct carrying water from Chapúltepec was cut and the siege began. Ten thousand Indian allies and thirteen small ships or launches were assembled on the lake for the long war against Cuauhtémoc, Montezuma's successor, and the inhabitants of what had once been the most powerful city in all Mexico. Cuauhtémoc and his warriors vowed to fight to the death, and fight they did. Cortés and Marina pleaded with them time and time again to save themselves, to stop their insane resistance, but their words went unheeded.

At last the Castilians realized that only by destroying the city stone by stone and filling in the hundreds of canals would victory be theirs. While the work of destruction proceeded, the launches were used with great effectiveness to prevent food from reaching the starving Mexicans, and after two months of siege, Spanish soldiers began finding pieces of chewed bark and roots in the streets. The hunger became so intense that late one night a crowd of eight hundred Aztec women and children were captured when they came out of hiding to search for food. Finally, on August 13, 1521, the starving city fell, and Cortés became captain-general and sole ruler of the Aztecs.

Cortés turned immediately to the task of rebuilding the city and of governing the kingdom that he and Marina had won for Spain. Sometime in 1522 Marina gave birth to Cortés's son Martín, one of the first Mexicans to be born of Spanish and Indian parents.

Strangely, the birth of little Martín seems to have marked the end of Cortés and Marina's intimate relationship. His great successes caused Cortés to lust after titles of nobility. A Spanish nobleman, Cortés reasoned, could hardly continue living with an Indian woman, even if she were a princess. In short, Cortés's gentle helper of preconquest days became a serious handicap. Just three months after the fall of Tenochtitlán he sent for his wife Doña Catalina Suárez de Marcayda from Cuba. In public Marina continued to serve Cortés as his interpreter, and her loyalty to him never wavered. In return Cortés gave her enough land, vassals, and gold to insure her physical comfort for life.

Reconstruction of the Mexican capital began immediately. European-style buildings soon rose over a foundation of broken idols and temple stones, and broad streets replaced the Aztec canal system. Cortés dedicated himself as intensely to the government and economy of Mexico as he had to its conquest. Yet once he turned away from Marina, his fortunes changed for the worse. Within a few months of her arrival, his young wife, Doña Catalina, died mysteriously in the night. Seizing her death as an opportunity to discredit Cortés, enemies of the conquistador whispered that he was to blame.

The following year, in October 1524, Cortés led a large force to Honduras to quash a rebellion against his rule. A more difficult journey could not have been imagined, either for Cortés or for Marina. She was still his primary interpreter and had become a major force in the Indians' conversion to Christianity; her presence was therefore a necessity on the long, dangerous expedition.

For reasons that have never been fully explained, Cortés arranged for Marina to marry his lieutenant Juan Jaramillo, a hero of the siege of Mexico and a "Castilian knight." The marriage took place at Orizaba soon after the party left Mexico City, and Marina gave birth to a daughter, María Jaramillo, a year and a half later as the torn remnants of Cortés's army sailed back to Mexico.

Marina, by now a person of wealth and standing in Mexico, did not live long after returning to the city she had worked so hard to win. In 1527 or early in 1528 Marina died—perhaps from smallpox, perhaps from the effects of the dreadful trip to Honduras. Her short life lasted only about twenty-four years, and her memory was not honored after her death. Indeed, the two men she admired were the first to belittle her. In Cortés's long, narrative letters to Carlos V he mentioned her only twice and called her merely "a native Indian girl." Her husband Juan Jaramillo seemed to forget her so quickly that he remarried a few weeks after her death and tried in later years to disinherit their daughter María. In the Castilian code of values, an Indian woman, however loyal, intelligent, and beautiful, was of little worth in comparison with the glitter of gold and the attractions of noble Spanish blood.

Yet Marina did not appear bitter about her fate. A few years before her death, during an unexpected meeting with her mother and half-brother, she spoke openly of the path her life had taken. Instead of seeking vengeance, she forgave her mother for giving her to the Xicalangos so long ago. No happier fate could be imagined than her own, she said, adding that she would rather serve her lord and master Cortés and her gentleman husband Jaramillo than be the greatest princess of all Mexico. It was with humility, without bitterness, that this young Indian woman viewed her role in the conquest—a feat whose greatness remains undiminished by time.

# II
# Inés de Suárez,
# 1507-1572?

ATIVE AMERICANS AND European invaders fought desperately during the wars of conquest. Quarter was neither
given nor expected in a struggle whose outcome shaped
the destiny of two continents. At length the Europeans, with
their superior military technology, hammered Indian peoples
into submission and imposed European social structures upon
them. What emerged was a highly stratified, hierarchical society
with theoretical roots extending back to the Roman Empire.

An institution of fundamental importance in early Spanish
America was the *encomienda*, a royal grant of Indian labor that
was awarded to conquistadores for their service to the crown. *Encomenderos*, the holders of such grants, were obliged to school the
Indians in Spanish ways, teaching them to become good vassals
to the king. The *encomienda* worked poorly in practice. The conquerors and their descendants usually took what they could from
the Indians and offered little in return. They paid lip service to
royal law, often disobeying it with a shrug and the admission
*"Obedezco pero no cumplo"* ("I obey the law in principle but not in
practice"). No wonder the society that developed in Latin
America was one of vast inequalities. Spanish settlers and their
children, or Creoles as they came to be called, formed a
nominally autonomous, landed elite. Mixed bloods stood lower in
the social structure, and at its base were the Indians and enslaved
blacks.

And what was the role of women in this stratified social system? Their place was the home, though few outside the highest aristocracy could afford the luxury of remaining homebodies. The case of Inés de Suárez is illustrative. When faced with the choice of eking out an existence as a proper widow, or seeking adventure with handsome Pedro de Valdivia, she unhesitatingly chose the latter. She thus became a protagonist in the drama that earned Valdivia fame and ultimately a ghastly death in the south of Chile. As with many other unconventional women of Latin American history, the least important aspect of her role has been most remembered. But when the story is told objectively, Inés de Suárez stands as high as her consort: not only was she a chief participant in the conquest of Chile, but she survived it and went on to become a grande dame of Hispanic society in the land she helped tame.

Sixteenth-century travelers who embarked for the New World at Sevilla usually began the voyage with eager expectancy. Behind them lay the old, confining life of Spain; before them, the Americas, a land so recently discovered that its power to arouse hope seemed limitless. Within a day after their ships slipped past the sand bar at the mouth of the Guadalquivir River, the travelers' eagerness and high spirits gave way to a dreadful realization that between Spain and the New World lay a vast purgatory known as the Atlantic crossing. Trapped in small, narrow ships, protected from the ocean's ominous might by tar caulking and a few planks, only the foolhardy failed to ponder their imminent danger.

Seasickness came first, with days and nights of nausea. Men and women too ill to move sprawled on the deck and longed to return to Spain or, better yet, to die at once. By the time seasickness subsided and appetites returned, the supply of fruit and vegetables was spoiled, and passengers resigned themselves to a diet of salt meat and biscuits, made less palatable by the scarcity of water. During hot summer months the heat and stench from below drove passengers above deck where they and their lice and fleas roasted in the merciless sun. Time passed slowly; gambling, conversation, and even prayer did little to fill the long days. In addition to the physical discomforts, there was always fear—fear of storms, of being becalmed, of pirates. Not all survived the hardship of crossing. Those who died, defrauded of their hopes, were buried at sea, to rest forever in the salty depths of the Atlantic.

Among those who successfully crossed in 1537 was Inés de Suárez, one of the few women—women made up less than 10 percent of all travelers—making the journey that year. When she glimpsed the coast of the New World for the first time, Inés was thirty years old. Had she been a man, she would have been considered to be in the prime of life. But a woman of thirty was thought old, past marriageable age and usually worn by childbearing. By chance Inés de Suárez, although married for a number of years, had borne no children, and she retained the energy that might have been expended in more traditional ways. Free from ties at home, splendidly healthy and spirited, she left Spain without a tear and set off in search of her husband, a soldier of fortune living somewhere in the New World.

The fleet that carried Inés anchored first in the Gulf of Paria, lying between Venezuela and the island of Trinidad. Undaunted by the steamy heat of that northeastern extremity of South America, she gazed at the low coastlines to the east and west and by night beheld in wonder the flecks of light sparkling in the gently swelling water. She thought at first that those millions of minute lights were stars reflected in the dark waters, but soon she realized that tiny phosphorescent sea plants were responsible for the strange effect. If these bejeweled waters were any indication, then the New World would prove more bizarre, more wonderful than she had dreamed possible.

Inés de Suárez found no trace of her husband in Venezuela, only vague rumors that he had gone to Peru. She decided to follow him there. In Venezuela she learned much about Peru, about its rich mines, fertile land, and dense population of Indians busy paying tribute to the conquering Spaniards. Peru was a powerful magnet that drew adventurers from Mexico, the Caribbean islands, and Panama, not to mention Spain itself. In 1538 Inés joined that hardy procession, traveling by ship to Panama, then by foot or horseback across the isthmus to the Pacific, first seen by

Europeans only twenty-five years earlier. There she again boarded ship, a rude vessel constructed in Panama or Nicaragua, and at last reached Peru.

A deep uneasiness pervaded Lima when Inés de Suárez arrived. Only two years earlier the Spanish had narrowly escaped defeat when Manco Inca Yupanqui besieged Cuzco and trapped Francisco Pizarro in Lima. Then, in the spring of 1538, war again broke out, not between Spanish and Incas but between the forces of Pizarro and those of Diego de Almagro, partners in conquest turned into enemies by greed and mistrust. Almagro suffered defeat, and in July Hernando Pizarro ordered him garroted in a Cuzco dungeon. Hundreds of Almagro supporters still roamed the Peruvian highlands spoiling for renewal of the conflict.

As a recent arrival and a woman, Inés de Suárez was not expected to take sides in such struggles. That was her only advantage, for her position in an armed camp placed her honor, if not her life, in constant jeopardy. Although many men treated her respectfully, others assumed she was easy prey. To them her answer was always "no"—a "no" accompanied by the glint of a polished steel dagger and, if need be, by a timely call for help. Inés was not flattered by less than honorable attentions; she had not come to the New World to indulge some rowdy soldier's lust. As a married woman descended from a family of some standing in her native Plasencia, her sights were set high. Like other Spaniards from Extremadura Province (Pizarro himself among them) who came to win wealth and glory through conquest, Inés hoped to have a share in the riches of Peru. She hoped to find her husband well established, perhaps already an *encomendero* or a respected captain of Pizarro, a leader of men. The men who approached her were brushed aside like minor irritants as she went on her way to far better things.

In Lima Inés learned that her husband had last been heard of in Cuzco, where he had perhaps helped defend that large, wealthy city first from Manco Inca's warriors and then from Almagro's forces. Realizing that she would never have a moment's peace until she found him, Inés decided to travel the six hundred miles to the Incan capital. Sometime in 1539 she reached that high, mountain-ringed city and discovered that she was a widow. Her husband had died after the siege of Cuzco, and all Inés had to show for her months of travel was the confirmation of her widowhood.

The *cabildo*, or town council, of Cuzco recognized the services of Inés's dead husband by awarding her a small dwelling and a few Indians to provide a modest income. This was hardly the fortune she desired, but Inés was confident that she could soon improve her position. She displayed an independence of spirit that few could equal. Eager for hard work, even the manual sort so despised by Spanish *hidalgos*, or aristocrats, ambitious and highly practical, Inés was spurred to action by bad luck and disappointment. She settled into her new home with some pleasure, for she relished the chance to set up a kitchen of her own and to raise a few chickens and sheep, perhaps a pair of goats and pigs. For the first time in two years, she enjoyed wholesome, carefully prepared food. Unwilling to depend on her Indians to support her, she established herself as a nurse and soon found great demand for her services. Cuzco was almost bereft of European-style medical care, and while native medicines and Indian women skilled in their application were available, the Spanish mistrusted them and tended to label indigenous cures as witchcraft. Inés trained her Indian servants, or *yanaconas*, to help her and soon had a thriving business dispensing first aid and, if all else failed, consolation to the ill and wounded.

Although her life had improved considerably since the days of hard travel, Inés still was very vulnerable. A woman who hoped to be reunited with her husband could defend herself in his name, but a widow had only her own strength, moral and physical, to protect her. The little dagger continued to be her faithful companion. She kept it polished and wore it conspicuously at her waist to discourage men who understood violence far better than pleas of the defenseless. Inés was able to convince most suitors of her lack of interest. Others she simply avoided by never going out alone during the day and staying at home after dark. But among the multitude of adventurers who roamed Cuzco was a certain Fernán Núñez who was not so easily put off. Although she rebuffed him at every opportunity, he refused to admit defeat. Late one night, when most people were already in bed, windows securely shuttered against the cold mountain air, Núñez and a pair of servants approached Inés's little house. They banged on the door and she, accustomed to late-night visitors in search of first aid, moved sleepily to open it. By the time she realized who waited in the shadowy street, it was too late. The three men barged through the door, slamming it shut behind them. While Núñez watched, his lackeys seized Inés and tried to overpower her. Defending herself with fingernails and teeth, she struggled against their superior strength.

Soon her cries were heard and the door flew open again. There in the doorway stood an elegantly dressed man of military bearing who glanced around the room and barked a command to his companions outside. The odds suddenly reversed. Núñez's henchmen released Inés and retreated awkwardly through the gathering crowd. In spite of her rage and excitement, Inés recognized her rescuer. He was Pedro de Valdivia, Pizarro's famous lieutenant, hero of the recent battle against Almagro's forces. For a moment Valdivia gazed at Inés, noted the long, chestnut hair hanging loosely over her shoulders, glanced at the simple white nightgown that modestly outlined her slender body, and then scanned her face with its haughty Spanish nose and darkly luminous eyes. His chivalrous instincts fully aroused, Valdivia turned on Núñez and promised that Núñez would pay with his life should he so much as look at Señora de Suárez again.

Perhaps the first thing Inés noticed about Pedro de Valdivia in the days following their late-night encounter was the ease with which he imposed his will on friend and foe. He was a natural leader, equally adept at persuasion and command. It was logical that she, so vulnerable, was attracted to that strength. For the first time since her marriage, Inés de Suárez began to think favorably of a man—one whose position, bearing, and gentlemanly manners all recommended him. And Valdivia was more than ready to return the favor. Like Fernando Cortés, Valdivia was at heart a lusty soldier, as fond of women as he was of adventure. The warm and grateful glances of a beautiful Spanish woman, that rarest of creatures, were not things to be taken lightly. The initial attraction was soon strengthened by respect. Inés, like Valdivia, was descended from a noble family of rural

Spain. And, again like Valdivia, she boasted great courage and independence of spirit. Inés and Valdivia were well matched, and it was only a matter of time before their relationship became an intimate one.

Only one problem disturbed the liaison of Inés de Suárez and Pedro de Valdivia—Valdivia was married, eternally bound by holy sacrament to Marina Ortiz de Gaete, whom he had left behind in Spain almost five years before. His marriage, like that of Inés, was childless. Although he stayed in touch with his wife and sent her money, Valdivia was not eager to send for her, and she was justifiably reluctant to leave home for the dangers and uncertainties of the New World.

Pedro and Inés were in a difficult position. Had Valdivia been free, they would probably have married. Since he was not, they decided to ignore the inflexible rules governing such matters, although it meant Inés's reputation would suffer irreparable damage. They hoped that somehow Valdivia's constancy and protection would shield her from unpleasantness, for he was without doubt one of the richest men in Cuzco. So valuable had been his support of Francisco Pizarro in the mortal struggle with Almagro that only a few months earlier Pizarro gave him the right to exploit the entire Canela Valley, its Indian population, and the Porco mines as a reward. The estate was more than enough to make three men rich, and it rivaled Pizarro's own holdings in wealth. The income Valdivia could expect to earn from his *encomienda* amounted to almost half a million pesos a year, perhaps more.

A few months as landowner and overlord were sufficient to convince Pedro and Inés that luxurious monotony was no less boring than the penurious monotony both had experienced in Spain. Valdivia protested that he had not come to the New World to fight for a mere five years, then hang up his sword and retire. Surely that great continent had room for one more conquistador of the stature of Fernando Cortés, of Francisco Pizarro, of Jiménez de Quesada. Never did Valdivia doubt that given lands to conquer and obstacles to overcome he could join that select company. And if the fire of conquest raged unchecked in Valdivia's veins, Inés was no less alert to the call of adventure. Both were ambitious on a grand scale. Mere wealth could not satisfy them, so they searched for a new kingdom to conquer and chose at last the untamed lands to the south: Chile.

When Francisco Pizarro heard that Valdivia wanted to lead an expedition to Chile, he was dumbfounded. It was impossible to understand why Valdivia should abandon holdings equal to Pizarro's own and devote himself to so risky an undertaking. Several years earlier Diego de Almagro, with ample money and five hundred men, had tried and failed to conquer Chile. The native population—the Picunches, Mapuches (or Araucanians as they came to be called), and the Huilliches—had taken courage from Almagro's failure and was not likely to submit easily to a second expeditionary force. For these and other reasons, Chile was the least promising of all the regions to be claimed for the glory of King Carlos V.

In April of 1539 Pizarro was at last persuaded to let Valdivia attempt the conquest of lands lying between the Copiapó River and the Straits of Magellan. With the grant came a series of problems that Valdivia later described in a letter to the king:

> When the Marquis Don Francisco Pizarro gave me this under-
> taking, there was no one willing to come to this region [Chile], and
> those who were most reluctant were those who accompanied Com-
> mander Don Diego de Almagro, and once they abandoned it,
> [Chile] became so infamous that they avoided it like the plague;
> and even many people who thought well of me, and who were
> taken to be sane, began to doubt my sanity when they saw me
> spend my income on an undertaking so far from Peru.

But Valdivia seemed to take courage from adversity. He was unruffled by the reluctance of investors to take a chance on the venture, and he was unconcerned that scarcely seven soldiers planned to leave Cuzco with him in January 1540. He believed that more soldiers, drawn especially from the defeated Almagro faction, would join him as the expedition moved slowly south.

Inés was not quite so confident. Indeed, for a time she feared she might be left behind altogether. As the only woman and, it was whispered, his mistress, Inés was the object of increasing gossip. In order to silence the malicious rumors, Valdivia asked

Francisco Pizarro to grant her a license to accompany the expedition as a *criada,* a domestic servant and nurse, who would oversee the Indian carriers and manage Valdivia's domestic affairs. Inés would go not as Valdivia's favorite but in an official capacity, as a legitimate and indispensable member of the expedition.

A few months before their departure, an obstacle far more serious than any other appeared in the person of Pedro Sancho de Hoz. An untrustworthy character, a former secretary to Pizarro in the early years of conquest, Sancho de Hoz returned from a trip to Spain with a document from Carlos V purportedly giving him the right to conquer Chile. Although Pizarro had never learned to read, he soon discovered that the king had given Sancho permission to make an exploratory expedition by sea down the coast of Chile as well as certain rights to territory south of the Straits of Magellan. There was no legal conflict between Valdivia's commission and Sancho's. But Pizarro feared that Sancho de Hoz's supporters in Spain might cause trouble at court if his unfounded claims to a piece of Valdivia's expedition were not respected. Therefore, on December 28, 1539, Pizarro called both men to his house, where they signed a binding agreement. Valdivia would lead the expedition to Chile as already planned, and Sancho de Hoz would become a partner in the undertaking by providing within four months a number of horses and two shiploads of equipment. Valdivia lost no sleep over the contract, but Inés worried about Sancho, whose opportunistic character she read so clearly.

There was little time even for worry in the last days before leaving Cuzco. A thousand Indian servants—*yanaconas*—were assembled to carry supplies for the pitifully small force, for neither Spanish soldiers nor their precious horses could be expected to carry baggage. Inés saw to it that chickens, goats, and pigs were gathered for the journey, that seeds and grain were carefully packed, and that food and remedies were in good supply. After all, the expedition was not merely one of conquest but one of settlement. Valdivia and Inés hoped to build a kingdom, establish cities, and attract Europeans to populate the countryside. Wealth and conquest were not the only elements in their ambition; settlement on a grand scale came first. The seeds and livestock were almost as important as swords and guns, for the former would feed settlers and their descendants long after—so Inés hoped—arms had become unnecessary.

Valdivia had been correct in his belief that Almagro's discredited supporters would join him. Realizing that they would never be welcome in Pizarro's Peru, the *almagristas* were forced to seek their fortunes in Chile under Valdivia's command. In the first days a number of men joined the group, each with his own servants and supplies. But by April 1540, after four months on the road, Valdivia's expedition had grown to only twenty men. Further progress was impossible without reinforcements, so the expedition halted in Tarapacá in the hope that more men would come to join them.

At last the long-awaited soldiers arrived: first a group of sixteen, then a force of seventy men loosely organized under Francisco de Villagra. The new arrivals transformed Valdivia's expedition. They swelled his forces to more than one hundred armed men, each of whom had invested his money and his future in the undertaking. Not one had received aid from Pizarro; the Spanish government of Carlos V, for whose glory the expedition had been undertaken, had contributed neither money nor encouragement. Each soldier was an independent adventurer who was prepared to finance his own way—by going into debt if necessary—and who hoped, by his daring, to win *qué comer*, roughly translated as "something to eat" and, by implication, wealth. The desired reward was tribute: tribute paid by Indian populations whose land produced abundant food and livestock, whose mines glittered with gold and silver, and whose labors would produce wealth effortlessly for each *encomendero* and his descendants.

In May 1540 Valdivia and his expedition left Tarapacá and began the dreaded desert crossing. Between Bolivia and the Copiapó Valley lay the Atacama Desert, an endless stretch of sand and pebbles along Chile's northern coast. The region was virtually uninhabitable. Scorched by a blazing sun during the day and chilled by the night's cold, the expedition traveled four painful leagues a day. Grumbling was common among those free-spirited soldiers. On one occasion Inés warned Valdivia that a young soldier named Escobar was making trouble for his captain

Juan Guzmán. Fearing rebellion, Valdivia decided to make an example of Escobar and ordered him hung for disobedience. Pleas for clemency were ignored. The rope was placed around the terrified Spaniard's neck and then pulled taut. His body rose into the air, his face turned purple, eyes bulged. Then, as the last shuddering breath escaped the man's tortured throat, the rope snapped and he slumped gasping to the ground. Saved by the grace of God, Escobar was freed immediately and ordered to Spain, where he spent his remaining years as a monk. Idle complaints and hints of revolt were for a time effectively silenced.

Early in June the expedition stopped two days north of Atacama la Chica. Leaving chief of staff Pero Gómez in charge, Valdivia and ten soldiers continued on to Atacama la Grande to secure supplies for the expedition. There Valdivia met Francisco de Aguirre, Rodrigo de Quiroga, and some twenty-three men who had been awaiting the expedition for two months.

While Valdivia was away from camp, another addition, much less welcome, joined the expedition. Late at night, Inés was awakened by intruders in the tent she shared with Valdivia. Alarmed, she sat up and cried, "Who are you? What are you looking for?"

A voice answered, "Where is the captain?"

Inés, now fully awake, answered, "He's not here. What do you want of him? Who are you? Tell me who you are."

By that time, the guard was alerted and came to the tent bearing lights. Seeing that Valdivia was indeed absent, the intruder replied, "Señora, I am Pedro Sancho de Hoz."

Inés, seeing the sinister way in which Valdivia's long-awaited partner had chosen to arrive, was immediately suspicious—even more so when she noticed that Sancho and his friends carried daggers in their boot tops. But she said only, "Now, sir, is this how a man like yourself enters someone else's house? It seems strange to me!"

"As I am the captain's servant," answered Sancho, "Señora should not be surprised."

Inés decided to let the matter drop and, after conferring privately with Pero Gómez, sent for Valdivia. Then she ordered supper for the men to keep them from taking flight before Valdivia could return, and the next morning the expedition moved on as usual. Sancho soon confirmed Inés's suspicions of the night before. Seeking out the most dissatisfied members of the expedition, he claimed to be its true leader and promised land, Indians, and special rewards should the men switch their allegiance to him. Revolt was squelched when Valdivia and the new reinforcements arrived the next day. Valdivia followed Inés's lead and, hiding his true feelings, greeted Sancho de Hoz with warmth. But as soon as the expedition arrived in Atacama la Grande, he had Sancho and his accomplices seized and thrown into jail. The truth behind their midnight arrival—for they had plotted to murder Valdivia as he slept—was soon revealed. A gallows was built in the main square, but Valdivia had little desire to hang a man whose friends at court might cause him trouble. So he agreed to banish three of the plotters to Peru and to allow Sancho de Hoz and another to remain with the expedition. Sancho was kept under guard until August 1540, when he signed documents releasing Valdivia from their partnership and renouncing his claim to the territory of Chile. Sancho de Hoz would continue on the expedition, no longer enjoying any claim to partnership in it.

After the expedition left Atacama la Grande, they experienced the desert in all its harsh intensity. What little food was normally to be found there had been hidden or destroyed by Indians hoping to discourage the Spanish from continuing south. Supplies ran disastrously low. Hunger and thirst threatened the expedition with slow death. Inés discovered that certain parts of the desert produced an edible cactus called *tuna*, or prickly pear. The *tuna* protected them from thirst for a while, but soon even that red, watery desert fruit grew scarce. Finally, one night after camp was set up, Mass had to be suspended because the faithful, their tongues leaden with thirst, were unable to speak the necessary responses. At that moment, sensing the despair around her, Inés called some *yanaconas* to her and ordered them to begin digging in the dry desert sand at her feet. Down they dug, each shovelful as dry as the first. Then several feet down, the sand seemed to turn darker and heavier. A few more feet and hoarse cheers rose from the ragged crowd. Pure, cool water bubbled from the sand. By some incredible coincidence, or by a miracle, Inés had found a freshwater spring deep in the Atacama Desert—not a paltry one, but the source of enough water to satisfy the *yanaconas*, soldiers, horses, and even the livestock. The spring was called Jagüey Inés, Inés's Pool, and its timely discovery spared the solitary expedition miserable defeat.

Progress through the desert was marked by brief skirmishes with Indians. Once the desert was behind them, however, Indian attacks became more frequent, and the Spanish were forced to maintain a constant alert as they moved through the northernmost reaches of the lands they would soon conquer. Confronted by bands of warriors at narrow passes, fighting pitched battles every time a detachment scouted territory ahead, harassed by ambushes, the Spaniards could proceed only because of their horses and the immense superiority of their arms and armor. As they approached the Mapocho Valley, Valdivia realized that the time had come to found a settlement. After eleven months of deprivation and threatening encounters with the desert and hostile warriors, his exhausted forces clamored for the *qué comer*, the rewards they had come so far to win.

The valley of the Mapocho River was ideal for their needs. It boasted rich soil, a large population of Indians, and a system of irrigation that the Picunche Indians had built to carry water from the Mapocho to lush green fields up and down the valley. Fresh from spring rains, with crops coaxed into extravagant growth by the warm December sun, the valley offered blessed relief to the homeless, exhausted Spaniards. Their new city, Santiago del Nuevo Extremo, was founded on February 12, 1541, between two forks of the Mapocho River. The one-eyed soldier Pedro de Gamboa, Chile's first surveyor, carefully laid out the city according to Carlos V's instructions. A plaza was staked out first, and streets extended from it at right angles in a grid pattern. Each of the 126 blocks was a perfect square, 350 feet on a side, divided into four corner lots. It was to be many years before the five hundred original lots were occupied.

The Picunches, hiding their distrust of that handful of foreigners, worked with them to build the new city. Wood-frame houses with straw roofs rose quickly on street corners. Around the plaza foundations for more ambitious structures were laid: a cathedral on the west; government buildings, a jail, and the residences of Valdivia and his officers on the north, south, and east. These buildings were built of stone and adobe and furnished with chairs, tables, and cots of rough-hewn wood.

While Santiago was still little more than a military camp, Valdivia appointed a town council, Chile's first *cabildo*. By setting up that municipal body, Valdivia in no way intended to lessen his own absolute power. Instead, he hoped to share responsibility for his actions with members of the *cabildo* without giving them any real authority. The *cabildo*'s subservience to Valdivia was obvious to everyone in the small community and seemed quite proper to most. Those who wanted some action taken on their behalf knew they must persuade Valdivia before presenting their requests to the *cabildo*. The requests were many. In Santiago's first decade, no matter was too trifling to escape attention. Even prices were fixed, so demand for commodities and services—food, horseshoes, tailoring, and so on—would not drive prices to scandalous heights. But Valdivia could not be equally disposed to the needs of everyone, and those who sought a favorable response soon learned to approach him through his most trusted adviser, Inés de Suárez.

Inés had become adept at reading the pulse of the colony. She was in close touch with the *yanaconas*, with the men whose wounds and illnesses she treated, and, above all, with Pedro de Valdivia's interests as leader of the colony. Valdivia trusted her judgment, her infallible common sense, and listened to her opinion on many matters. She, in turn, relished her role as go-between. When petitioners turned to her for help in winning Valdivia's favor, she would set up an informal meeting with Valdivia after dinner. Sometimes, if the night air was cool, Valdivia and Inés would retreat to the comfort of their bedroom while their guests, perched on chairs around the bed, pressed Valdivia for support. Successful petitioners often expressed their gratitude by giving Inés gifts. Although she felt her actions benefited the colony as a whole, there were those who resented her influence.

From the first, Valdivia was eager to find favor for his infant colony at the distant court of Carlos V. Of course, nothing ensured a colony's favor at court so much as gold. Fertility of soil, a com-

fortable climate, and abundant livestock meant nothing to the
king. What he desperately needed was money—gold and silver to
carry on his constant military campaigns in Europe. Valdivia understood this, and as a loyal servant, he set out to satisfy that
need. After a series of military successes in the Aconcagua Valley,
the Spanish learned the location of the Marga-Marga gold mines,
the same mines that had produced tribute for the Incas long before the Spaniards arrived. Under the direction of two mining experts who commanded a labor force of twelve hundred male Indians, gold for Carlos V began to trickle from the mines. Not far
from Marga-Marga, on the beach of Concón, shipbuilders went to
work on a vessel to carry the king's share of Chile's wealth to
Peru.

The general happiness caused by discovery of the mines and
construction of the first ship was soon darkened by tragedy. In
August 1541 an Indian attack reduced the ship to blackened,
smoking timbers and took the lives of thirteen Spaniards and numerous Indian mine workers. Only one Spaniard and a black
slave escaped the slaughter. The attack was a warning of things to
come. The wily Michimalongo, a *cacique* of the Aconcagua Valley, assembled a huge force of warriors in the Mapocho Valley
and waited for a propitious moment to attack Santiago. That moment was not long in coming. In early September Valdivia, accompanied by close to ninety horsemen, left the city in order to
subdue an encampment of Indians to the south. Remaining behind to guard Santiago were Alonso de Monroy, thirty-two
horsemen, less than twenty infantrymen, the *yanaconas*, and Inés
de Suárez.

Long before dawn on September 11, the city was awakened
by desperate cries from the sentries. An immense number of warriors, nearly ten thousand in all, was creeping up on all sides,
prepared to slaughter the foreigners as they slept. The Spaniards
and loyal *yanaconas* armed themselves and faced the attack. All
day Michimalongo's divisions came, attacking in waves while
the Spaniards, resisting fatigue, pain, and fear, fought desperately. Inés and her servants moved back and forth along the lines
of battle with food, water, and first aid for men and horses alike.
Inés watched with mounting concern as the vastly outnumbered

defenders were slowly beaten back toward the central plaza. As the sun sank in the sky, Indian warriors threw torches on the wood and straw houses of Santiago, burned stores of food and utensils, and destroyed the carefully tended livestock. Inés surveyed the situation. Two Spanish soldiers and hundreds of *yanaconas* lay dead. Almost no one—not even Pedro Sancho de Hoz, who had fought valiantly with the rest—had escaped injury. Of the outstanding fighters, Alonso de Monroy, Francisco de Aguirre, and Rodrigo de Quiroga were seriously wounded, and an overwhelming exhaustion sapped the defenders' strength.

But in the center of the plaza, trapped in a makeshift stockade, were seven Indian *caciques* who had been captured several days earlier. Inés ran to Alonso de Monroy and proposed a plan: all seven prisoners should be decapitated at once and their heads tossed at the attacking forces as the Spaniards followed with one last cavalry charge. Monroy vigorously opposed the plan. Those captive chiefs, he argued, were their only hope for bargaining with Michimalongo. Other officers too opposed Inés's plan. But realizing the desperate nature of their situation, and how unlikely it was that any of them would remain alive long enough to bargain, Inés finally persuaded them to support her. As the light began to fade and the red flames of Santiago's burning houses flickered against the sky, Inés went to the stockade and, shouting over the war cries of the attackers, ordered the guards to behead all seven imprisoned chiefs. Seeing that no one was willing to start the grisly work, Inés grasped a sword and with strength born of necessity beheaded the first captive. She was joined in the butchery by several others, and the sodden heads soon hurtled through the air, thudding at the very feet of the attackers. Those who were able, Inés among them, mounted their horses and rode out for the final desperate attack.

The plan succeeded, the Indians retreated in sudden confusion. But four days later, when Valdivia returned to Santiago, he found nothing but cinders and ashes where his city had stood. The few houses that had escaped the flames were virtual hospitals, and wounded horses, nursed as lovingly as the men, rested around the perimeter of the plaza. Turning to Inés for an account, Valdivia watched as she showed him all that remained of their livestock and seed: two young sows and a boar, a hen and a rooster that Inés herself had saved, and two handfuls of wheat. All their tools, their clothing, food supplies, and the seeds stored carefully for sowing in October were destroyed. They had only the clothes they wore and the arms they carried to protect them from the elements and further attacks.

For the next two years Santiago was scarcely more than an armed camp. Bands of soldiers rode through the surrounding countryside day and night, patrolling for Indians and discouraging attack. The wheat was planted and tended with untiring care. Adobe houses rose over the ashes, and Valdivia began the construction of a thick adobe wall that soon formed a fortress four hundred feet square in the center of the city. Much of the work was done by the long-suffering *yanaconas:* "They were," said Valdivia, "our very life." The colonists survived at first on meal made from a variety of oat that grew wild in the valley. Several of the hungry Spaniards, it was rumored, actually ate cicadas in an effort to quell their insistent hunger. Most, however, tried to be content with coarsely milled grain. By early 1542 Valdivia realized that he must take action to get needed supplies and reinforcements from Peru. Calling on the citizens of Santiago to contribute their wealth to the common good, Valdivia was able to send Alonso de Monroy and five others on the long and dangerous journey. With them went the best horses, a quantity of gold, and the hopes of the entire colony. They were not seen or heard from for almost two years.

During those long months of isolation and constant vigilance, Santiago was gradually pulled together. Under Inés's careful husbandry the livestock reproduced almost miraculously so that four years later Valdivia bragged of ten thousand pigs and chickens as numerous as blades of grass. The fertile soil of the valley produced more wheat than anyone had dared expect and, although most of December's crop was saved for seed, by winter Santiago had bread once again. But many commodities could not be produced in the valley, even by that resourceful band. Mass had to be suspended for lack of wine. Clothing was of the most elementary sort, made of rags and animal skins, and Inés, Valdivia, and the others suffered almost as much from the lack of decent clothing as they did from hunger. Although some people owned money and gold, very little could be bought to satisfy the colonists' desire for a touch of luxury to alleviate the grinding labor and constant dangers of their lives.

Early in the year after Santiago burned, Valdivia and the *cabildo* began the troublesome process of *repartimiento:* assigning groups of Indians to deserving members of the expedition. They knew next to nothing about inhabited regions in central Chile. No one knew how many Indians lived along the Mapocho River or in other major valleys; no one could guess how long it would be until Spaniards could live in peace among the indigenous people of Chile. Still the men clamored for some reward for their services, and the process of *repartimiento* began. Some sixty men and Inés de Suárez received *repartimientos* in early 1542. The Indian population lived between the Copiapó Valley in the north and the Maule River in the south and were identified with the name of a *cacique* where it was known. It was Valdivia who decided which members of the expedition were most deserving of reward, and he had a tendency to reward his most trusted officers and friends, Inés among them, with the choice *encomiendas* near Santiago. Although the Spanish now considered themselves lords of the land and its indigenous population, the grim reality of their position remained unchanged: they lived in a besieged city, far from help, surrounded by Indians who preferred to die in battle rather than pay tribute.

At last, in September 1543, a ship arrived from Peru loaded with iron goods, military supplies, and, most important, clothing. It brought news as well—news of the new governor of Peru, Vaca de Castro, and news of Alonso de Monroy's incredible journey in search of help for the suffering colonists. Lines of supply were finally opened between Chile and Peru. Father Rodrigo González said Mass for the first time in four months, and tailors worked into the night to satisfy the demand for fine new clothes. In December a total of seventy men lead by Monroy began to arrive in small groups, intimidating Indian divisions camped close to Santiago and driving them several leagues from the city.

Peace, a new experience for the hardy citizens of Santiago, settled upon the city. Life was still not what it was in most other settlements of the viceroyalty of Peru. Only one Spanish woman resided there, though many men had begun *mestizo* families with their *yanacona* mistresses. In fact, not one marriage between a Spanish man and woman had yet taken place, nor had a properly married couple yet established a household. Nevertheless, with the urgent problems of food and security solved for the moment, the city turned to secondary pursuits. In Inés's case it was a pursuit of knowledge. She was by turns teacher and student, teaching the catechism and Spanish customs to the *yanaconas* and daughters of local *caciques,* and in less busy moments learning to read and write under Father Rodrigo's tutoring.

For the first time in many years Inés and Valdivia indulged their taste for elegant clothing, cut from bolts of expensive cloth brought by sea from Peru. Inés replaced her worn, patched skirts and plain shawl with dresses of rich fabrics embroidered with gold and silver threads. Her sleeves hung in perfect folds from the shoulder, and a multicolored shawl of the lightest wool protected against the chill. Touches of white lace graced her throat, and on Sundays her high headdress was draped with a delicate mantilla. Valdivia was not to be outdone. When not arrayed in armor of burnished steel, he dressed impeccably in rich velvet doublet and knee breeches, a long, heavy cloak, and polished boots of the softest leather. A high lace ruff, starched to a martial stiffness, pressed up against his chin. He kept his hair short but, as if to compensate for its severity, carefully cultivated his narrow goatee and a luxurious moustache that curled up at each end. To celebrate their new plumage, Inés and Valdivia encouraged a festive spirit among the citizens of Santiago by appearing at public fiestas, entertaining friends, and attending musical events with some frequency. Those who wondered at times whether Inés's place in Valdivia's affections was less secure than before only had to witness the way their eyes met over their wine goblets or to hear them murmur "I drink to thee" as they lifted their glasses.

During those years the energies of the colony were absorbed in expeditions to the south and settlement in the north. Valdivia and his lieutenants were confident of success in their plans for expansion. Familiar with the conquests of Mexico and Peru, they expected the Indians of Chile to resist for a time, perhaps even several years, and then give in to the Spaniards' superior military strength. This was, in fact, the case in the regions already settled by them. Even the indefatigable Michimalongo and his Picunche warriors saw the futility of further resistance and became stalwart supporters of Valdivia.

But far to the south, between the Itata and Tolten Rivers, lived a group of Indians, the Araucanians, who were more ferocious than any other tribe in the Americas, save perhaps the Carib and the Apache. Relatively recent arrivals themselves, possibly immigrants from the pampas of Argentina, they carved out a small area between the Picunche lands to the north and those of the Huilliches to the south. Not until February 1546 did Valdivia and sixty heavily armed horsemen first engage the Araucanians. Although they routed them twice in two days, the Spanish prudently left the region under cover of night, leaving brightly blazing campfires to hide their retreat. This incident was the first skirmish in a long war that was to be waged by ten successive generations of Araucanians over a span of three hundred years. The intensity of the war and its incredible duration made it unique in world history. Unfortunately, Valdivia did not take full measure of the Araucanians, and he consistently underestimated their intelligence and fighting ability, a mistake for which he later paid with his life.

After his return to Santiago, Valdivia decided to take action on mounting complaints about the *repartimientos* that had been made four years earlier. He agreed that there were many *encomenderos* and too few Indians to make their holdings profitable. Valdivia thought the matter over for nearly three weeks, consulting extensively with Jerónimo de Alderete and Inés de Suárez. Finally he reduced the number of *repartimientos* from sixty to thirty-two, preserving intact the rights of his advisers and intimates, and in several cases markedly improving them. He realized that the arbitrarily dispossessed *encomenderos* would be irate, but to their outraged demands for fair treatment Valdivia reacted with mounting impatience. It was *his* colony, after all, and he had acted in everyone's best interests. Those who lost out this time would receive rich *encomiendas* in the well-populated but still unsettled south. But several men rejected this promise and again approached Valdivia. Irritated by their insistence, he threatened to hang them if they didn't keep their peace.

If his handling of the *repartimientos* did little to endear Valdivia to the citizens of Santiago, his bizarre actions of December 1547 made him even less popular. Late that year he decided to aid the king's chief representative to strife-torn Peru and to lobby for the governorship of Chile. But Valdivia could not afford to underwrite such a voyage himself, and the colonists would never have donated the large sums he needed. Finally, Valdivia announced that Jerónimo de Alderete would sail to Spain by way of Peru in order to represent Chilean interests at the court of Carlos V. He then told the citizens of Santiago that for the first time anyone who wished to leave Chile could do so. Sixteen men made plans to sail with Alderete, some hoping to buy goods in Peru for profitable resale in Chile, others expecting to sail home to Spain. They liquidated all their holdings, disposed of household goods, and collected as much gold and money as possible from business partners and friends.

On December 6, after their possessions were loaded aboard the ship anchored in Valparaíso harbor, the men returned to shore for a banquet hosted by Pedro de Valdivia. During a long address, Valdivia wished them all well and with misty eyes reminded them of the years of sacrifice and hardship they had shared. He hoped they would speak well of him wherever they went and asked each of them to declare before the notary there present how much money he was carrying so that an account of Chile's wealth could be kept. Warmed by Valdivia's kind words and the meal they had just eaten, the prospective travelers gathered around the notary, as Valdivia moved casually toward a rowboat that waited on the beach. When their captain leapt into the boat the men suddenly realized what was afoot. Valdivia intended to take the ship and their money to Peru, leaving them behind homeless and destitute. A few of the reluctant donors jumped in the water and tried to swim after the rowboat but were clubbed when they got too near. The rest saw that pursuit was hopeless and remained on shore shouting curses at the receding boat.

Valdivia left Francisco de Villagra in charge of the colony as its lieutenant governor. Both men feared trouble as soon as word of Valdivia's trick reached Santiago, so Villagra rode back to the capital that same day. Their fears were well founded. Within twenty-four hours a revolt led by Pedro Sancho de Hoz boiled to the surface—a revolt so widespread that dozens of men, many of them previously above suspicion, were implicated. Quick action by Villagra squelched it, and the ringleaders were put to death. Sancho de Hoz, who had been pardoned so many times, was hanged while Pedro de Valdivia's ship still rode at anchor in Valparaíso Bay.

What Inés de Suárez thought of Valdivia's absence is not known, but she probably was aware of his plans and even urged him to go. The wait was nonetheless onerous. They had endured so much danger and adventure together that her passive role must have been hard to bear. News trickled slowly from Peru, and she welcomed each bit of information about his odyssey. Inés learned, months after it happened, that Valdivia had arrived safely at Callao in mid-January; that he had immediately taken charge of the king's forces and led them in routing the last Pizarro rebellion in April. She rejoiced when she heard that Valdivia had finally been named His Majesty's governor and captain-general of Chile and confidently awaited his triumphant return.

But formal accusations of misgovernment, drawn up by his numerous enemies in Santiago, followed Valdivia to Peru and formed the basis of judicial proceedings to determine whether he was fit to govern Chile. Some fifty-eight charges of misconduct were considered—charges that included his handling of the *repartimientos*, his questionable methods of fund raising, and, not least, his irregular relations with Inés de Suárez. Valdivia defended himself on each count. Those who had lost their first *repartimientos*, he protested, would soon receive far richer grants in Chile's populous south. All moneys that had been taken from Santiago's citizens were in reality debts that would be repaid by Valdivia himself. And the accusations having to do with Inés de Suárez were nothing but malicious rumors. He explained that she went to Chile by license of Don Francisco Pizarro and was much loved by the people for her good deeds. True, she lived in his house, but there was nothing wrong in that because Doña Inés was his *criada*, his servant. After almost a month of deliberations Valdivia was declared innocent of wrongdoing on all but one count. He was reaffirmed as governor and permitted to return to Chile, but in his hand he carried a document that read:

> It is ordered that Pedro de Valdivia, His Majesty's governor and captain-general of the provinces of Chile, cease immodest relations with Inés Suárez; that he not live with her in a single house, nor enter nor stay with her in a suspicious place; that from now on, all suspicion of carnal relations between them be put to rest; and that, within the first six months after his arrival in the city of Santiago of the province of Chile, she be married or sent to these provinces of Peru, where she may reside, or that she go to Spain or other places, wherever she may choose.

Word of the sentence reached Inés sometime in December 1548. She reacted first with fury. How dare they bandy her name about in such a way! How dare they intrude in her private affairs! Hadn't every man she knew been guilty at one time or another of "immodest relations"? Why should she bear the full weight of the sentence and perhaps suffer banishment when Valdivia shared equally in their illicit love? Later, when she was able to contemplate her fate more calmly, Inés recognized the sentence for what it was: a sop thrown to Valdivia's enemies by his powerful supporters. It was some time, however, before she could think clearly about her own future. When that moment came she was certain of one thing: she could never leave Chile. Santiago was her home. She was one of its leading citizens and one of its wealthiest as well. In Peru she was infamous; in Spain she was nobody. Far better that she should lose Valdivia forever than accept banishment.

By the time Valdivia's ship arrived in Valparaíso Bay, Inés had decided on an acceptable course of action. Within a short time she married Rodrigo de Quiroga, one of Valdivia's outstanding captains and a close friend of both Inés and the governor. By so doing she regained the respectability she had sacrificed ten years earlier and incidentally established one of the wealthiest households in all Chile.

Valdivia and Inés seemed to have settled into a comfortable sort of friendship. In January 1550 he gave Inés some land on Cerro Blanco Hill so that she could build and maintain the Church of Our Lady of Monserrate. Rumor had it that he soon found a replacement for Inés among the Spanish women who had come with him from Peru. But two years later, bowing to an explicit command from the king, he liquidated several of his holdings and sent for his wife, Doña Marina, who still languished in faroff Spain. He never lived to see her, for in December 1553 he became the most important casualty of the Araucanian Wars.

In a sense Inés suffered less at Valdivia's death than did Chile. She was by then quite independent of the governor. Not so the colony, which suffered through several years without a legitimate leader. Calamity seemed to feed on itself: insecurity in government was compounded by three years of drought and savage epidemics. The Araucanian wars raged unabated, and the Spaniards' initial advantage evaporated when the Indians learned to fight on horseback with European weapons. But the will to impose Spanish ways on that alien land remained strong. Just as Inés had often taken the lead during the earliest years, so did she now lead the effort to superimpose Spanish culture on Chile.

In the last decades of her life, Inés de Suárez became the doyenne of Santiago's gradually increasing population, and every year she acted with greater piety and generosity. In 1558 she and Rodrigo de Quiroga established a Dominican chaplaincy at the hermitage of Our Lady of Monserrate, where Mass was said each Friday for the soul of Pedro de Valdivia. While her husband was away in Arauco and Tucumán and during his years as governor, Inés supported the church in its efforts to provide religious instruction to indigenous residents of Santiago and the new generation of *mestizo* children. Rodrigo de Quiroga's only child, his daughter Isabel, was herself a *mestiza*, born out of wedlock. Inés made sure that she did not reach adulthood unable to read and write as she, Inés, had, and in 1566, with Inés's support, Rodrigo de Quiroga recognized Isabel as his full and legitimate heir.

Valdivia's widow provided a sharp contrast to Inés in wealth and prestige. Doña Marina Ortiz de Gaete arrived from

Spain only months after Valdivia's death. Expecting to find herself a wealthy woman, she discovered with chagrin that Valdivia had left her debts of some 200,000 pesos for which she was responsible under law. In 1555 she received permission from the king to earn what income she could by sending Indians out to work as day laborers. But it was scarcely an easy existence, for in addition to her financial burdens, she suffered abuse at the hands of those who had been roughly treated by Valdivia. Inés tried to help Doña Marina from afar, fearing that Valdivia's legitimate wife would not welcome the attentions of his paramour, especially when that lady was a leading personality of the colony.

One day early in 1572 Inés de Suárez stepped through the iron gates of her house and, accompanied by the governor and a cluster of servants, walked slowly down the street and across La Cañada stream. She was dressed in black; a heavy mantilla covered her gray hair; and her shoulders were rounded with the weight of sixty-four years. As a small crowd gathered around her, Inés laid the cornerstone of Santiago's first permanent church building, the Church of San Francisco. The hands that had bound so many wounds, that had been bathed more than once in the blood of battle, now carried out the duty of philanthropist and local dignitary. The record shows that it was her last public act. When she died, Chile mourned its first lady's passing, oblivious of the controversy that had swirled about her decades earlier.

Succeeding generations of Chileans forgot Inés de Suárez the social arbiter of the early colony. The historic Inés was replaced by the heroic and scandalous mistress of Pedro de Valdivia. Yet to dwell solely on her role in that turbulent decade of conquest is to slight the greater significance of the woman. Like the cornerstone she laid near the end of her life, Inés de Suárez was one of the builders of early Hispanic Chile.

# III

# The Nun Ensign, 1592-1650?

L ATE IN THE sixteenth century America poured forth her treasure with an abandon that reshaped the economy of Spain and of Western Europe as well. The ingots of silver and gold, the pieces of eight and doubloons quickened the commercial pulse of Europe and helped usher in a new age of commerce and industry.

The New World was no less transformed by her wealth. Gold on the Caribbean coast of South America, rich silver mines in Mexico, and the fabulous silver lode of Potosí in Upper Peru produced cities fabled for the ostentation and excess of their inhabitants. Streets of these boom towns teemed with adventurers from all parts of Spain's far-flung kingdoms. Catalans, Italians, Flemings, Portuguese, Basques, and Greeks jostled and competed in an atmosphere of unfettered freedom. Fortunes were made in a day and lives lost overnight. It has been said that the privileged European population of frontier Spanish America offered "a wanton challenge to death born of sheer intoxication with life."

Women as well as men joined in the chase after riches, suffering all the same dangers in equal, and sometimes greater, measure. When gender proved a hindrance many simply disguised themselves as men. Records of the era yield many such examples. *The Annals of Potosí* chronicle the case of two maidens who for fourteen turbulent years traveled over Peru dressed as men, re-

turning home only at the point of death and announcing to incredulous relatives that they died chaste. The same source tells of the beautiful Doña Clara who, dressed as a soldier, fought beside her brother in the wars between Basques and Castilians. Only as the enemy prepared to behead her did she escape by revealing her identity.

No tale of unconventional womanhood can rival that of Catalina de Erauzo, a nun and a proud Basque. After she fled the convent, Catalina donned men's clothing and mingled with the vagabonds traveling Spain's highways. Making her way to America, she earned the esteem of her peers through sheer audacity and mastery of the martial arts. She was breveted ensign on the field of battle and later, when her true identity was discovered, became famous as the Nun Ensign.

The Nun Ensign's story is one of high adventure spanning an epic phase in the expansion of Iberian civilization. It also provides an unfolding microcosm of a rude society-in-flux. Because Catalina was Basque, she held regional loyalties far transcending her sense of "Spanish" citizenship. She and the many others from Spain's diverse empire sowed seeds of regionalism in an American soil already geographically conditioned to receive them.

Another theme running through Catalina's odyssey is that of ecclesiastical privilege and the related one of church-state conflict. Time and again Catalina sought and received religious sanctuary, thus escaping punishment by the secular arm of government. Often those granting sanctuary were her own Basque countrymen. Finally, when appeal for clerical intercession could not save the hot-blooded ensign from punishment by the secular state, Catalina played her unbeatable trump card: not only was she a woman and a nun, but, most incredibly, she was a virgin!

The history of Catalina de Erauzo arouses conflicting emotions: admiration for her rejection of a stereotype that frustrated her, amazement that she succeeded at the heroic masquerade, horror at her thirst for blood. Finally, one is bound to be a bit skeptical that she experienced all the adventures attributed to her in the sources, and one may wonder whether some details were not tailored to fit the picaresque convention that had by her day captured the Spanish imagination. But there can be no doubt that

Catalina the Nun Ensign lived; nor can it be disputed that she was one of the most remarkable women of her age.

Catalina de Erauzo was fifteen years old when she stole the key to the outer door of the convent. Her stern aunt, the mother superior of San Sebastián's Dominican Convent, had ordered her to bring the heavy ring of keys from her cell, and Catalina, realizing that freedom lay in possessing one of them, slipped it from the ring and dropped it into the deep pocket of her novice's habit. The dream of many long nights seemed suddenly possible, and the half-conceived plans of escape crystallized. From a blue wool overskirt she cut and sewed a pair of knee breeches and transformed a coarse green petticoat into a doublet with long sleeves. The remodeled clothes cost her a mere three days' work. On the third night Catalina put on her disguise and, without a moment's regret, cut off her long, black hair. The nun's habit that had confined her since earliest childhood lay abandoned on her cot. Scarcely daring to breathe, she opened the door to her cell and crept into the hall, then down the stairs to the side entryway. Turning the key in the high iron-hinged door, she opened it and, casting a wary eye at the moon riding high over the convent garden, made her way to the outer gate and at last stepped into the street beyond.

In those first few days of freedom, Catalina traveled south from San Sebastián, a provincial capital in the heart of Spain's Basque country. Her goal was Vitoria, another Basque city lying almost sixty miles inland. As she walked, she practiced the small gestures and forms of speech that went with her new identity, replacing the feminine words she had used all her life with masculine ones. Her body, free from the heavy skirts and tight bodice of her nun's habit, soon relaxed into the swinging stride of the long-distance traveler. By the time she arrived in Vitoria, her convent paleness had been burned away by the sun, and with it every trace of the femininity that had held her captive since birth. Longing for anonymity, she exchanged her illustrious Basque name for a more common one that was far less likely to betray her. Catalina de Erauzo y Pérez de Galarraga thus became Antonio Ramírez de Guzmán, a name as rootless as its new owner was determined to become.

Hunger was the first by-product of her new freedom. Little grew in the Basque countryside of early spring to satisfy her appetite, and by the time she approached Vitoria, her courage was much augmented by the demands of an empty stomach. On arrival, the new Antonio went directly to the home of a distant relative, Don Francisco de Cerralta. Her disguise easily protected her true identity, and for a few weeks she did odd jobs in the Cerralta household. Soon, however, the taste for trouble that had so exasperated the nuns of San Sebastián reappeared on a more ambitious scale. Tempted by her master's purse lying unguarded on a table, she seized it and took refuge on the open road.

The few weeks' success as Antonio Ramírez gave her confidence in the new role, and she traveled the highways of Spain with new boldness toward Valladolid, a city some 130 miles from Vitoria, close to the heart of the Iberian peninsula. In Valladolid she became a page in the household of the duke, Don Juan de Idiaquez, a member of Spain's highest nobility. Principal among her duties was to accompany the ladies of the house to Mass, the irony of which was not lost on her. For seven months Catalina lived in Valladolid, learning to be an adequate servant and demonstrating skill for seeking out trouble. She started arguments with the other servants and gambled away the nights in the servants' quarters. These tendencies, so alien to young ladies of that day, were quite appropriate in the duke's page, who was considered agreeably high-spirited. All was well, in fact, until Catalina's own father came to call on the duke. Fearful that she would be discovered, she stayed only to hear him tell the story of his daughter's escape from the convent.

Catalina was almost seventeen years old when she fled Valladolid. She was large-boned for a girl, athletic, strong, and gifted with an abundance of physical energy that had caused her many a problem in the close environment of the San Sebastián convent. But it was her Basque audacity, above all else, that kept her small hands and hairless face from becoming features that called her "masculinity" into question.

For two years Catalina wandered the Basque provinces of northern Spain. She stayed for a while in Bilbao, but soon got into a fight, injuring her opponent with a carefully thrown rock. Authorities jailed her for the month that it took the wound to heal.

Somehow she maintained her disguise during the days in prison —and fought back the impulse to gain release by confessing her sex. She realized too well that such a confession would lead her back to a prison of a different sort, constructed not of iron bars but of long, heavy skirts, endless household chores, and cloistered confinement. So she endured the ignominy of prison without revealing her strange secret to anyone.

Free once again, she journeyed almost one hundred miles to the city of Estella de Navarra. There she found employment as page to one Carlos de Arellano, in whose household she lived for almost two years. During that time she perfected a style that complemented her youthful good looks. Her original knee breeches and doublet were replaced by an elegant black suit trimmed in silver, high boots of crimson morocco leather, and a soft, broad-brimmed hat, bright red and adorned with a single black ostrich feather. The "handsome Antonio," dressed in that red and black costume, attracted the admiration of many a Spanish maiden. Catalina enjoyed their attentions and began to adopt a swagger, an exaggerated braggadocio, that fed on her natural boldness.

By 1610 she had lost herself in the life of the rogues and vagabonds who roamed the heart of Spain. Like the *pícaros* who peopled Spain's popular literature of that era, Catalina lived by her wits and paid homage only to her own freedom. The fraud she lived was her most prized possession, for it permitted her to shape a destiny totally different from the one prescribed by society. Most important, by dressing as a man, she could contemplate an active role in the greatest adventure of her day: the one to be had in Spain's New World colonies.

For a full century the New World had served as an escape valve for the Spanish population. Spain offered neither wealth nor honor to the average person, while the New World offered both to those with sufficient energy and endurance to fight for it. Simple adventurers escaping bonded servitude, second sons of noble families, friars and priests anxious to convert an entire continent to Christianity, and soldiers of fortune in search of a battle —these were the men who flocked to the New World. And with them, distinguished only by an accident of biology, went Catalina.

Her decision to leave Spain was easy to make. She could never be satisfied to spend her days as some nobleman's servant chafing against the limitations of a calcified social system. Then too, she had long heard stories of Basque youths who left for the New World and returned wealthy. Her brother Miguel de Erauzo, a dozen years her senior, had gone to the New World when Catalina was very small, and even her friend Friar Lope de Altolaguirre, chaplain of the San Sebastián convent, had abandoned his religious vows in favor of New World adventuring. Convinced that her future too lay in those outer fringes of Spain's empire, Catalina packed her things and took the road north to San Sebastián and the coast. There once again, she walked the streets of her childhood and entered the cool, dimly lit chapel of the Dominican convent, her plumed hat in one hand, a well-polished sword of Toledo steel swinging at her side. As Mass began she noticed a familiar, mantilla-clad head bowed a few feet from where she stood. Catalina recognized her mother, but Doña María glanced only briefly at her daughter and saw not a trace of the young novice who had run away three years before. All ties with her parents irrevocably cut, Catalina boarded ship and sailed down the coast to the great Spanish port of Sevilla. There, on Easter Monday, 1610, she boarded a second ship, sailed down the Guadalquivir River, through the marshy delta lowlands, and out into the broad Atlantic.

Catalina stayed with her ship, a galleon named the *Santa María*, until it reached Panama. There, having pocketed the purse of a careless passenger, she jumped ship, crossed the isthmus, and sailed south along the Pacific coast of South America. Her destination was Peru, the vast kingdom that reached from Quito and Nueva Granada in the north to Chile and Rio de la Plata in the south. From among the hundred Spanish cities of that great empire, Catalina chose the small coastal town of Paita, more than five hundred miles north of Lima.

Soon after her arrival she was employed as a shopkeeper by Juan de Urquiza, a Basque like Catalina and one of a small army of merchants and landowners who, blessed with characteristic Basque industriousness, were busy accumulating wealth throughout Peru. Catalina served her master well and was rewarded with two new suits, several Indian servants, and an allowance of three pesos a day. After a time, however, these physical comforts and the routine of minding the store for Urquiza began to bore her, and she became increasingly touchy and quick to pick a fight. Urquiza, misinterpreting the cause of his friend Antonio's restlessness, suggested in a fatherly manner that he court the lovely Beatriz de Cárdenas, a lady whose enthusiasm for romance Urquiza already knew well. Beatriz, a frequent visitor to the store, had often admired the masculine Antonio, while Catalina, seeing her own interest in Beatriz returned, became bolder in her advances, even accepting invitations to visit Beatriz at night.

As Catalina became tangled in the sticky web of love, she slipped into indiscretions of a different sort. One night at a local cantina, a man named Reyes pulled his chair in front of hers, and Catalina, her temper rising, ordered him to move. Words were exchanged and Reyes refused to budge. Furious, Catalina took her sword to the barber to be sharpened and then returned to confront Reyes. In the ensuing brawl, Catalina laid open Reyes's face and stabbed one of his friends for good measure.

Pleased with her first taste of armed combat and with the insignificant jail term that it earned her, she thirsted for further encounters. However, her success in the boudoir had just the opposite effect. As her lover Beatriz became more aggressive, Antonio became more reticent. At length Beatriz locked Antonio in her room, opening the door only after exacting a proposal of marriage. The delight of Beatriz was hardly shared by her fiance: Catalina was terrified. Romance was delightful, and flirtations were stimulating; even duels over the love of a beautiful woman were pleasant entertainment. But marriage was, to say the least, out of the question. Finally, in an act of charity that he was never fully to appreciate, Catalina's employer Urquiza sent her to open a shop in the walled city of Trujillo, 250 miles down the coast.

The transfer to Trujillo was a welcome release from the affectionate Beatriz, who was making wedding plans even as Catalina plotted her escape. Trujillo offered little peace, however, for Reyes and two companions soon followed Catalina, eager for revenge. In a matter of days the confrontation became unavoidable, forced to a head by universal obedience to a code of honor that claimed life itself as surety. As the brawl began, Catalina and a friend managed a good defense against the three men from Paita. Finally, urged on by the shouts of onlookers and her own excitement, she ran Reyes through with her sword. Companions of the dead man ran to local authorities and accused Catalina of murder, demanding that she be punished. But Trujillo's magistrate, Ordoño de Aguirre, was a sympathetic man. Like Catalina he was a Basque. He recognized the incident for what it was—an affair of honor—and permitted her to seek sanctuary in the cathedral of Trujillo. There, safe from civil authorities and from further revenge, Catalina sent word of her troubles to Urquiza, who washed his hands of her—although not before sending pocket money, two new suits, a letter of recommendation, and his best wishes.

Several weeks later, Catalina slipped out of Trujillo and traveled down the coast to Lima. At that time, and indeed throughout the ensuing century, Lima was the primary seat of government and center of trade for the entire South American continent. It boasted large, impressive buildings that housed the viceroy, the archbishop, and the continent's finest university. Fed by a constant flow of silver from the mines of Potosí, Lima was a plump and prosperous city, full of ostentation and vainglory, peopled by soldiers of fortune, professional bureaucrats, and grasping merchants.

Soon after arriving in Lima, Catalina presented her letter of recommendation to a businessman named Diego de Solarte, who hired her on the spot—and Solarte's daughter promptly fell in love with Antonio. For nine months Catalina worked for Solarte, barely enduring the boredom and confinement of city life. Convinced that Lima promised little more than another unwelcome betrothal, she let her thoughts turn to the possibility of new adventures. Had the nights not been sweetened by secret trysts with Solarte's daughter, it is doubtful that she would have suffered Lima's bourgeois society as long as she did. When word of his daughter's infatuation at last reached Solarte, he threw Catalina unceremoniously into the street and closed the door firmly behind her. With no reason and less desire to stay in Lima, Catalina persuaded some gambling companions to travel to Cuzco, where they could enlist as soldiers in the Indian wars of Chile.

When Catalina and her friends left Lima in early 1613, the Indian wars in Chile were a smoldering fire consuming the constant stream of soldiers sent from Peru. Only the roughest, most rootless of Spain's sons were drawn to that battlefield. Unlike Alto Peru, or Bolivia, the colony established by Pedro de Valdivia seventy-four years earlier offered neither silver nor easily exploited Indians. Chile had become an agricultural colony, and the irrigated valleys that spread out from Santiago supported vineyards and orchards, domestic animals, and crops of wheat, maize, and other grains. Chile's farms never contributed great wealth to the Spanish crown. In fact, the colony had a negative impact on the viceroyalty's ledger books due to the long, costly wars between the Spanish and the Araucanian Indians. South of Santiago, in a region bounded on the north by the River Maule, lay the Araucanian territories that constant battle had failed to secure for the Spanish empire. Far different from the Incas of Peru, the Araucanians were nomads, intensely warlike and independent, and they resisted Spain's encroachments far into the nineteenth century. Chile's principal attraction for the soldiers who traveled over high *cordilleras* and coastal deserts to reach it was the chance to win glory on the field of battle.

Drawn by the prospect of adventure, Catalina, now twenty-one years old, left Lima to go to Cuzco. Although the distance was 360 miles by direct line, the trail ran well over 500 miles through Peru's Andean *cordillera*. From the parched valleys around Lima, the travelers journeyed east to the low foothills of the craggy mountain range and then up into highlands dotted with Indian hamlets. The Pariacaca Mountains southeast of Lima were so desolate that Catalina and her party carried all necessary supplies with them—even firewood for cooking. Some 120 miles from Lima, they entered the Jauja Valley, inhabited by Indians whose labors in the rich fields provided Lima with fresh fruit and vegetables. From Huancayo in the Jauja Valley on to Cuzco, the viceroyalty maintained wayside inns every fifteen or twenty miles, a typical day's journey apart. The inns were staffed by somber highland Indians whose forced labor provided travelers with firewood, straw to sleep on, and hot meals.

Catalina's small band traveled on from Huancayo to Huan-cavélica, where the mercury used in extracting pure silver from silver-bearing ore was mined. Then, fording rivers and climbing steep mountains, they reached Huamanga, later called Ayacucho, a large, prosperous center of trade surrounded by fertile farms. Past Huamanga they skirted high mountain peaks and threaded narrow paths chipped out of the rock-faced cliffs rising from the Apurimac River. In order to cross the Apurimac chasm they had to use the wooden bridge that provided the only passage from Lima to Cuzco. All efforts to build a stone bridge at that point had failed, as the piles of cut rocks lying futilely on either side demonstrated. So well traveled was that road and so vital the Apurimac bridge, that an engineer was stationed there to maintain its wooden timbers and planks. Yet so insecure was the 350-foot structure that the mules and llama trains, sometimes made up of sixty or seventy beasts of burden, were painstakingly unloaded, while black and Indian carriers transported their packs across the chasm, piece by piece. Once they crossed the Apurimac, burdened only by their few possessions, Catalina and her friends traveled on to Cuzco, completing a journey of seemingly endless miles and as many dangers.

Cuzco, the capital of the Incas, was more than four centuries old when the Spaniards arrived there. Surrounded by mountains, at a heady altitude of eleven thousand feet, Cuzco served the southern colonies as the source of troops needed for the wars with the Araucanians. Catalina and her friends joined the forces of Gonzalo Rodríguez, almost sixteen hundred strong, as members of Bravo de Saravia's "One Hundred Lances." Mounted on horse-back, dressed in black and red finery and fully armed with knife, sword, and lance, Catalina as Antonio was an impressive picture of military might. She was doubtless the only woman among the soldiers. Her weapons caught the sun's rays and caromed them crazily about. As excited horses pawed Cuzco's fine dust into a cloud, the formidable force left the city and began the long journey to Chile's battlefields.

It was November 1613 and late spring when the soldiers arrived in Concepción, then ruled by Governor Garcia Ramón, whose fame as an iron-willed commander had spread throughout the continent. Located close to the Pacific, on the banks of the

Bío-Bío River, Concepción was a frontier settlement, distinguished by its importance as a center of military operations and by the fact that a bishop resided there. On all other counts it was an inhospitable place. Its muddy streets were lined with gambling houses, and its nights were pierced by clashing swords and the muffled cries of soldiers playing their deadly games.

Catalina fell in with a group of hard-drinking Basques and soon became known as one of the worst of the lot. Not long after arriving in Concepción, she learned that the governor's secretary was another Basque, Captain Miguel de Erauzo, none other than her own brother. She quickly searched him out but was careful not to reveal her true identity. They spoke only of their common ancestry and of the mutual sympathy existing between sons of the same Spanish region. Antonio and Miguel became constant companions who ate together, gambled together, and, after petitioning the governor for Antonio's transfer to Miguel's company, fought together.

Barely two months after the arrival of troops from Cuzco, word of serious Indian attacks arrived from the regions south of Concepción. Colonists from Nacimiento, Temuco, Villarrica, and the plains east of Valdivia straggled into Concepción with word of greatly increased Araucanian activity. Then came the news that *Cacique* Huenchullán, leader of Indian forces near Temuco, had surrounded the fort at Villarrica. The entire region south of Concepción was about to fall to the Araucanians. Governor García Ramón mobilized Concepción's fighting force of three thousand men and ordered it to the plains of Valdivia, more than two hundred miles south. Camp was established there, and the Spanish troops undertook forays into the surrounding countryside.

Fifty soldiers made up Miguel's company, and among them was his sister, known to them as Antonio Ramírez de Guzmán. Receiving their orders to march, the company broke camp and traveled eastward toward the foothills of the Andes. For several days they saw no one and heard nothing but birdsong and the sound of their own horses' hooves. On the third day a young Indian, mounted bareback and seemingly alone, appeared from a stand of trees, rode swiftly up to Captain Miguel, and thrust his lance into the ground. Even before the lance had stopped quivering, the Spanish were set upon by an Araucanian force of twice their number. The Spanish managed to hold their own for a time, shielding themselves from the enemy's lances and arrows and charging again and again into the Indians' ranks, hacking at them with their swords. Spaniards fell from their horses, their bodies bristling with arrows. Many died instantly as an Indian lance found a vital spot; others, severely wounded, lost consciousness and lay helpless under the feet of the plunging horses. One soldier, wounded by ten lances, dragged his failing body to a protected place and, drawing a cross with his own blood, kissed it and died.

As the Spanish were driven back, Catalina realized that they were close to disaster. Seized by sudden inspiration, she rode among the remaining soldiers shouting the ancient battle cry of Catholic Spain: "Santiago! Santiago and attack!" She was a fearsome sight. Bleeding from the shoulder and from several arrow wounds, her face covered with dirt and sweat, and her sword flashing in the dusty air, she turned the tide of battle. The Indian line wavered and finally broke. As suddenly as they had appeared the Araucanians were gone.

Captain Miguel wept with fury as he surveyed the wounded survivors. Of his fifty soldiers, thirty were dead and not one of the living was uninjured. On that same bloody battlefield he promoted Catalina to the rank of ensign, recognizing that only his companion's heroism had saved them.

Catalina's promotion was upheld by Governor García Ramón when the survivors limped into camp several days later. During the months following her foray Catalina participated in several other skirmishes, on one occasion capturing and mutilating the son of one of the Araucanians' most important leaders by cutting off his hands. Their numerous reverses convinced the Araucanians that further attacks were futile, and they withdrew, some to the eastern slope of the Andes, others south to the cold lake district far beyond the reach of even the most fearless Spaniard. The Indian retreat and the onset of winter brought peace to frontier Chile. Catalina and her comrades undertook the painful and tedious journey north. Hundreds of veterans nursed wounds, and many whose horses had perished struggled along on foot. By the time the men reached Concepción, they were more than eager for the pleasures denied them in the field.

Boasting a new rank and outfitted with new clothing bought with combat pay, Catalina returned to the grimy gaming rooms of Concepción. She continued to take meals with Captain Miguel, but friction developed when her battle-ripened handsomeness turned the head of Miguel's own mistress. For a time Catalina stayed away, seeking amusement in other gambling dens and cantinas, where she became notorious for the quickness of her temper. The most innocent comment was enough to provoke her anger and send her sword from its scabbard. One night, months after returning to Concepción, a drinking companion innocently remarked that the ensign's latest love had the smile of a toad. Enraged, Catalina buried her sword in the erstwhile jokester and dashed into the street, leaving him convulsed on the floor. She hid in an alleyway and fell on the man's friends as they raced after her, fatally wounding two of them. The triple murderer was finally subdued and dragged before the governor for judgment. Incredibly, García Ramón chose to ignore her crimes and released her with a mere reprimand, claiming that he needed all the skilled fighters he could find. He probably assumed that justice would be dispensed by friends of the victims.

Thanks to the protection of her Basque comrades and her own fame as a swordsman, Catalina was able to remain in Concepción after the murders. Her enthusiasm for battle continued undampened, and she was often a member of scouting expeditions into the surrounding countryside. As the Araucanians recovered from the blow dealt them at Valdivia, news of renewed attacks reached Spanish authorities with increasing frequency. An expeditionary force was sent south, stopping briefly at the encampment of Nacimiento and then continuing to the center of hostilities.

As several hundred Spanish troops neared the plains of Purén, three thousand Indians attacked from all quarters, filling the air with battle cries and a hail of arrows. Closing ranks at the order of field commander Gonzalo Rodríguez, the mounted soldiers began the sallies and sword thrusts that slowly wore their attackers down. Four times during the course of the battle, Catalina's mount fell dead under her; each time she leapt to the back of a riderless horse and continued the attack. Although the Spanish lost their commander and many men, heavy Indian losses forced their withdrawal. After that initial battle, the Indians resorted to ambushes and continual attacks on scouting parties.

The Spanish army remained in the Valley of Purén for six months, often clashing with the enemy in skirmishes. It was during one such fray that Catalina lost her chance at further promotion in rank. After the death of Gonzalo Rodríguez, she had taken command of a company of soldiers, leading them on frequent excursions into Indian territory beyond Purén. On one such sortie, Catalina captured and summarily hanged a Christian Indian named Don Francisco Quispiguancha. Unfortunately for both, the governor wanted Don Francisco taken alive to Concepción, and in executing him the ensign had overstepped the bounds of her authority. The captaincy that she had long desired was given to another.

The expedition to Purén was Catalina's last. Soon after returning to Concepción, her proclivity to violence passed the bounds tolerated by even that lenient frontier colony. At a party given by the governor, Catalina was drawn into a petty squabble; words were exchanged, then insults; and soon swords so recently bloodied in battle were drawn against friends. Catalina caught an opponent off guard and fatally wounded him. The governor himself witnessed the murder and ordered her capture. Surrounded, Catalina leapt to a table and through a bank of windows.

Once outside she fled down the dark street and into an alley where she stopped to listen for sounds of pursuit. Suddenly a man's voice came to her from the shadows ahead: "Antonio! This way!" Believing herself surrounded, she lunged at the dark figure and felt her sword sink into his chest. The man fell forward, and a familiar voice choked out the words "Traitor, you have killed me!" Her brother! She had murdered her brother Miguel! Dazed yet fearful that she might be captured and hanged, she left her brother's body and ran the length of the alley to the chapel of the San Francisco convent. Like the embassy of a foreign nation, the chapel was beyond the reach of the governor and his civil authority. Once inside she was safe from capture.

For eight months she claimed the sanctuary of the convent.

Quito

Paita

PERU

Trujillo

Lima
Callao
Jauja
Huancayo
Huancavelica
Huamanga
Apurimac R.
Cuzco

Parrococa Mts.

PACIFIC OCEAN

ALTO PERU

Lake Titicaca
La Paz
Cochabamba

Lake Poopó
Charcas
Potosí

# Peru and Alto Peru
NOT TO SCALE

The passage of time eased Catalina's grief and made it possible for her to plan an escape. One moonless night when the guard posted outside was less than vigilant, she left the convent and walked swiftly to a sheltered spot where a friend waited with a horse and arms. She mounted the horse and with a terse farewell headed northeast toward the Andean *cordillera* and, beyond that, the city of Tucumán.

She traveled alone for several days, then fell in with two renegade soldiers who were as anxious as she to leave Chile. Together they rode deep into the mountains, climbing higher and higher until they reached cold country. The provisions they had with them were soon exhausted, and there were few homesteads to offer hospitality in that desolate region. Even water was scarce, and, as they climbed, everything but the coarsest grasses and the hardy *frailejón* ceased to grow. As the days passed, the travelers grew desperate for food. They killed and ate their horses one by one, until they were forced to continue on foot. The journey began to exact its toll. First one, then the other of Catalina's fellow travelers died. Before moving on alone, she searched the corpses and found eight pesos, a gun, and a small supply of ammunition. Her clothes torn, her boots long since worn through, Catalina traveled on, driven by her will to survive.

At last, many months since her escape from Concepción, she saw what must have seemed a mirage. Down the slope a herd of sheep grazed in front of a rustic shelter. A slender line of smoke rising from its chimney signaled the end of her ordeal. The two shepherds whose hut she had stumbled on scarcely concealed their amazement when Catalina appeared, shouting hoarsely and dragging the heavy gun behind her. They were even more amazed when Catalina told them how she had survived the thousand-mile journey from Chile to their hut on the fringe of Tucumán province. The shepherds fed her a little hot soup, bound her bloody feet, and took her to a nearby estate for rest and care.

Tucumán was only slightly less remote from the viceregal capital of Lima than the Chilean settlement Catalina had recently abandoned. Yet, unlike Chile, Tucumán was an essential link in the silver chain binding the New World to the king's treasury in Madrid. For Tucumán and its neighbors Córdoba, Salta, and Jujuy

La Paz

ALTO PERU

Atacama

Desert

PACIFIC OCEAN

Atacama la
Grande

Jujuy

Tucumán

Copiapó

Picunches

ANDES

Córdoba

Concón
Marga-Marga Mines
Valparaíso

Aconcagua Valley
Mapocho Valley

Santiago

Maule R.

Itata R.

Concepción

Arauco

Purén

Araucanians

Tolten R.

Temuco

Villarrica

Valdivia

Huilliches

Chile
1550-1650

NOT TO SCALE

provided the mules that were the single most important form of transportation in the New World. In exchange, the towns received a share of the silver that their mules carried from the Andean fastness over dangerous trails and down to the coast.

The comfortable estate where Catalina recuperated was the property of a *mestiza* widow whose pocketbook bulged with mule-train riches. Doña Encarnación had one child, a daughter of marriageable age, and the welcome she gave Catalina was not entirely disinterested. Believing Catalina to be, as she claimed, the Ensign Antonio Ramírez, a battle-scarred veteran of the Indian wars, Spanish-born and unmarried, Doña Encarnación was overcome with delight. After scarcely a week had passed she asked Catalina to become foreman of her workers and administrator of the estate. In exchange it was understood that Catalina would promptly marry into the family.

The ensign pretended great happiness but secretly lamented the fact that Doña Encarnación's daughter was a singularly homely young woman. For several months she managed to please everyone, solicitously wooing the unfortunate heiress while at the same time resisting a dash to the altar. During that time, Catalina became acquainted with a priest who, like Doña Encarnación, had an unmarried dependent in need of a husband. Catalina found herself besieged from two quarters. Favors, gifts, and special attention flowed from both, and only a bit of quick thinking now and then was needed to keep her duplicity a secret. The priest was as generous as was Doña Encarnación, giving her an excellent dowry that included a velvet suit, a dozen shirts and stockings, collars of fine linen, and two hundred pesos. Catalina adopted a posture of humble gratitude toward her solicitous patrons, but she realized that the situation was volatile. Thus she was prepared when an annoyed Doña Encarnación finally insisted that the wedding be celebrated immediately. That same night Catalina slipped away as she had so many times before and rode off on muleback, leaving behind her two sorely disappointed benefactors.

The trade route from Tucumán to Potosí was six hundred mountainous miles long, and on the way Catalina fell in with another solitary traveler. Thus accompanied, with ample provisions and several mules to carry her, she traveled the weary miles to the rich highland region of Potosí, arriving there late in 1621.

The Potosí that greeted Catalina was a large, unfortified city lying over the finest silver mines in the New World. Its varied population of more than 100,000 was made up of Spaniards from eleven different regions or "nations" of Spain and their *criollo* children, Indians, blacks, and all possible combinations of these groups. The wealthiest residents lived in elegant stone houses, several stories tall, and all, even those of modest means, commonly ate from silver plates and dressed in the finest brocades, laces, and linens. In Potosí a Sunday afternoon stroll became occasion for the display of jewels and finery, and the simplest celebration became a week-long carnival, with elaborate floats, open-air plays, and religious processions that wound endlessly through the streets. Yet that same exuberance had a darker side: a casual affront festered for a lifetime; a quarrel between friends easily became a neighborhood brawl; and political jealousies among groups became cause for civil war.

Conflict verging on civil war was epidemic when Catalina arrived in Potosí. Two warring factions had clashed again and again over a period of twenty years. On one hand were the Basques—merchants, administrators, and elected officials—who carefully maintained their position of preeminence during Potosí's richest years. More silver merchants, more craftsmen, more mayors and magistrates, and more officers of the mint and the royal treasury were from the Basque countries than from any other region of Spain. Jealousy and suspicion born of this disproportion were widespread. Yet the Basques did little to placate their fellow citizens and seemed instead to use their positions to their own advantage. Other groups, among them Andalusians, Extremadurans, and Castilians, wanted to destroy Basque power. Basque-owned businesses suffered frequent boycotts; courtship of Basque daughters by young men from other groups was discouraged; and civil disobedience and more violent forms of protest were common.

It was only a matter of time until Catalina became involved in the ongoing warfare. She was hired by the Basque Juan López de Arguijo, a merchant who was in the highly profitable business of carrying food supplies into Potosi. As one of López's principal overseers, Catalina was responsible for twelve hundred pack ani-

mals and eighty Indian carriers who plied the route from the agricultural plains of Cochabamba to Charcas and on to Potosí,
more than 13,200 feet above sea level. In Cochabamba she commonly bought eight thousand bushels of wheat for four pesos a
bushel, had it ground, and then transported it to Potosí, where it
was worth four times its lowland rate. Her work with López
quickly earned her a reputation as an efficient worker by day and
an incurable brawler by night. The frequent attacks on Basques
gave her constant cause for swordplay. In those clashes she
earned an informal rank of sergeant major, and for two years she
played a double role: supervisor or *capataz* of López's teamsters on
one hand and defender of Potosí's Basque power structure on the
other. And everywhere she went in Upper Peru—Charcas, Cochabamba, Piscobamba, La Paz—she carried along the fiery temper that injury, loss, and tragic death were unable to curb.

By 1623 Catalina had made so many enemies that she was
forced to leave Potosí. The ensign was thirty-one years old when
she left Upper Peru in search of protective anonymity in Lima.
But her reputation preceded her. In Cuzco she was arrested for a
murder she did not commit, and five full months passed before
witnesses at last absolved her of responsibility in the crime. Soon
after her release, however, she did in fact commit murder, stab-
bing the bandit El Nuevo Cid for daring to steal money she had
won at cards. Wounded and pursued by the bandit's friends,
Catalina fled Cuzco, hoping to lose her enemies on the road to the
capital. On the way, she was stopped by three soldiers who recognized her as the infamous ensign Antonio, but she was able to
bribe them with three gold doubloons and hastened on to the city
of Huamanga. El Nuevo Cid's friends were close behind, however, and they trapped her in a squalid gambling den on one of
Huamanga's back streets. No sooner had the first of Catalina's ad-
versaries fallen than soldiers arrived to break up the fight. Catalina was seized and dragged to jail.

This time she had no easy escape, no strings to pull, no influential friends to arrange a timely pardon. Word of her outrageous
past had followed too closely on her heels and previously lenient
authorities could no longer wink at such gross lawlessness. Soon
all Huamanga heard the news: the ensign Antonio was to be
hanged.

On the morning of what was to be her last day, Catalina was taken from her cell to an anteroom where the priest waited to perform final religious rites. A portable altar stood to one side, and after a perfunctory confession, the priest began Mass, placing the Host carefully on the ensign's tongue. To his horror, the prisoner leapt to her feet, took the Host from her mouth, and ran into the street, Host held high, crying "Mercy, mercy!" The crowd gathered around the scaffold was aghast. No one dared seize her, so awful was the sacrilege she was committing. Instead, they followed her down the street, into the central plaza and watched as she dashed into the cathedral. Once inside, secure in the comforting shadows of the church, Catalina knelt at the high altar and returned the Host to the priests. Then she submitted docilely while the ritual cleansing was performed. The hands that had touched so sacred an object were washed with holy water, then scraped and passed through fire. By the time the process was complete, word came that the saintly bishop of Huamanga, Friar Agustin de Carvajal, wished the condemned prisoner brought to him. Civil authorities had already demanded return of the fugitive, but Bishop Carvajal demurred. He wanted to interview the notorious ensign.

The bishop looked up from his desk as Catalina entered. Accustomed to judging people from all ranks of society, he examined the figure before him, noted the stiff military bearing, the proud head and slender neck, the sun-blackened, clean-shaven face, the hard, suspicious eyes. This man was obviously a fighter, a loner, probably dangerous, but not totally beyond reach of the bishop's spiritual guidance. He dismissed the priests with a gesture, and in a deep, kindly voice spoke of life and death, of sin and salvation, of the horrors of hell and the glories of heaven. Then he began asking questions—direct, unavoidable questions—his eyes fixed on the scarred face. Who are you? he asked. Where are you from? What brought you to Peru? Suddenly Catalina fell to her knees, overwhelmed by the vision of damnation surely awaiting her. One by one the long-hidden details of her true identity poured forth in a confession that left the bishop shocked and bewildered. Nothing short of a perverse miracle could account for the transformation of a bride of Christ into the feared and lawless swordsman—perhaps swordswoman—who stood before him! Anxious to verify that most incredible detail, the bishop took Catalina by the hand and led her out of the cathedral. Hushed whispers became a confused babble when the bishop and the outlaw pushed through the crowd and proceeded to a nearby convent. Then a shocked silence descended as both figures stepped inside, closing the high wooden doors behind them. While the bishop conferred privately with the prioress, ten quaking nuns examined the ensign. One of the nuns finally entered with the astonishing news: the murderous Antonio was a woman and a virgin!

On the strength of that awesome revelation, Catalina's crimes were forgiven. Surely no woman could be hanged for murder, especially if she were both a nun and a virgin. But neither could she be permitted to leave the cloister. Dressed awkwardly in nun's habit, she was held a virtual prisoner in the Huamanga convent while the bishop tried to decide what to do with her. He sent detailed messages concerning the "Nun Ensign" to Pope Urban VIII in Rome, to King Felipe IV in Madrid and to the San Sebastián Convent from which she had escaped sixteen years earlier, seeking advice on the peculiar case.

For several months, Catalina awaited some word on her future, while outside the convent walls her bizarre exploits were the only topic of conversation, especially among those who had known her as Antonio Ramírez. After five months Lima's Archbishop Lobo Guerrero called her to the capital where she arrived escorted by six priests, four nuns, and five swordsmen, none of whom, she protested, would be a match for her in a street fight. Given a choice of the convents in Lima, she picked the largest, the Holy Trinity Convent of St. Bernard, where she continued to await word from Spain. After two long years a report arrived from San Sebastián explaining that Catalina de Erauzo had indeed been a novice there but had never taken perpetual vows. The archbishop gave her permission to return to masculine dress and made arrangements for her to travel to Spain where Felipe IV, a king more interested in novelty than government, wanted to see her.

Catalina left the New World on November 1, 1624, hoping to receive a pension from the king and absolution from Pope Urban. Word of her peculiar history preceded her, and in Madrid she was forced to dodge mobs of curious people. She had an inconclusive audience with the king and shortly after submitted patiently as Francisco Pacheco, a great artist of the period, painted the portrait that hangs today among those of illustrious Basque sons in a San Sebastián cafe.

Several months passed during which Catalina wrote a long petition to the king, recounting her many courageous activities and requesting a pension in return for years of faithful service in the royal army. Felipe doubtless mused that the petition was more a picaresque novel than a true account of Catalina's adventures. Nevertheless, he awarded her a pension worth four times the usual ensign's wages as well as a bonus of thirty ducats, payable by the royal treasuries of Peru, Manila, or Mexico. Although much less than she had hoped, the pension was adequate. Realizing that further requests were useless, she proceeded with plans to visit Rome.

In 1627 she was finally received by the Pope, who found her story as intriguing as did Felipe IV. After hearing her story he gave her ecclesiastical permission to wear men's clothing. Armed with papal dispensation, Catalina returned to Spain en route to the New World. On July 21, 1630, she departed Sevilla for Mexico. There, far from the enemies of her youth, free from the social restrictions she had endured in Spain, and with a measure of financial security, she settled into the way of life most suited to her. Dressed in the Spanish style, a silver-handled sword and matching dagger at her side, she became a muleteer on the royal highway from Veracruz to Mexico City and spent the remainder of her days transporting goods between the coast and the capital.

The last account of Catalina de Erauzo was recorded in 1645 when a Capuchin friar wrote that he had seen her in Veracruz where she was universally respected for her fearlessness and piety. About her subsequent death little is known. Whether she died by the sword or expired peacefully at age sixty, as various writers have suggested, will perhaps never be determined. Far more important than her way of death, however, was her way of life. More than any other woman of her time she shaped her own destiny. Escaping from the narrow role assigned her from birth, she became an abiding symbol of that bizarre and extravagant age.

# IV
# Sor Juana Inés de la Cruz, 1651-1695

SPAIN AND HER far-flung kingdoms were under attack from every quarter by the seventeenth century. Ships of the Dutch and English harassed her vessels on the high seas, and Protestant settlers from those same countries began carving out settlements on American soil long claimed by Spain. In 1643 the formerly invincible Spanish infantry was beaten by the French at Rocroi—a defeat as shocking as that of the "Invincible Armada" some half-century earlier. Deteriorating conditions within Spain paralleled the unrelieved disasters occurring outside the country. The American gold and silver that helped make Spain supreme in the previous century ended up in northern Europe, where it served to fuel economic prosperity there. The short-lived bonanza had wrecked the national economy by driving up prices, leaving the ordinary person worse off than ever before.

Unable to halt the military and economic reverses outside her territory, Spain adopted a defensive foreign policy. Great fortresses were built at strategic points throughout the empire and effort was made to enforce the closed economic system known as mercantilism. The defensive measures were not only military and economic but intellectual as well. The Spanish way to knowledge had long rested on the belief that all truth was revealed by God through the teachings of early church fathers. Yet truth by

73

revelation was increasingly under attack by thinkers from the rising nation states of Protestant Europe, who, like the French philosopher René Descartes, advocated scientific observation as the best way to arrive at knowledge. Should the Cartesian method contaminate Catholic Spain's kingdoms, the religious wisdom of the ages might come into question. To guard against that appalling possibility, church and state collaborated to police the thoughts of the people. The Holy Office, or Inquisition, became the watchdog and censor whose duty it was to ferret out any person who failed to think along acceptable lines.

Under such conditions it seems incredible that creative intellectual activity was possible, but ironically the troubled seventeenth century witnessed a spectacular outpouring of the Spanish genius. The incomparable *Quijote* of Cervantes was published in 1604; many of Lope de Vega's two thousand dramas appeared during the first thirty-five years of the century; and the intricate poetry of Luis de Góngora set a style that was extensively imitated in the Spanish-speaking world. In Spain's distant Mexican kingdom the remarkable nun Juana Inés de la Cruz won a place among those Spanish luminaries by crafting lyric poetry rivaling any in the Spanish language. Confronted by obstacles that would certainly have overwhelmed a lesser genius, Sister Juana Inés struggled for a lifetime against the limitations placed upon her by the besieged civilization that produced her in spite of itself. Today it is not only for her poetry but for her heroism in the face of conflict and opposition that Sor Juana is remembered with affection, even awe, by her admirers.

It was summer of 1664, and the marqués and marquesa of Mancera, only recently arrived in Mexico City, still marveled at the intense blue of the skies of New Spain. The marqués of Mancera had served Felipe IV of Spain as ambassador to Germany and Venice and, in recognition of his faithful service, had been appointed twenty-fifth viceroy of the kingdom of New Spain. The viceroy was the king's own representative in Spain's New World possessions with power inferior only to that of the king himself. Mancera was pleased that the new position was important—and one that he was eminently qualified to occupy.

Soon after their triumphant entrance into Mexico City, the marqués and his beautiful wife, Doña Leonor Carreto, began to make their tastes and interests known within the viceregal court. The marqués was eager to find aides who could serve him faithfully as counselors and entertain him with intelligent conversation. Doña Leonor, too, wished to surround herself with companions who could sweeten the long hours with poetry, art, music, and learned discourses on questions of religious or historical interest. Accustomed to the sophisticated and intricate pastimes of the age, both were eager to recreate in Mexico the elaborate court life they had known as members of Europe's highest diplomatic circles.

During her first months in New Spain Doña Leonor received a petition from the family of a young Creole girl, Juana Inés de Asbaje, begging that she be admitted to the viceregal court as a member of the marquesa's retinue. Such requests were not uncommon. In fact, Doña Leonor received petitions almost daily from families of young ladies who hoped to find suitable husbands—preferably rich and Spanish-born—in the heady atmosphere of the Mexican court. But in the case of Juana Inés de Asbaje, the request was quite different. Instead of a husband the Asbaje family sought viceregal protection for Juana as though she were a precious jewel or rare book in need of safekeeping.

Her curiosity aroused by this unusual petition, the marquesa asked for further information about Juana Inés. To her delight, she found that the child was a prodigy, a young genius who had begun to read at age three and who, when she was eight, had learned Latin in a scant twenty lessons—or so her tutor claimed. At that same age she won a prize for a poem, called a *loa* and written in complicated style, celebrating the sacrament of Holy Communion. Doña Leonor was not discouraged by the fact that Juana's family was poor nor by the suspicion that her parents may not have been legally wed. It was enough that the girl was of pure Spanish blood, supremely intelligent, and poetically gifted.

The first meeting between the gracious marquesa and Juana, then thirteen years old, convinced Doña Leonor that Juana Inés would be a delightful and valuable companion. She was as pleased by Juana's adolescent beauty—her pale skin, dark eyes, and long dark hair—as she was by the young girl's gentle manners and elegant speech. Doña Leonor understood immediately that Juana's family was right: only in the sophisticated atmosphere of the viceroy's court would Juana's talents develop and receive the applause they so obviously deserved. Outside, unprotected by wealth or high birth, Juana would be subject to constant criticism from the church and society—from the church because learning was considered a threat to faith, and from society because women were believed to be inferior to men and were expected to act the part. Indeed, Juana would never have been happy in ordinary society. While still a small child she had shown such an overwhelming desire to learn that she begged to be disguised as a boy in order to attend the university. This bizarre idea made her family dispair of ever turning her into an ordinary child. In Mexico of the 1600s, women of the advantaged classes were expected to remain at home, shut away from the evils of the outside world. But for the marquesa of Mancera, this might have been Juana's fate.

In late 1664, Juana packed her belongings and left the home of relatives for her new residence in the viceregal palace on Mexico City's huge central plaza. The change must have been a dizzying one. From quiet isolation she passed directly into the rarefied atmosphere of New Spain's intellectual and political center. Fortunately for her own sake, Juana was armed with two talents that ensured her success. The first was the powerful intelligence so admired by her contemporaries. If, as it was believed, all knowledge was contained in certain church-approved works, here was a mind capable of reaching into those dusty volumes and pulling out great quantities of truths that were guaranteed not to harm the soul longing for salvation. Juana's conversation, her writing, and her contributions to learned discussions at the viceregal court were laced with long and gracefully appropriate quotations from her readings.

Her second talent as a skilled and sensitive poet guaranteed her a place of honor in the viceregal court. For Juana, writing in verse was, if anything, easier than writing in prose. And since the niceties of court life, and much of its entertainment, were carried along on a cushion of poetry, Juana's singular talent was much in demand. Every occasion, ordinary or extraordinary, religious or secular, called for a sonnet at the very least. The exchange of gifts brought forth a poetic exercise of one kind or another. Love, death, illness, graduation, and birthdays were similarly remembered in poems in honor of the person involved. These poems, often called poems of protocol or occasional verse, are peppered throughout the more serious works of Juana Inés, much of their value lost as soon as the occasion that inspired them had passed.

The court of the marqués and marquesa of Mancera attracted outstanding figures from New Spain and from abroad. Those distinguished by wealth or power, by beauty or noble birth, by intellectual renown or artistic achievement gathered at the table of the viceroy and participated in the social life of the court. Elaborate plays were performed, many of them by acting companies from Spain. Feasts, glittering balls, and opulent dress were commonplace. Learned debates and poetry contests provided entertainment for those fortunate enough to spend time at court.

Juana lived surrounded by the luxury and frivolous play of the Manceras' court for five years. During that time she enjoyed the unceasing affection of Doña Leonor, an affection she wholeheartedly returned, and was able to continue her studies by reading works that had not been available to her before. Spanish plays of the Golden Age, the works of Cervantes, Quevedo's somber satire, the intricate verses of Góngora and perhaps even the prohibited writings of Descartes were read by the worldly members of the viceroy's court in Mexico.

It would be hard to believe that Juana, young and increasingly beautiful, was not enchanted by a way of life deliberately designed to amuse and to banish boredom. Secure in her favored position, pampered and sought after for her talents, Juana Inés was already famous throughout New Spain by the time she was seventeen.

That same year, at an age when most of Juana's peers were concerned only with romance and entertainment, the marqués of Mancera arranged for her to prove once and for all whether she truly deserved her fame as a well-educated, skilled debater. To that end he arranged a public examination of Juana by some forty professors who taught at the University of Mexico. The debate would be an oral test of Juana's knowledge of theology, philosophy, mathematics, history, poetry, and other disciplines. She, denied all formal education because of her sex, would face the questions of those who had enjoyed the best education then available. Years later, after Juana's death, the marqués of Mancera wrote a description of that historic confrontation. "As a royal galleon would defend itself from the attack of a few small boats," he wrote, "so Juana Inés fended off the questions, arguments and replies that all of them, each in his own field, put to her." Her self-education thus displayed, her fame soundly defended, Juana Inés had the grace to claim that her great triumph had caused her only the slightest satisfaction.

Even as belle of the viceregal court Juana Inés was faced with a problem of such gravity that it was to plague her, unsolved, throughout life. Where in the closed and restricted society of seventeenth-century Mexico was Juana Inés to find a life congenial to her talents and tastes? She, and her sisters throughout the Hispanic world, had but two choices. She could marry, or she could become a nun, married in effect to the church. No other option was open to her. Her family lacked the wealth to support her in her scholarly pursuits, and she was barred by her sex from earning her own living. Faced with a choice between marriage and the church, and encouraged by her confessor, Jesuit priest Antonio Núñez, Juana Inés at last chose the convent. As she wrote many years later, "I became a nun, because even though I realized that state was (in many superficial ways) repugnant to my temperament, given the total disinclination I felt toward marriage, it seemed the most fitting and decent thing I could do, especially since I wished to insure my personal salvation."

Shortly before her sixteenth birthday, Juana had left her dear marquesa and entered the Convent of the Discalced (Barefoot) Carmelites, a strict religious order that had the advantage of owning a large library of some twelve thousand volumes. The young novice found it hard to adapt to the change from viceregal opulence to the cold severity of the Carmelite order. Barely three months later, in November 1667, Juana Inés fell ill and was taken out of the convent by her viceregal protectors. For fifteen months she recuperated at the marqués's palace. Yet the harsh experiences of the Carmelite convent failed to divert her from her course, and in February 1669 she entered the convent of San Jerónimo, a far less rigid order located in the heart of Mexico City.

Convent life in Mexico was not the other-worldly existence that one might expect. With the exception of a few orders like the Carmelite, most convents were comfortable places that offered a routine not much different from that of a large, well-to-do household. Nuns were permitted to have private rooms customarily called cells but not as austere as that word implies. They were also allowed to have personal servants and even slaves, and this practice was carried to such an extreme that one large Mexican convent reported that five hundred servants were in attendance on a mere one hundred nuns. Yet these practices were not treated severely when brought to the archbishop's attention. The convents served much too important a function in a society that offered so little to its female members. It was recognized that many who entered the convents were unmarried daughters of well-to-do parents who had no convenient place to live and who may or may not have had true religious vocations. No one seemed to expect outstanding saintliness from such nuns, nor did it seem a waste that a great number of them spent their lives singing in choirs, doing embroidery, cooking sweetmeats, and receiving visitors.

Those aspiring to the religious life were required to bring a dowry when they entered the convent. This, and the celebration similar to a wedding feast that followed the ceremony of taking the veil, placed most convents financially beyond the reach of poorer women. Juana Inés's dowry was provided not by her own family but by Don Pedro Velázquez de la Cadena, a wealthy resident of Mexico City, and Juana's confessor, Father Núñez, was only too happy to host a party in honor of the young nun. Sor Juana Inés de la Cruz, as she was called from that day on, did not enter the convent as an ordinary nun. Protected by her friends the viceroy and Doña Leonor, on good terms with Don Payo de Ribera, the archbishop of New Spain, and already famous throughout the colony for her poetry and intellectual prowess, Sor Juana began her convent life as something of a celebrity. The dowry provided by Don Pedro Velázquez was ample, and Sor

Juana never suffered from lack of money. Visitors flocked to the convent locutory, a comfortable sort of living room, where Sor Juana participated in learned discussions and courtly conversation with highly placed friends and admirers. Requests for poems arrived often, and the exchange of delicacies and small gifts was constant. Among the gifts that Sor Juana valued most were the books and scientific instruments that she received from friends beyond the convent walls.

Even after she had taken the veil, Sor Juana remained a kind of poet laureate of the viceregal court. On occasions of secular importance it was she who was called upon to write official poems, and often she was paid for that service. Should someone noteworthy die, it was she who composed sonnets in honor of his memory. When New Spain commemorated events in the life of the Spanish monarch, it was she whose words rang out with proper dignity and respect. Sor Juana carried out her function as official poet with great skill and surprisingly, given the themes she had to deal with, some originality.

From her first days as a nun, Sor Juana realized that communal life would create conflicts between convent routines and her private "inclination," as she called her scholarly vocation. Taught from earliest childhood to expect criticism of her intellectual interests, she had nevertheless hoped for some miraculous change in either herself or the world that would finally let the two live together in peace. By entering the convent, she wrote, "I thought I could escape from myself, but—woe is me—I brought myself with me and I brought my worst enemy in this inclination, that I cannot tell if heaven gave it to me as a gift or a punishment." Her drive to learn did not loosen its hold over her after she took religious vows. In spite of the noise of convent life, the lack of privacy, and the routines that governed her activities from early morning until night, Sor Juana managed to steal many hours from her religious obligations, and, by candlelight, while others slept, she "read and read some more, studied and studied some more, with no other teacher than those very books."

In the effort to satisfy this inner drive and at the same time fulfill her obligations, she scrupulously obeyed the convent regulations. She tried to be patient and friendly to her sisters, and she accepted the routine duties of the convent stoically. When her studies were interrupted by voices from a neighboring cell or when she had to help with kitchen duties, Sor Juana generally controlled her impatience. Yet she longed for a more private life with no distractions and no interruptions, free from the restrictions that were often placed on her. Humble as she tried to be, there were times when her control snapped. A few years after she became a nun, the San Jerónimo Convent elected a prioress who, whatever may have been her spiritual virtues, was uneducated and, in fact, quite ignorant. Once, after suffering her in silence for a while, Sor Juana burst out with "Be quiet, Mother, you're such a fool!" So offended was the mother superior that she wrote a formal complaint to Archbishop Payo. The archbishop, one of Sor Juana's admirers, merely scribbled in the margin of the letter, "If the Mother Superior can prove the contrary, justice will be done."

In 1673, the marqués and marquesa of Mancera were called back to Spain. The loss of such kind and interesting patrons must have been difficult for Sor Juana. For nine years the Manceras, and especially Doña Leonor, had been far more important to Sor Juana than her own family. Then, only a few days after the Manceras' departure from Mexico City, Doña Leonor suddenly fell ill and died. On receiving word of that untimely death Sor Juana wrote three sonnets later published under the title "On the Death of the Marquesa de Mancera."

No one can doubt that Sor Juana, then barely twenty-two years old, grieved over the death of Doña Leonor—"Laura," as she was called in the poems. Yet by the time Juana had put her feelings into verse, they became lost in the metaphors and difficult syntax that were the bread and butter of seventeenth-century poetry. No single voice of sorrow cuts through that elegant façade; instead, strangely impersonal images of loss dominate the poems:

> And love laments its bitter fate,
> For, if before, ambitious to enjoy your beauty,
> It searched for eyes to see you,
> Now those eyes serve only to weep.

And:

> *She was born where the red sails of the east*
> *Run swiftly as the rubicund star is born,*
> *And she died where, with ardent sighing,*
>
> *The deep seas give burial to its light;*
> *And it was fitting to her divine flight*
> *That like the sun, she traveled 'round the world.*

Sor Juana's poetry, even when her own feelings were most caught up in it, seemed restrained by the styles then popular. Far from being isolated from the tastes of Spain, she had ample access to the works of many Spanish poets and especially to the elaborate, technically dazzling works of Luis de Góngora. She was seduced by the colorful, unexpected verses of the great Castilian poet and in her own favorite poem, "Primer Sueño" ("First Dream"), confessed openly to imitating Don Luis's famous poem "Soledades" ("Solitudes"). For the Mexican nun, writing in verse was as natural as writing in prose, and the rhymes that flowed from her pen lent themselves easily to the demands of baroque style, as the intricate and difficult poetry of the period is usually called. Intellectual and complicated plays on opposites—love and hate, beauty and death, fame and envy—abound in her poems. Delicate, but often impersonal, images and metaphors fill her sonnets, ballads, and romances with variety and color. Sor Juana was able to take these elements, so often abused by her contemporaries, and blend them into praiseworthy verse.

Of her seventy-five sonnets, twenty-two are about love—not as passion or emotion, but as a theme, something to think about. Take, for example, these lines, translated with words as close as possible to the original Spanish:

> *Who ungrateful leaves me I as lover seek;*
> *Who lovingly follows me I unthankful abandon;*
> *I adore him faithfully who mistreats my love;*
> *And I mistreat him who faithfully seeks my love.*

Or:

*Feliciano adores me and I despise him;*
*Lizardo despises me and I adore him;*
*I weep for him who ungratefully rejects me*
*And him who cries tenderly for me I in turn reject.*

So many of Sor Juana's love poems follow this intellectual, rather than emotional, pattern that scholars have debated whether she was writing about love at all. Yet there are other poems, written about a lover's absence or spoken directly to the beloved person, that seem as personal and as fragile as any love poem ever written. An example of these is the following one that Sor Juana entitled "In Which a Suspicion Is Satisfied with the Rhetoric of Tears."

*This afternoon, my love, when I spoke to you,*
*When I saw in your face and in your manner*
*That I could not persuade you with my words,*
*Then my heart begged you to believe me.*

*And Love, that helped me in my efforts,*
*Overcame what seemed impossible;*
*For among the tears that my pain spilled out,*
*My heart, undone, was itself distilled.*

*Enough of such severity, my love, enough;*
*May despotic jealousy torment you no more,*
*Nor low suspicion invade your quiet*

*With silly shadows, with empty clues,*
*For in that liquid humor you saw and touched*
*My undone heart in your hands.*

It is tempting to think of Sor Juana, the lovely young nun, as a refugee from a sad love affair suffered while she lived at the viceregal court. Yet, despite the temptation of that theory, her temperament—even her own words written in later years—support the claim that her one true love was learning.

That love of learning proved to be the foundation of a friendship that lasted throughout Sor Juana's life. For the death of her beloved marquesa and departure of the marqués of Mancera did not leave her entirely alone. Among the visitors who came regularly to talk with Sor Juana in the locutory was a man, about six years her senior, who shared many of her problems and interests. Don Carlos Sigüenza y Góngora was highly unusual in tradition-bound New Spain because of his rather gruff independence of mind and love of the new scientific methods of observation. Don Carlos won the professorship of mathematics and astrology at the University of Mexico when he was in his twenties and then launched himself into a lifelong effort to learn everything he could about the stars, Mexican history, geography, and scientific methods of investigation. As he pursued his studies, Don Carlos also struggled to make ends meet. Unlike Sor Juana, who enjoyed financial security provided through the church, Don Carlos was forced to accept a broad variety of jobs throughout his life, among them chaplain, mapmaker, official of the Inquisition, and professor. In addition, Don Carlos found time to write poetry, motivated by the fact that poetry was the most common literary form of his time and by the fame of his well-known ancestor, Spanish poet Luis de Góngora.

The friendship between Sor Juana and Don Carlos was a fruitful one that both valued highly. Their frequent meetings in the San Jerónimo reception room were filled with discussions of new developments in science and with readings of their original compositions. Don Carlos was Sor Juana's contact with intellectual trends that were developing far off in Europe; and she was his superior in writing lyric verse. Don Carlos never failed to express his admiration for "Mother Juana Inés," who, he claimed, could equal or surpass any poet or scholar of the age. She, for her part, was enchanted to have so learned a friend, especially one who was a descendant of the great Luis de Góngora.

Don Carlos's influence on Sor Juana was extensive. The new scientific methods that so fascinated Don Carlos came as an affirmation of the practices her own curiosity led her to follow. Toward the end of her life she described an incident that clearly showed her belief in the power of observation as a guide to knowledge. Once, she wrote, the San Jerónimo convent was assigned a mother superior who held that "study was a thing for the Inquisition to deal with" and who ordered Sor Juana to abandon her books. Such an order could not be ignored, and Juana Inés was not permitted any contact with her studies for a full three months. Yet she continued to study by observing "all the things God created" and reflecting with equal concentration on a spinning top, a game played with pins, and an egg frying in oil. As she wrote, "Well, what could I tell you about the natural secrets I have discovered while cooking. ... If Aristotle had ever done any cooking, how much more would he have written!" Ordinary observations such as these carry as much weight, she claimed, as all the church-approved knowledge contained in her library.

The "natural secrets" she learned from the behavior of ordinary objects were sought out in accord with Descartes's command—in total opposition to the Church. Forget everything you ever learned, wrote he, and through minute and painstaking observation rebuild your system of knowledge from the foundations up. This indeed was an idea "for the Inquisition to deal with," but Sor Juana could no more abandon her fascination with direct observation than she could quell the rhymes that came to her at every moment, even during her dreams.

Sor Juana's life was filled with her poetry, books, scientific observations, and those friends who sought her company in the locutory. Among those who came to see her was Don Payo de Ribera, the archbishop who had defended her against the anger of her offended superior. The genial cleric became viceroy as well as church leader in 1673 and served in this dual capacity until 1680. During his reign as archbishop Sor Juana wrote him a poem, friendly and familiar in tone, asking him to perform for her the long delayed sacrament of confirmation. The verses are full of word play and references to mythological characters, forms that might seem out of place—even disrespectful—had the request come from anyone but Sor Juana.

> *Illustrious Don Payo,*
> *Beloved prelate of mine . . .*
> *I call you mine, so without risk*
> *That with the echo of your name*
> *I already have the convent*
> *Quite free of rats.*

The humor and confident familiarity of these lines written to a man who was the supreme civil and religious authority of New Spain show that Sor Juana knew how to enjoy her favored position.

Within the convent itself her place was no less favored. Her sisters recognized her abilities by twice unanimously electing her prioress, a position she refused to take. For nine years, however, she served as bookkeeper of the convent and maintained its archive as well. In addition to these duties, Sor Juana studied music and created a system of musical notation that unfortunately has been lost. The musical instruments displayed in her cell did not lie idle, but were put to good use performing original compositions for the pleasure of her friends and convent sisters. Carols, written for Christmas, the Assumption, and other religious holidays, were performed publicly by the convent choir, and many of them were published the same year they were written.

The San Jerónimo convent thus benefited from the presence of the famous nun. She, on the other hand, continued to suffer from the daily irritations and constant interruptions of convent life. But even these were minor compared to the criticism she received because of her talent and erudition. "Who wouldn't believe," she wrote, "that I, so broadly praised, have not sailed, with the wind at my back and on a sea of milk over the palms of general acclaim?" Quite the contrary, she added. Any outstanding talent only seems to make one an easy target for the jealousy of those who are less favored. And what better target than a woman and, worse, a simple nun whose intellect was far superior to that of most of her contemporaries?

As time went on, the criticism and jealousies that followed her like a dark shadow came to plague her more and more. She felt herself increasingly defenseless and unprotected not only from her petty critics but also from those who, sincerely or not, criticized her under the pretense of loving concern for her spiritual welfare.

From this viewpoint, her friendship with sophisticated persons of the nonreligious world must have been comforting to her. Those friendships, however, were few. The vast majority of the 400,000 people who lived in Mexico City in the 1680s were poorly educated and painfully provincial. The most cosmopolitan element of the population was the 70,000 persons who were of pure Spanish descent or were from Spain itself; and of that total 30,000 were women. Within that relatively small population, the possibility of finding persons who could accept Sor Juana's gifts uncritically was extremely remote. Consequently, the extraordinary nun lived most of her days in isolation from kindred spirits. To most church people, among them her confessor, Father Núñez, her intellectual pursuits were mildly scandalous; to most men, except of course Don Carlos Sigüenza y Góngora and a few others, Sor Juana was, if not a threat to their own achievements, at least a peculiarity; and to women the nun must have seemed incomprehensible. Trapped between the criticism of some and the awe of others, Sor Juana longed for some sympathetic person to take the place left vacant when Doña Leonor, the kindly patroness of her adolescence, died.

In 1680, her place was suddenly filled. In that year the twenty-eighth viceroy of New Spain, the high-born count of Paredes, arrived to take over the government of Spain's New World possession. With him came his beautiful wife, the countess of Paredes, who soon became Sor Juana's intimate friend.

Sor Juana's affection for the beautiful countess, "Lysi" as she called her, shows clearly in the many poems dedicated to her. From the first moment of her arrival, the countess praised and inspired Sor Juana's poetry, and it was she who asked Sor Juana to gather her poems together so that they could be published. Every act carried out between them, every event, was punctuated by a poem, and the gift of her collected poems was no different:

> *The son that the slave-woman has borne,*
> *Belongs under law*
> *To the legitimate master*
> *Whom his mother obeys . . .*

. . . . . . . . . . . . . . . . . . . . . . . . . . . . . . . . . . . . . . . . . . . . . . . . . . . . .

> *Thus, Divine Lysi, these scribblings,*
> *Sons of my soul, born of my heart,*
> *Are rightly returned to thee*

*And their imperfections cannot prevent it*
*For they are lawfully thine,*
*These, the thoughts of a soul that is thine alone.*

Poems mark the birth of Lysi's child, the birthdays of the count, the giving of a gift and, above all, the beauty of the countess herself. "The heavens are the plate/ On which is engraved thy angelic form," wrote the nun in one of her ballads honoring the countess. The humility and courtliness of these poems, written by one woman to another, seem strange but not inexplicable given Sor Juana's almost complete emotional insulation. "Lysi" was the unique, yet wholly proper, object of the nun's affections, and so it was to her that those emotions poured.

The year that the count and countess of Paredes arrived coincided with the appearance of the Great Comet of 1680,* whose fiery path cut across the skies of Europe and the New World. This heavenly apparition caused widespread alarm among the people of both continents. It was commonly believed that comets were a dreadful sign of disasters to come, a superstition rejected by the handful of scholarly people who were excited, rather than frightened, by the chance to observe the phenomenon. Among the few such cool-headed souls in New Spain were Don Carlos Sigüenza y Góngora and Sor Juana Inés. Motivated by the desire to calm widespread fears, Don Carlos published a pamphlet in which he proclaimed the innocence of comets and the virtues of scientific and mathematical methods in studying the heavens. The pamphlet almost immediately became the focus of a battle waged between those who believed in the ominous nature of comets (one person described comets as being composed of perspiration and vapors that rise from corpses) and those who used mathematics to prove that comets behaved naturally, according to rational laws. Sor Juana participated in the debate indirectly by giving her support to Don Carlos.

Sor Juana was deeply involved in this and other issues and events of her day. The limitations of convent life were balanced by her friendship with powerful people who visited her and

---

*Later named Haley's Comet, after the English astronomer who observed its passage.

brought her news of the secular world outside the convent. Pirate raids, intrigues in the viceregal court, the latest sermon, gossip about love affairs, and scientific debates were all fair topics for conversation in the San Jerónimo locutory. Thus there are among Sor Juana's poems a series of verses dedicated to pleading certain causes that came to her attention. In one such poem she begs the countess to free an Englishman imprisoned in Mexico City; in another she asks that a widow be given protection from those who wanted to sell her house. At one point she wrote to the viceroy:

*Suffer my stubborn insistence*
*That you listen everyday*
*To these continual petitions,*
*Now that these my constant requests*
*Have already become litanies.*

Sor Juana's readiness to plead the cause of others reveals a sharp sense of justice, a sense of fairness, that was perhaps most offended by her society's treatment of women. From her earliest years, Sor Juana had suffered because she was born a woman. This fact bound her to her sisters who, although less gifted, were no less afflicted by prevalent social beliefs. Principal among them was the church's idea that women might study but should never teach. As a result, there were few schools for women and no women teachers in New Spain. Should a young girl's parents decide to give her some education, they were forced to hire a male tutor who might easily take advantage of his student. "What is wrong," wrote Sor Juana, "with allowing a mature woman, learned in letters and wholesome in conversation and habits, to take charge of the education of young ladies?" Sor Juana modestly denied being accomplished enough to teach. But there is little doubt that she would have supported the establishment of schools for girls run by women had such a radical idea been proposed to her.

The injustices suffered by women in the name of romance caused Sor Juana no less indignation than the lack of educational opportunities. The infamous double standard that has historically plagued male-female relations did not escape her notice, and she described it with deadly accuracy:

*Ignorant men who accuse*
*Women wrongly,*
*Without seeing that you cause*
*The very thing you condemn,*

*If with unequaled fervor*
*You solicit their disdain,*
*Why do you expect them to be virtuous*
*When you encourage them to sin?*

*You combat their resistance*
*And then, gravely,*
*You say it was their weakness*
*That accomplished your end.*

. . . . . . . . . . . . . . . . . . . . . . . . . . . . . . . . . . . . . . . . . . . . . . . . . .

*Whose is the greater guilt,*
*In a sinful passion,*
*She who falls to his lure*
*Or he who, fallen, lures her?*

*Or which is more rightly to be reproached,*
*Although both are guilty,*
*She who sins for pay,*
*Or he who pays to sin?*

Sor Juana's poems, this among them, were widely read during her lifetime and in the centuries following her death. It is not known what, if any, results were gained by her pleas for just, reasonable treatment of specific individuals as well as women in general. Her words, however, have survived as witnesses to her sensitivity to these injustices.

In 1686 Sor Juana's friends the count and countess of Paredes returned to Spain, to be replaced in 1688 by the count of Galve, who reigned as thirtieth viceroy of New Spain during the remaining years of Sor Juana's life. The beautiful countess took many of Sor Juana's poems with her and had them published in Madrid in 1689. The title of this first book of verses, *The Castalian Flood*, or *Inundación castálida*, is an appealingly baroque reference to the Castalian spring that flowed from Greece's Mount Parnassus and was considered the source of poetic inspiration. In harmony with this metaphor, Sor Juana was called the "Tenth Muse," a not uncommon compliment paid to female poets of that elegant age.

As Sor Juana's fame spread to Madrid and praise began to flow back to New Spain, her own situation became more troubled. As the ninth decade of the century came to an end, the kind nun of San Jerónimo began to suffer more acutely from loneliness and poor health. The departure of her beloved Lysi coincided with Don Carlos's travels away from Mexico City. Without the unfailing protection of the former and the intellectual support of the latter, Sor Juana bent before the critics who constantly worried her with their advice. With no family or intimate friends to turn to, the lonely nun expressed her complaints in verse: "By persecuting me, world, what do you hope to gain?" Later she penned these poignant lines: "Let us pretend that I am happy,/ Sad thought, a while." While in this frame of mind she suffered the blow that finally broke her will to resist her critics.

Early in 1689, the bishop of Puebla, Don Manuel Fernández de Santa Cruz, visited with Sor Juana in her convent and found that she was familiar with a sermon written many years before by the famous Portuguese Jesuit Antônio de Vieyra. The conversation that followed was the kind that scholars of that era dearly loved. All the erudition, the finely trained memories and powers of subtle reasoning were brought to bear on Vieyra's thesis: that none of the learned saints of the church—St. Augustine, St. Thomas Aquinas, and St. John Chrisostomo—could name Christ's greatest work without he, Vieyra, being able to mention an even greater one. Sor Juana, in the weeks after the bishop's visit, no doubt irritated by Vieyra's decades old boast, rebutted him in a piece entitled "Crisis of a Sermon." She then sent it to Bishop Fernández, who was so impressed by her clever reasoning that he published the argument under the title "Athenagoric Letter of Mother Juana Inés de la Cruz." The title was highly complimentary, comparing its author to Athena, the goddess of wisdom and war. Had the bishop left their exchange at that, the lonely nun would have been pleased and quite encouraged. Instead he chose to apply, in private, a heavy dose of criticism.

In a long letter that he signed "Sor Filotea de la Cruz," the bishop applauded her skills in scholastic debate but urged her to devote her talents to more spiritual pursuits than she had in the past. "Turn away from your scientific and worldly interests," he urged, "and devote yourself to holy activities as becomes a nun." "Don't forget," he continued, "that holy writings contain divine wisdom, which is far superior to all the books written by men." The letter, although critical, was composed by one who truly admired Sor Juana and wanted, in his own way, the best for her. The bishop concluded with these lines: "All this is wished for you by one who, since he first kissed your hand many years ago, has loved your soul, without distance or time proving able to cool that love, because spiritual love never suffers the shock of change nor does pure love admit any changes but those toward growth. May the Lord hear my pleas and make you most saintly and keep you in all prosperity."

The letter left Sor Juana distraught. Although gentle in outward appearance, the criticism was nevertheless harsh. For three months she brooded over her course of action. Should she remain silent and accept the bishop's advice without comment? This was the course recommended by Don Carlos, who warned her that the Inquisition might become involved if she protested. Should she ignore the letter and continue her life of study and verse? This was impossible; she was bound by vows of obedience to the church and had already created far too many problems through her independence of mind. Or should she answer his criticisms and, using all her powers of reason and debate, defend herself against them? At last she wrote her "Reply of the Poetess to Sor Filotea de la Cruz," the famous *"Respuesta"* that has survived as one of the finest essays ever written in Spanish.

From the *"Respuesta"* comes much of what is known about Sor Juana's life and thoughts. Biographical details and lucid descriptions of her ideas and attitudes are woven around a central theme: that women no less than men have the right to intellectual freedom. In arguing this case she calls herself "a poor nun, the least important creature in the world," but claims nonetheless that she has as much right to her opinions as Father Vieyra— "such a Man," she calls him—has to his. She defends her intelligence and thirst for study as divine gifts, "at least I see them celebrated as such in men," gifts that denial and penance could not destroy. Her verses, although not dedicated solely to spiritual themes, are innocent of any evil, she writes, and they were written mainly at the behest of others. Even the Mother Church could not reproach her for her poetry, since the works of many saints, hymns, and the Bible itself all include verses. Drawing on everyday examples, subtle comparisons and straightforward details, mixed together with reference to Greek mythology and quotes from Latin scholars, she bravely defended her position—but lost the battle.

Following the exchange of letters, her old confessor, Father Núñez, pressured her to change her way of life. Her involvement in secular affairs was totally unacceptable to him, and he convinced her that her very salvation was endangered by those activities. Suffering from poor health and the strain of mounting criticism, Sor Juana's spirit broke. It is ironic that as she was suffering her greatest personal crisis, her friend the countess of Paredes published a second volume of her poetry in Madrid. In an orgy of repentance for her "sins," Sor Juana sold her library of some four thousand books and her musical and scientific instruments, and quietly gave the money to the poor. After days of confession in which every sin, real or imagined, was resurrected, she dedicated herself with feverish enthusiasm to penitence. Drawing blood from her own veins she wrote in the great ledgers of the convent "I, the worst in the world, Juana Inés de la Cruz."

Sor Juana devoted her remaining two years to the most severe forms of religious penance. Famous before for her learning, beauty, and poetic talent, she earned a new kind of fame for the mortification of her own flesh. Father Núñez tried to moderate her excesses, saying that "Juana Inés does not merely run toward virtue, but rather flies." Her earliest biographer, Father Calleja, was equally pleased with this abrupt turnabout. He wrote that she gave away her books as though she were turning off artificial lights at sunrise.

The year of 1695 was one of plague and famine in Mexico, and hundreds of persons jammed the hospitals and places of charity. Against the advice of her friends, Sor Juana devoted herself to the care of nuns who suffered from the highly infectious plague. In her weakened state, she herself soon caught the disease and died. Her forty-four years of life had been remarkably productive, even within the limits of her time and position. Yet she died with little sense of her own lasting worth. In the empty cell after her death was found an unfinished poem written to thank those from faraway Europe who had praised her poetic work. Wondering how her verses had attracted the attention of great European writers, she wrote, shortly before her death:

> *I am not who you think,*
> *Rather from afar you have given me*
> *Another being with your pens,*
> *Another breath with your lips.*
>
> *And different from myself,*
> *Among your pens I wander*
> *Not as I am, but instead*
> *As you imagine me to be.*

In this belief the learned nun was wrong: she was properly perceived by those who praised her. The tragedy of her life was that in the final years she lost sight of her own worth in the mists of Baroque custom and prejudice that even her greatest efforts could never fully dispel.

# V

# La Pola, 1795-1817

THE EIGHTEENTH AND early nineteenth centuries were times of great ferment throughout the Western world. Ideas given form by Newton and Descartes culminated in the radical individualism of Voltaire, Rousseau, and Benjamin Franklin—great iconoclasts of an iconoclastic age. Men and women began to speak out against ancient social evils and against political institutions that ran counter to the new philosophies that bubbled in the centers of European thought and action.

Spanish America was remote from Europe but hardly insulated from these trends. A dynastic marriage at the turn of the eighteenth century had linked Spain to the French House of Bourbon, and with Bourbon influence came a long series of imperial reforms disturbing to patterns of thought and action grown ossified over the centuries. Then came the phenomenon of revolution in Anglo-America, France, and nearby Haiti, and suddenly Spain's hegemony over her American colonies seemed tenuous indeed. Final impetus to Spanish American revolt came in 1808, when Napoleon Bonaparte invaded Spain and imprisoned the Spanish royal family. Into the void created by absence of legitimate authority stepped the Creoles, a group long resentful of the way *peninsulares* rode roughshod over them.

When it seemed that French arms had sealed Spanish fate early in 1810, Latin Americans struck almost simultaneously at

points as distant as Mexico City, Santafé de Bogotá, Caracas, Buenos Aires, and Santiago de Chile. Independence was declared all over Spain's vast continental empire.

The early euphoria of independence soon faded and, like the trials of Job, grave afflictions plagued the Spanish Americas. The Creoles were unaccustomed to governing and fell to squabbling among themselves over a number of critical issues: Should the new government be centralist or federalist? Should power be vested in the hands of one person or should it be placed in an elected assembly? What should be the territorial boundaries of the new states? What role should the church play in the new scheme of things? In the midst of these and other thorny problems came Napoleon's defeat in 1814 and the return of King Fernando VII, an absolute monarch convinced that all who had rebelled against him must be severely punished. If the central issue before 1814 was whose view would prevail in the new governments, afterward it became who would escape with his life before implacable royalist armies.

Northern South America bore the brunt of the furious Spanish onslaught. As rapidly as they sprang to life the young rebel governments disintegrated. The years from 1815 to 1817 were bleak ones for Spanish-speaking revolutionaries everywhere. This was nowhere more apparent than in the area of Nueva Granada. The wars of independence devastated large areas, and in Spanish-dominated regions unending purges of the patriot ranks drove those who escaped execution underground or into exile. Only a few were not intimidated. Following is the heroic tale of one who would not be silenced and who paid accordingly. The facts surrounding Policarpa Salavarrieta's brief life and exemplary death are among the best known in the annals of patriot martyrdom. Still, her story is far from unique. In that heady age of revolution and republicanism hundreds of men and women actively resisted the Spanish, suffering swift and sure retribution.

The heat of June on one evening in 1805, and the promise of a clear night ahead, drew Policarpa out of doors to sleep in the hammock on the patio. She lay there quietly, listening to the distant noises that drifted over the roof—voices in the street outside, snatches of melody from a *tiple* next door, the steps of an occasional passer-by. Just as she dozed off, little Bibiano, her three-year-old brother, toddled out to join her in the relative coolness of the hammock. The two were asleep in a moment, and soon the village of Guaduas slept among its mountains and thick stands of bamboo in the landlocked heart of Nueva Granada.

It was the gentle swaying of her hammock that awakened Policarpa—that, and the frenzied crowing of roosters behind the house. She thought at first that someone had bumped into her in the dark, but instead of slowing, the swaying became more pronounced, almost violent, and a strange rumbling sound swelled up from deep within the earth. Earthquake! She jumped from the hammock, lifted her still sleeping brother, and dashed into the street. There she found her father and brothers already on their knees praying aloud as screams and shouts rose from all sides. Policarpa knelt with her family and in the midst of the panic comforted little Bibiano, who sobbed with fright.

Several hours later, when the sun at last climbed the massive *cordillera* east of Guaduas, the villagers assessed their losses. The houses of mud and bamboo had sustained some damage; several had collapsed; and the hostel built to accommodate travelers between Santafé de Bogotá and the Magdalena River was in need of considerable repair. It was not until late in the afternoon that they learned how close they had come to disaster. Messengers en route to Santafé, the viceregal capital high on the *sabana* of Bogotá, told of the terrible damage suffered at Honda. The earthquake had shaken that important river port with such violence that only a few structures were left standing. Its two major churches and the convent of San Francisco were reduced to rubble, and many were dead and injured.

In the days following the earthquake, as Guaduas worked to repair its damaged buildings, Policarpa and her sister Catarina, shadowed as always by little Bibiano, sought out their friends to ask where each had been and what each had felt when the earthquake struck. In the evenings small groups of girls gathered in the plaza, linked arms, and promenaded slowly around and around, chattering about that major intrusion in their otherwise tranquil lives. Every day for three days special Masses were said, and religious processions wound through the dusty streets to reaffirm the bonds between the Catholic deity and frightened mortals who had been emphatically reminded of their own fragility.

Gradually, as cracked walls were patched and the injured healed, Guaduas regained some of its self-confidence and resumed its normal rhythm of life. Early every morning, breakfast of hot chocolate and bland *arepas,* patties made of ground white corn, was followed by Mass. Shops opened; the men rode out to work on *fincas,* or farms; and women swept the dirt floors of their two- and three-room houses, collected eggs in the long grass out back, and carefully spread wet, soapy clothes to bleach in the sun's rays. Policarpa and her sister added some elementary schooling to that domestic regimen and as they grew older spent their afternoons learning to cut and sew clothing, first for themselves and their brothers, later for paying customers. After dinner the family said the rosary and then, weather permitting, went to the plaza to see and be seen by their neighbors. Later, as dusk deepened and candles flickered under the eaves of the houses, they gathered to sing the rhythmic songs of the region, accompanied by guitar and *tiple,* and to spin unending threads of talk that bound each person to his fellows and all to events beyond the borders of family and village.

Guaduas in the early nineteenth century was not quite the somnolent rural village it seemed, and all things considered it was not a bad place in which to grow up. Policarpa had moved there from Santafé in 1802, the year her mother, a sister, and a brother had died during a virulent outbreak of smallpox. Joaquín Salavarrieta, Policarpa's father, settled his children in a small house two blocks from the central plaza. There, Policarpa soon discovered, she could observe the movement of the major personages of the viceroyalty of Nueva Granada. For Guaduas was located a day's journey east of Honda on the major route between Cartagena on the coast and the viceregal capital. It was founded to serve as a way station between the long, hot river voyage from Cartagena and the arduous ascent to the plains of Bogotá, high in the Andean *cordillera.* Archbishops, viceroys, royal couriers, and other travelers rested in Guaduas for a day or two, some for as much as a week, before continuing on their way. Thus Policarpa had ample time to find out where each traveler was going and why. Mail from the coast passed through regularly and Guaduas heard of great events before the capital itself, a fact reflected in those evening conversations that encompassed matters of local interest, affairs of the viceroyalty, and even events in faraway Spain.

A bond of genuine loyalty and affection linked the people of Guaduas to the crown of Spain. When word came on June 10, 1808, that Fernando VII had been crowned king, the Salavarrieta family, the residents of Guaduas, and others living in Nueva Granada rejoiced. Bells pealed, a special Mass of thanksgiving was said, and for three nights the village was illuminated by candles at every window and door. Scarcely two months later the news of Fernando's imprisonment by Napoleon Bonaparte reached Guaduas and, by August 19, Santafé. During long conversations in the patio, the younger Salavarrietas talked excitedly about Napoleon and his brother José Bonaparte, the usurper who now occupied the Spanish throne. They abhorred the French and endlessly discussed the occupation of Spain by Napoleon's troops. In September the arrogant Spanish captain Sanllorente passed through Guaduas on his way to Santafé to raise money for the captive king. Two weeks later he came through again, bringing his coffers loaded with half a million pesos in donations and carrying pledges of loyalty to Fernando VII, the "beloved captive."

American-born Spaniards, the *criollos*, of Santafé, like those of Guaduas and other villages in Cundinamarca province, reacted much as their Spanish cousins, rising up in defense of the captured king and refusing José Bonaparte's seductive promise of increased liberty and local autonomy under his rule. Policarpa and her brothers shared that sense of loyalty to Fernando VII, but they were neither blind nor deaf. They could see the effects of inferior government imposed on Nueva Granada by Spanish officials, and they could hear the words of a small *criollo* minority who knew of the experiments in representative government in North America and who had read the egalitarian treatises of French political philosophers. Their doubts about Spain's ability to rule were aggravated by the behavior of certain *peninsulares*, snobbish Spaniards who routinely belittled American-born Creoles. Gossip from the capital classed the viceroy, Don Antonio Amar y Borbón, with those self-aggrandizing Spaniards. The unfortunate man was bereft of administrative talent and deaf besides, and his popularity suffered from his wife's exaggerated conceit. Santafé's wealthy Creoles saw little basis for their claim to social superiority and, like the Salavarrietas, suffered from an odd double standard in their attitude toward Spain. They tended to expect the worst of the Spaniards sent to govern them even while they continued to believe the best of their imprisoned king.

Policarpa's barely developed ideas, at first nourished only on bits of news and gossip, soon received a far more solid diet of radical thought. Her older brothers José and José María Salavarrieta left Guaduas for Santafé, where they became monks of the Augustinian order. There they came under the powerful influence of Fray Diego Padilla, twice named provincial of the order in Nueva Granada and a fearless proponent of freedom from Spain. By 1809 Fray Diego had published some fifty pamphlets and preached innumerable sermons on the subject. José and José María became willing converts to the cause, and through them Policarpa received copies of Fray Diego's tracts and learned as well of the radical proposals of Antonio Nariño and other patriots.

Still, Policarpa and others who were gradually withdrawing their sympathies from Spain were startled when news of revolution in Quito reached the province of Cundinamarca in September 1809. The news threw Spanish officials into a panic. Their position could not have been more precarious. The king, the source of their authority, was still imprisoned, leaving them without support in the restive colonies. And now the worst had happened: revolution had broken out in a part of Nueva Granada itself. Hoping to contain it, royalist priests and government officials in every town and village preached loyalty to Spanish officialdom and extolled the virtues of peace and tranquillity.

Although nothing untoward happened in the important province of Cundinamarca, representatives of the Spanish crown and the population of *peninsulares* experienced well-founded anxiety. In every town, *criollos* watched the course of Quito's short-lived revolution and, when it was stamped out a few months later, many a secret patriot, Policarpa among them, mourned its failure. The impulse toward revolution did not diminish after the premature revolt in Quito. Instead it built quietly toward the day it would burst forth full-grown in Nueva Granada.

On January 26, 1810, Policarpa celebrated her fifteenth birthday. Matured by the responsibilities that she had assumed at an early age, intelligent and forthright, La Pola, as she was often called, moved easily between the houses of her wealthy customers in Guaduas and the humble dwellings of friends and neighbors. She had ample opportunity to observe all levels of society. The social differences among racial groups in Nueva Granada were clearly visible, for they corresponded to the degree of pigmentation. Indians and *mestizos*, blacks and mulattoes were confined to menial jobs and generally denied higher education. Their place in the social order was rigidly fixed, because marriage between people of different races was specifically outlawed. *Criollos* were much more fortunate than the lower castes. Policarpa knew that her brothers would never have been permitted to become friars if her parents had not been legally wed and generally believed to be of pure Spanish blood. After all, a person of mixed blood could not aspire to study law or enter the church. The new races formed by mingling the Old World and the New were relegated to the "low and mechanical occupations" of farm laborer, artisan, domestic worker, primary school teacher, and surgeon, among others.

This arbitrary state of affairs did not particularly bother Policarpa. She accepted the privileges of her own class, but she bridled at being thought inferior to Spanish-born whites. Instinctively she rejected the idea that any Spaniard, no matter how ineffectual, was superior to all *criollos* by virtue of his place of birth. How ridiculous, she thought, that an old, indecisive man like Viceroy Amar y Borbón should be sent to govern Nueva Granada when there were far more capable men than he among the *criollo* elite. Yet intelligent and ambitious Creoles generally had to be content with positions in the local *cabildo* or with lower offices in the church. Only a very few rose to high positions reserved for the Spanish-born. The deep sense of injustice felt by *criollos* like

Policarpa and the *peninsulares'* obvious disdain for them destroyed whatever affinity might have existed between Nueva Granada's two most privileged classes. The consequences of these resentments were soon manifest.

On July 21, 1810, a pair of horsemen rode down out of the eastern *cordillera* and dismounted in the plaza of Guaduas. The message they bore had an impact almost as powerful as that of the great earthquake five years earlier. Their unsettling news flew from person to person, down side streets and out to the fringes of town. Women sent children to the fields for their fathers and brothers, and by evening the entire population of Guaduas knew of the astounding events taking place in Santafé. Only the day before a quarrel between *criollos* and a *peninsular* had led to mass riots, and within a matter of hours the existing royal government was abolished, and a Supreme Junta made up of prominent Creoles replaced it.

The principal actors in that drama called it a revolution, but dispassionate examination showed it to be less far-reaching. Although the junta called for a constitution incorporating principles of liberty and independence, its new president was Viceroy Amar, and its supreme source of authority continued to be Fernando VII, that "august and unfortunate monarch." The oath of office, sworn on the New Testament by junta members, included these words: "We swear by the God who exists in the heavens . . . to carry out religiously the Constitution and will of the people . . .; to spill the last drop of our blood to defend our sacred Catholic, Apostolic, Roman religion, our beloved monarch Fernando VII and the liberty of the homeland. . . ." The shackles thrown off on July 20 were not those of domination by Spain. Instead, Santafé's *criollos* threw off their inferior colonial status and demanded equality to other kingdoms of Spain, under the crown of Fernando VII.

While the Creole population of Cundinamarca province rejoiced, attended Mass, rang church bells, set off firecrackers, and organized balls and other celebrations, events pressed the enthusiastic new government closer and closer to complete independence from Spain. The first tie to be severed was the position of viceroy. So unpopular were Viceroy Amar and his wife Doña

Francisca Villanova that mobs demanded their imprisonment. Doña Francisca, who embodied all the negative qualities of the *peninsular*, was attacked by a mob of women who scratched, spit, and screamed at her as she was escorted to jail. By the second week of August, the junta realized that Viceroy Amar must follow other royal officials back to Spain.

Policarpa pushed to the front of the crowd when the heavily guarded viceroy and his wife reached Guaduas. Their drawn faces peered fearfully through the windows of the coach as if they expected Guaduas to be as dangerous a place as Santafé had suddenly become. La Pola gazed back from the silent crowd and watched as those symbols of arrogance climbed down uncertainly from the carriage and disappeared into their lodgings. In a few days they were gone, retracing the route they had followed in 1803 when, with great pomp and ostentation, they had arrived from Spain fully invested with royal authority.

Fernando VII's continued captivity was destructive to Nueva Granada's allegiance to the crown. As the months and years passed, more and more *criollos* doubted whether Fernando VII would ever be restored to the throne of Spain. Napoleon seemed invincible. News of the Spanish resistance that sapped French strength rarely reached Spanish America. Slowly all hope of a prompt restoration faded, and in July 1813 Cartagena, Antioquia, and finally Santafé declared complete independence from Spain, a country they now believed to be little more than a French satellite.

Guaduas complied with the junta's command that militias be formed in towns and villages throughout Nueva Granada. Don Joaquín Salavarrieta was active in that undertaking, and Policarpa lamented the fact that she could not join the enthusiastic young men who paraded through the streets, brandishing their weapons and shouting "viva" to the new government. Honda, too, organized a militia, counting among its most vociferous members young Alejo Sabaraín, son of the commissioner of the royal mines of Mariquita and an acquaintance of the Salavarrieta family.

After independence was declared, the weightiest question facing the government was what form it should take. Bitter disagreement developed almost immediately. Santafé, long accustomed to its special position as the viceregal capital, supported the centralist system, hoping to retain preeminence over the various provinces. Other cities, notably Cartagena, felt that Santafé was a poor excuse for a capital, landlocked, perched more than a mile and a half above sea level, almost inaccessible. Under Cartagena's leadership, the United Provinces of Nueva Granada supported a federalist system similar to that of North America. Santafé did not give up without a fight, however, and under Antonio Nariño's leadership campaigned for the centralist cause. Thus it was that Alejo Sabaraín's first battle was a local one that pitted one Nueva Granadan faction against another. The town of Ambalema, bordering Honda to the south, was at first allied with the federalist provinces that encircled Cundinamarca. Soon after independence, the Honda militia invaded and defeated Ambalema on orders from Santafé. Alejo found the victory most satisfying. The brief glories of battle obscured for him the underlying tragedy of internal dissension. He forgot that no blood had been spilled when Nueva Granada broke its ties with Spain and that the first deaths in battle were inflicted by one group of patriots on another. The significance of such fierce discord was apparent only to older, more objective patriots, who were filled with alarm and foreboding.

For four years, Nueva Granada squandered its wealth and energies on internecine squabbles. Then in early 1814 word came that Fernando VII had been restored to the throne of Spain. Royalists rejoiced, confident that Nueva Granadans would rally to their rightful king. Others, those who had wearied of the constant bloodshed of the *"patria boba"*—the foolish fatherland—welcomed the news as well. Even many ardent supporters of independence in 1810 were quietly hopeful that a strong, legitimate government would soon be reestablished. These groups believed that the experiment in local government had failed; and they complained that constant conflicts had disrupted commerce and trade and disturbed the tranquillity of their lives. In short, much of the steam had gone out of the revolutionary movement. The few committed patriots were exhausted by factional strife, and Nueva Granada was in no condition to defend its new liberty against the retaliation and "reconquest" that was certain to come.

By October 1814 news of a Spanish invasion of Venezuela reached Cundinamarca. In a last desperate attempt to unify Nueva Granada, the foremost patriot general, Simón Bolívar, and his federalist army seized Santafé and sent troops to Honda and other centralist towns lying along the Magdalena River. Unity, such as it was, came too late. Spanish Commander Pablo Morillo and his army arrived on the coast of Venezuela in early 1815. Even as Bolívar tried to subdue centralist regions in Cundina-marca, Morillo, the "pacifier," encircled Nueva Granada with a noose of steel. Cartagena, Popayán, then Socorro, and, without a shot fired in its defense, Santafé de Bogotá fell before Morillo's army. By May 1816 all of Nueva Granada was in Spanish hands and Morillo's grim reign of terror had begun.

Fear filled the darkened houses of Santafé, the sunlit patios of Guaduas, and all the other small towns of Nueva Granada. The Santafé patriot José María Caballero wrote in his diary: "There is no family which has not cause for tears, there is no man who has not suffered, even those who were loyal to them [the Spanish] and who thought of themselves as faithful royalists. I cannot say more, because pain presses in on me and fills me with a kind of desperation, and thus I am silent, and tell not what I have suffered . . ."

But some patriots refused to withdraw into silence and paralyzing fear; their spirits could not accept the finality of Morillo's terror. Even as patriot leaders were shot or hanged in plazas all over the provinces, a strong underground resistance grew up under the very noses of the Spanish army. In Cúcuta, Socorro, Santafé, Guaduas, Honda, a few Creole patriots plotted secretly against the Spanish forces.

La Pola had watched with chagrin as the excitement of early independence was swiftly overcome by dread of Spanish retribution. But hers was not a fragile spirit, and she did all she could to oppose the Spanish. While most patriots chose the course of judicious silence, Policarpa encouraged vacillating Creoles, offered consolation to families whose sons were lost in battle, whose fathers lived facing the possibility of death or imprisonment. When the long lines of patriots, their hands chained together, their faces immovable landscapes of despair, began to arrive from Santafé on their way to Spanish dungeons, La Pola brought them refreshment and whispered words of sympathy. Among those sad emigrants were twenty priests, many of them highly placed in the church hierarchy. Policarpa was attentive to their needs, for the men were accustomed to soft living and suffered acutely from the physical hardships of the long journey. One of the captive priests was Fray Diego Padilla, the fiery Augustinian friar whose writings had reached the Salavarrietas six years before.

La Pola's most important contribution to the patriot cause was the support she gave Creole guerrillas, the vanguard of the resistance. Late at night she would answer a knock at the door, often finding José Antonio Olaya, José Ignacio Rodríguez, or some other guerrilla leader looking for rest and news. La Pola always had information on the movements of royalist troops between Honda and Guaduas and could report on the latest news from Spain. So reliable were Policarpa's reports and so fearless did she seem that those late-night visitors promised to find a way for her to make a greater contribution to the resistance.

Their promise was a timely one. By late 1816 La Pola had exhausted the possibilities for action in Guaduas. Moreover, it was known in town that her sympathies were antiroyalist and it became dangerous for anyone to be seen with her. Through her own connections with wealthy *criollos* in Guaduas, through the connections of her brothers in Santafé, and most importantly, through Olaya and Rodríguez's links to the Santafé underground, Policarpa arranged to leave Guaduas for the capital, where she could continue her work with a new degree of anonymity.

Not long after arranging the trip to Santafé, La Pola and Bibiano rode out of Guaduas. They started early, and long before the village stirred they were climbing the dusty foothills of the eastern *cordillera*. The first night they stayed with a patriot family in Villeta, then continued on the stone-paved highway that wound up through valleys, along cliffs covered with rich vegetation, and over ever higher ridges. At last they saw, spread below them, the *sabana* of Bogotá, almost seven hundred square miles of flat, fertile plain stretching north and south along a wall of moun-

# The Nueva Granada of La Pola

NOT TO SCALE

Cartagena

CARIBBEAN SEA

GULF OF MARACAIBO

Cúcuta

VENEZUELA

PROVINCE OF ANTIOQUIA

Magdalena R.

Medellín

Socorro

Tunja

PACIFIC OCEAN

Honda
Guaduas
Villeta

Sabana of Bogotá

Machetá

Santafé

Tolima

PROVINCE OF CUNDINAMARCA

Eastern Llanos

tains rising on its eastern edge. Chilled by the thin air, they
pushed on until dark and spent the night in a farmer's hut, one of
the squat, white, thick-walled dwellings dotting the *sabana*. After
a half day's journey over flat ground Policarpa and Bibiano at last
neared Santafé, the unpretentious capital whose red tile roofs and
more than a dozen church towers stood out against the dark
green mountains.

Santafé, a town of a few more than twenty thousand people,
showed signs of strain under the heavy-handed rule of Morillo
and his second in command, Juan Sámano. Sámano, a sixty-year-
old veteran of the southern campaign against patriot defenders,
was governor of Nueva Granada and commander of the king's
Third Division, a man better known for his cruelty and
intransigence than for sensitivity to human motives. Policarpa
and Bibiano entered the city by way of the San Victorino bridge,
and as they rode through the streets they saw troops everywhere.
On the façades of public buildings, where exuberant patriots had
plastered over the king's emblem a few years before, crude repre-
sentations of Fernando's coat of arms were now painted. The
Academy of San Bartolomé had been turned into headquarters of
the Battalion of El Tambo, and Policarpa guessed from the long
lines of women waiting in the street outside that it was used as a
jail as well. In the central plaza, newly paved by the forced labor
of patriots, she saw a gallows and a number of low benches for
those condemned to death by firing squad. And off to one side,
mounted on a thick pole, was a cage containing a patriot's head.

Somber sights of the occupied city accompanied them to
their destination, a house near the cathedral where Policarpa's
friends had arranged for her to stay. During the journey
Policarpa had carefully carried two sets of papers: one for the
Spanish guards at checkpoints on the highway, the other to
identify her to patriot collaborators. It was for the latter that she
reached as the wooden door opened and a young, pleasant-faced
woman led her down a narrow corridor to a small living room.
The young woman was Andrea Ricaurte, wife of a confirmed
patriot and close friend of José Ignacio Rodríguez who had arranged with her to receive Policarpa. She welcomed the two
travelers warmly, offered them hot chocolate, and urged them to

rest while they became accustomed to the altitude and the cool, thin air of Santafé.

Policarpa sensed that under the surface of Santafé's sullen tranquillity were enclaves of fierce resistance to Spanish military rule. Pablo Morillo bragged that he had broken patriot resistance; Juan Sámano followed his example by dealing severely with suspected rebels. Both were lulled into a feeling of confidence by the docility of most of Santafé's residents. But the patriots were far from silenced. The firm ground on which Morillo and Sámano believed that their reconquest stood was in reality undermined by tunnels of resistance. Not even the king's army was as loyal as its commanders chose to believe. After the major patriot defeats of 1816, prisoners of war were drafted directly into the ranks of the victorious royalist forces. By 1817 the battalions active on the *sabana* were composed of a high percentage of draftees. Almost a third of the soldiers in the Battalion of Numancia were former patriots; and the Battalion of El Tambo had many whose loyalty was at best doubtful.

During the first weeks after her arrival in Santafé, La Pola established a cover that would allow her to come and go as she liked. Her skill as a seamstress provided the perfect way to remain above suspicion as she moved freely through the streets, a basket swinging on her arm. Each morning she went to the home of one or another wealthy Creole family and spent hours sewing and listening to gossip about Sámano's cruelty and about patriot victories in the *llanos*. After long hours of sewing in the cool, high-ceilinged houses of well-to-do *criollos*, she would take a circuitous route back to Andrea Ricaurte's home, often passing an out-of-the-way corner where a young man stood idly tossing an orange into the air. Dressed sometimes in a gray woolen *ruana*, or heavy cape, sometimes in the long robes of a friar, the youth would quickly exchange his orange for the one hidden in her basket. In that prosaic way messages from Santafé began the long journey to patriot forces in the *llanos*.

For the first few weeks, La Pola performed only the most elementary chores of resistance. Gradually, however, she came to know all the principal figures in the Santafé underground, among them José María Arcos, clerk of the Battalion of El Tambo.

Many of the messages that found their way from Santafé to rebel forces in the *llanos* were reports of Spanish troop movements written in Arco's own hand. La Pola learned, too, of the major meeting places of patriot sympathizers, the countless shops and eating places where young recruits gathered, safe for a while from the watchful eyes of Spanish loyalists. During the hours of gossip in wealthy homes, she discovered which Creole families were patriots, which were split by divided loyalties, and which were hopelessly royalist. And she found out that the cloth merchants whose stores lined Royal Street were almost to a man enemies of the crown. They who sold the fine hand-woven fabrics of Socorro had ample reason to hate the Spanish and their cheap imported cloth. Little by little Policarpa learned who among Santafé's population sided with the patriots.

The central figures of resistance were Ambrosio Almeyda and his brother Vicente, as devoted to the cause of independence as they were wealthy. The Almeyda family owned a large hacienda on the *sabana* of Bogotá, as well as extensive holdings in Cúcuta, near Venezuela. Their *sabana* farm, "Tibabuyes," covered more than twenty square miles of rich land and lay just northwest of Santafé. Although they could easily have weathered the Spanish reconquest, they chose instead to enter actively into various plans of resistance. Their home in Santafé, a few blocks above the cathedral, quietly became a center of insurgency. Diffuse plans, some frankly impractical, and a loose network of spies and messengers were all that emerged from the gatherings in the Almeydas' sprawling house. Then in March and April 1817 events crystallized the Santafé resistance. In those months word came that the small, poorly equipped rebel force in the *llanos* had won a series of victories. The rebels managed to take several towns from the Spanish, in the process capturing and shooting royalist Colonel Julián Bayer. To the patriots in Santafé this news was more encouraging than it should perhaps have been. Ambrosio Almeyda became convinced that the *llanos* forces would soon invade Santafé itself.

From that hope grew a two-pronged plot. First, arms and men must be sent to buoy up the army in the *llanos*. The early, rather desultory attempts to encourage desertions from the

Spanish ranks must be stepped up and a safe escape route from Santafé to the *llanos* laid out. Policarpa, energetic, still virtually unknown in the capital, would coordinate those efforts. Second, the Almeyda brothers would use every means at their disposal—persuasion and bribery—to ensure that when the *llanos* army invaded Santafé, it would find the Spanish battalions full of patriots ready to join in the fight for independence.

Late in March 1817, as the underground resistance bolstered its strength in Santafé and in key towns on the *sabana*, Spanish officialdom celebrated the installation of the royal *Audiencia,* the judicial branch of government, in Nueva Granada. The royal seal, symbol of Spanish rule by law, was mounted on a silver platter, then strapped to the back of a horse whose reins and other trappings were of silk, silver, and gold. Government officials, astride richly harnessed horses, accompanied the seal through the streets while Santafé's citizens looked on. In a sense, the royal seal represented the best that Spain could offer: moderate government that could heal the wounds of 1810. But the seal of the *Audiencia* could do nothing while Viceroy Francisco Montalvo remained in Cartagena and Santafé languished in the clutches of Juan Sámano. The far milder law of the Viceroy was overridden by Sámano's cruel and arbitrary rule by decree and court-martial. So the executions continued, eliminating first the leaders of the revolution of 1810, then simple soldiers, deserters, and spies, and finally those merely suspected of giving aid to the patriot forces.

Fear and mistrust grew in the climate of ruthlessness cultivated by Sámano and his subalterns. Although wiser representatives of the crown might lament his cruelty, Sámano rarely modified his methods, and when he did, residents of Santafé reacted with hesitancy and suspicion. Such was the reaction to a general pardon Sámano announced on July 1, 1817. Amid fanfare, with music and parades, Sámano's aides rode through the streets announcing amnesty for all who had taken to the hills in fear of their lives. But many who heard the news doubted that Sámano was capable of pardon. "Nothing but a fishhook," Don José María Caballero noted in his diary. "Thus it has been in the past ... All those who turned themselves in ended against the stake, that is, they were shot by a firing squad. An infernal kind of pardon!"

Still, a few people benefited from Sámano's show of clemency. A number of prisoners of war were released that day, among them Alejo Sabaraín, La Pola's friend from easier times. Policarpa listened intently to his narrative of events dating from the time he left Honda to fight in Nariño's doomed southern campaign. His experiences, even for those who lived under Sámano's rule, seemed incredible. Alejo's career as a patriot soldier had lasted until the Battle of Tambo Ridge, slightly more than a year earlier, when remnants of the patriot army had flung themselves against El Tambo Fort. Sámano had been in command of the victorious Spanish troops, and his handling of republican soldiers was typical: some were absorbed into royalist ranks while others were condemned to death. Alejo had found himself in the latter group and actually faced the guns of the firing squad, when Sámano ordered them back to their quarters. If Sámano had intended that last-minute reprieve as a warning to young patriots, he was sorely disappointed. For Alejo Sabaraín dedicated himself even more firmly to the rebel cause and, on his release, sought ways to combat Sámano's forces.

At the same time Alejo joined the conspirators, a new feeling of urgency began to spread through Santafé's underground. Ambrosio Almeyda proceeded with his plans to subvert Sámano's army. Still convinced that *llanos* forces would soon liberate the capital, he arranged for three hundred horses to be brought up from the grazing lands of Tolima and kept on private land near San Victorino bridge. His agents worked their way through the barracks, talking to potential insurgents and promising them money, rank, and freedom should they turn on Spanish officials when the invasion began. Policarpa carefully extended her espionage network and laid out safe routes through the *sabana* and down to the *llanos*. Her contacts lived in every town along the escape route; some were women, others were priests or family men whose concerns seemed far removed from the political turmoil. With Alejo eager to join the patriot army in the *llanos*, she began arrangements for a group of deserters and civilians to escape from Santafé.

Disaster struck before her plans could be put into action. Late one night, after listening to an impassioned royalist harangue in battalion headquarters, one of Ambrosio Almeyda's contacts suffered a change of heart and confessed that he had been approached by patriots within the battalion itself. Questions were asked and names given. Spanish officer Pérez Delgado, whose oratory had loosened tongues throughout the ranks, soon learned that Ambrosio and Vicente Almeyda were the source of the conspiracy. He dispatched guards, and soon the brothers were under arrest.

The possibility of a revolt within the battalions unnerved the Spanish military command. The guard was doubled; persons of doubtful allegiance were closely watched and in several cases imprisoned. Because of the Spaniards' renewed vigilance, Andrea Ricaurte decided to move from her house near the central plaza to a smaller place up on the skirts of the *cordillera*, two blocks from the neighborhood called Egipto. Even though the Almeydas sat in jail, Policarpa decided to forge ahead with the plan she and Alejo had worked out.

On September 9, scarcely three weeks after the arrests, Sabarain and Arellano, a friend who had also been pardoned on July 1, met with José María Arcos and a handful of soldiers to make their escape. All were veterans of the hopeless southern campaign against the Spanish expeditionary force. All were confirmed patriots, even after a year of imprisonment and forced military service. When they left Santafé, Sabaraín carried a series of documents prepared by Policarpa, listing names of patriot supporters in Santafé and within the Spanish battalions. Arcos, too, carried information for the republican commanders in the *llanos*. In his own writing he described Sámano's plans and troop movements on the *sabana*, based on intelligence he had gathered as clerk of El Tambo Battalion. Carrying that invaluable information, plus their arms and ammunition, they began the journey north through the *sabana*.

Eleven days passed. Back in Santafé, Policarpa, Andrea, and Bibiano waited anxiously for word of Alejo's progress. On market day, they searched out their contacts from neighboring towns— women dressed in long black skirts, broad-brimmed hats and wool *ruanas,* who brought fresh produce from their towns to the capital. Yes, they nodded, the men had passed through four, six, seven days ago; yes, they had left safely.

On September 20, word came that Alejo and his companions had been captured deep in the hills that sloped down to the *llanos.* La Pola knew she was in imminent danger. If Alejo had not destroyed the papers he carried, she would be directly implicated in the plot. But before going into hiding, she had one last escape to arrange. Late on the evening of September 23, in the heart of El Tambo Battalion, a corporal named Torneros approached the guard outside Ambrosio and Vicente Almeyda's cell and ordered him off on an errand. When the guard returned, Torneros and the Almeyda brothers were gone. Every effort to find them failed. Well-placed bribes and Policarpa's network of sympathizers carried them safely north of Santafé to Machetá, where they stayed with Gertrudis Vanegas, one of La Pola's contacts, and began organizing a new guerrilla group. By the third week in September, Policarpa was in hiding in Andrea's house. Bibiano was her only direct contact with the outside, the only source of food and news.

Sámano began searching for La Pola soon after Alejo and his fellows were brought back to Santafé. The search was not easy. Few of his men remembered what she looked like, and few knew whom she lived with or where she worked. After all, there were more than eleven thousand women in Santafé, far more women than men, and many were young, dark-haired *criollas.* Days passed and Sámano's soldiers found no trace of her. Annoyed, Sámano assigned the search to Sergeant Anselmo Iglesias, an especially effective minion of the king. Iglesias knew that life in Santafé revolved around the small shops that stood on every corner, and he believed that La Pola, if she were still in the city, would eventually be traced from one of them. Methodically he interrogated shopkeepers in central Santafé, first those north of the cathedral, then those east and south of the plaza. Sometime in the second week of October, he found a shopkeeper not far from El Tambo Battalion who, for a price, admitted knowing Policarpa. Her brother came there every day or two, she told him. "Wait here long enough and you'll see him," she said.

Iglesias was more than willing to wait. For several days he

stood across the street, watching for the prearranged signal of identification. Late on the afternoon of October 13 or 14, he looked up and saw a boy about fifteen years old leaving the shop and heading down the street. Iglesias followed him at a distance until the youth, unaware that he was being watched, disappeared into a low doorway on a narrow side street.

An hour or two after Bibiano returned from his errands, the door of Andrea's house burst open and, before either woman could move, Sergeant Iglesias and an escort of soldiers stood in the small living room. All either woman could think of was the sheaf of papers lying on the kitchen table—papers that implicated dozens of *criollos* and included letters from the *llanos* commanders. Policarpa jumped to her feet and began a tirade against Iglesias and the Spanish army. Using the coarse language of the marketplace, she cursed them and heaped abuse on the names of Sámano, Morillo, the viceroy, and even Fernando VII. The men were thrown off balance by the violent verbal attack. While La Pola held their attention, Andrea slipped into the back room, quickly stuffed the pile of papers into the fire, and returned with her nursing babe in her arms.

In a few minutes Iglesias and his men regained their composure and placed Policarpa and Bibiano under arrest. Andrea Ricaurte escaped arrest because she was nursing a child and because careful search of her house revealed no telltale evidence of clandestine involvement. Bibiano remained in jail for three days; repeated beatings failed to make him say anything that might involve his sister and, incidentally, himself in espionage.

Policarpa was not so fortunate. Clearly implicated by the papers Alejo had carried at the time of his capture, she and fifteen others were held in the battalion prison. This time Sámano moved with dispatch. Deprived of the chance to try the Almeydas, he quickly assigned a prosecutor to Policarpa's case, and evidence was prepared and presented to the court-martial on November 10 and 11. Of the fifteen defendants, nine were sentenced to death, Policarpa and Alejo among them. Two days later, the condemned men and La Pola were moved to the chapel of the Academy of El Rosario, where they prepared to die.

Among the soldiers assigned to guard them that day was one

who had fought with Alejo and the others in the south. José Hilario López, a young soldier destined to become president of independent Nueva Granada, wrote an eyewitness account of the eve of Policarpa's execution. The sight of his comrades-in-arms and their words of farewell so moved him that he wept—strange behavior, to say the least, for a soldier in His Majesty's army. Making an excuse, José Hilario moved to a post outside the chapel door. La Pola saw him pass and noticed his tears. "Don't cry for us, little López," she said. "It will be a relief to get away from these tyrants, these wild beasts, these monsters . . ."

From his post he could see La Pola arguing with the priests who had come to advise her on her soul's salvation. Forgive your captors, they said; accept your fate with resignation or you will be forever damned.

To these exhortations La Pola reacted with scorn. Let my soul be lost, she cried. I cannot forgive those monsters of iniquity. My only consolation is the certainty that my death will be avenged. The horrified priests begged her to be silent, suspecting perhaps that she had lost her sanity under the pressure of nearing death. But the torrent of angry words never stopped until the dark of night, her last on earth, served to calm her fury.

On the morning of the executions, set for nine o'clock, La Pola resumed her diatribe against the Spanish, against the monster Juan Sámano, against Americans who blindly obeyed the Spanish. Three blocks separated the chapel of El Rosario from the central plaza where La Pola and the condemned men were to meet the firing squad. Gathered in that square were a multitude of citizens, both patriots and royalists, and soldiers who, Sámano hoped, would derive a moral lesson from the spectacle of death. Since La Pola was the first woman to be executed in Santafé, there were many whose curiosity brought them to witness so unique and macabre a drama, and it was upon them that she heaped her bitterest words. Policarpa walked through the crowd with firm step and, ignoring her priestly escort, cried out to the crowd, "Indolent people! How different would be our fate today if you knew the price of liberty! But it is not too late. Although I am a woman and young, I have more than enough courage to suffer this death and a thousand more. Do not forget my example!"

Sámano, watching from his balcony, signaled the drum corps to drown out the rest of her words. Soldiers led her to the bench, but she refused to stand on it, claiming that such a position was not proper for a woman. So saying she halfway knelt on it and carefully smoothed her skirts just before the soldiers blindfolded her and tied her hands together. Almost as a single shot, six bullets pierced her back, and Policarpa was silent at last.

La Pola's body was interred in the Church of San Agustín, but the fact of her execution refused to lie buried. Try as he would, Sámano could not put the ignominy of Policarpa's execution behind him. The vengeance she had foreseen was not long delayed. Within two years Spain's army fell in defeat and Sámano, dressed in peasant clothing, fled in cowardly retreat from Bolívar's victorious army, trampling beneath his horse's hooves the frightened royalists who filled the highway to Honda.

Years later, when chroniclers of the *patria boba* looked back on the foolish and heroic acts of that period, Policarpa stood out among the great martyrs of the Reign of Terror. The patriotic bravado of her last hours came to obscure the course of her life to that moment. Large parts of her final harangue were carefully preserved; the statue erected to her memory in Bogotá shows her seated, blindfolded, the moment before Sámano's guns cut her down; and her face is etched on Colombia's two-peso note. Yet the details of her life and her flamboyant individuality have been largely forgotten.

In a sense, La Pola has been transformed into a symbol of all the women patriots of the resistance. She is revered not so much for her own qualities and dramatic bravery, but because she alone, among the women who supported the underground with their deeds and sometimes their lives, had a national audience at the moment of death. The humbly born *criolla* of Guaduas, whose sharp tongue and almost irrational fearlessness made her Spanish guard cringe and priests blush, lives on as a national heroine who scarcely resembles the fiery, young woman she was in life.

# VI

# Leopoldina, 1797-1826

PORTUGUESE AMERICANS AND Spanish Americans won political independence at the same historical moment, but their
effectiveness in governing vast new territories was quite different. While their Spanish-speaking cousins fought among
themselves and fragmented their homeland, the Brazilians created a unified nation that in time dwarfed all others in Latin
America. The first act of this drama, and the story of the Austrian
princess who played an important part in it, is one of the most
fascinating of the Independence era.

Long before 1703, when the relationship was formalized by
treaty, Portugal was under the thumb of English commercial interests. With the coming of Napoleon Bonaparte a century later
the diminutive Iberian kingdom became little more than a British
satellite, relying heavily on her powerful ally for protection from
French armies. When Lisbon finally fell, it was a British fleet that
carried the royal family of Braganza to sanctuary in Brazil. After
Napoleon's defeat the Braganzas hoped to offset Britain's influence by allying themselves through marriage with the Hapsburgs
of Austria. Thus did Archduchess Leopoldina of Hapsburg come
to leave her beloved Europe for Brazil, where her husband,
Crown Prince Pedro of Braganza, awaited her.

Princess, and later Empress, Leopoldina was an ideal sovereign, performing all the duties required of her. In her short life-

time she bore numerous children, among them a son who inherited many of her virtues and who ruled Brazil with magnanimity for half a century. She served as regent on several occasions and was instrumental in persuading her husband to declare independence from Portugal, an act for which she has never received sufficient recognition. Because of her obvious fascination with their land, her affection for them, and her strength of character, the Austrian-born empress earned the respect and love of her subjects. This fact alone was of inestimable importance to the new nation, for Brazil was thus able to postpone for many years the struggle between monarchists and republicans that so devastated Spanish America in its national period.

A gloomy counterpoint to her success in other areas was Leopoldina's troubled personal life. She and her husband were like oil and water, she disciplined and intellectual, he impulsive and passionate. Though taught the meaning of *noblesse oblige* from birth, Leopoldina did not know how to defend herself from the coquette who mesmerized Dom Pedro and destroyed her happiness. But to her great credit she bore her triumphs and her tragedies with a strength of character that left no doubt that she was every inch a queen.

If Archduchess Maria Leopoldina, the daughter of Franz I of Austria, had ever harbored romantic notions about imperial marriages, the betrothal of her sister soon banished them. In 1810, when Leopoldina was just thirteen, Marie Louise was married to Napoleon Bonaparte of France, the man who had been Austria's greatest enemy for more than a decade. Stifling her aversion to the upstart emperor, Marie Louise bowed to her father's will and traveled obediently, if tearfully, to his bed. Napoleon had defeated her country three times and was now to be her husband. So much for romance.

The Hapsburgs had long used marriage as a tool of diplomacy. Leopoldina well remembered stories told of her great-aunts, daughters of the great Maria Theresa, who years before had submitted to their mother's elaborate matchmaking plans. There was Caroline, who shook uncontrollably as she married the gauche and sulking king of Naples; Amalia, wed against her will to the duke of Parma, who never developed beyond emotional adolescence; and Marie Antoinette, whose marriage to France's pathetic Dauphin ended under the blade of a guillotine.

Within the golden walls of Schönbrunn palace, Leopoldina's placid life belied the uncertain future that awaited her. Protected by Hapsburg power and its centuries-old absolutist traditions, surrounded by her personal servants and ladies-in-waiting, Leopoldina was encouraged to indulge her tastes, which were not frivolous by any means. She was fascinated by the natural sciences, mathematics, history, and travel; she collected coins and medals, studied insects, plants, and animals, read widely, and learned to converse in ten languages. Her devotion to intellectual pursuits was balanced by a love of the outdoors. Every day she rode about the palace grounds, from the ancient Roman ruins down shady promenades where trees towered above clipped hedge rows, and on through thick shrubbery to higher ground behind the fountains.

Leopoldina was not a fairy-tale princess. Unfashionably studious, her taste in clothes determined by the rigors of frequent horseback riding, Leopoldina was blond and plump, admirably robust, and endowed with the light blue eyes, weak chin, and bowed lower lip that characterized the Hapsburgs. She disliked the trappings of feminine allure: long trains, elaborate coiffures, jewels, and the rouged cheeks and painted lips that adorned ladies of the court. She felt that devotion to beauty was not only time-consuming but slightly profane, and the formidable Leopoldina avoided worldliness with great determination.

Life, serene and uncomplicated, flowed like a gentle Viennese melody. Indeed, music pervaded not only the palace but the city as well, for Leopoldina's Vienna was the Vienna of Haydn, Beethoven, Mozart, and unnumbered lesser geniuses. Never was a city so enamoured of operettas and concerts; never did a city produce so many musicians and attract so many composers. Even Leopoldina's father, the austere and conservative Emperor Franz, was a frequent performer in the court theater at Schönbrunn, where he played first violin in the orchestra. The archduchess absorbed a love of music from the air she breathed, from the melodies that rose from open-air concerts and escaped from the windows of middle-class homes.

In 1814 Marie Louise returned to Vienna with her son by Napoleon, the little duke of Reichstadt. Napoleon's luck had changed. Defeats first in Spain and then, disastrously, in Russia stripped him of power and of the marriage that bound him to the Hapsburgs' boundless prestige. Leopoldina listened to Marie Louise's whispered accounts of her ill-starred match and became justifiably uneasy when she learned of her own betrothal to the duke of Saxony. But events soon conspired to deprive the duke of his fiancée. Late in November 1816 a marriage contract was signed arranging the marriage of Leopoldina to Dom Pedro of Braganza, the ruling house of Portugal and Brazil.

The Hapsburgs were not entirely convinced that this match was a great improvement over the first. The Braganzas had ruled Portugal for almost two hundred years, so there was no question of their legitimacy. But the present ruler, Dom João VI, father of Pedro, had the dubious distinction of being the only European monarch ever to remove himself, his court, and the entire national government to an overseas colony. The incredible move was made late in 1807 as Napoleon's army, commanded by Marshal Junot, marched on Lisbon and threatened Dom João with the same fate suffered by his brother-in-law Fernando VII of Spain. Rather than submit to French rule, Dom João loaded the national treasury and thousands of courtiers and government officials onto ships provided by the British and sailed away to Brazil. Stranger still was that, once established in Rio de Janeiro, Don João seemed reluctant to return to Europe and even elevated Brazil to the status of a kingdom, coequal with Portugal.

Franz of Austria could scarcely conceive of leaving his gracious Vienna for any length of time, much less abandoning it for a wild, uncivilized colonial capital. Yet Dom João had done just that, and his son Pedro, only nine years old at the time of the voyage, was by now probably half Brazilian. The Hapsburgs worried about sending Leopoldina so far away to an uncertain fate. But Prince Metternich, Franz's wily counselor, supported the match, and the emperor at last agreed to it.

Within months Vienna was dazzled by the arrival of Dom João's special emissary to the Austrian court, the marquês of Marialva. Eager to impress the haughty Hapsburgs with the wealth of Portugal and Brazil, Dom João had instructed Marialva to spare no expense during the official courtship and marriage by proxy of the Hapsburg archduchess. This Marialva did with lavishness and flair. On February 7, 1816, Marialva, Portugal's ambassador extraordinary, arrived with an ostentation that brought throngs of onlookers to Vienna's streets and drew the highest nobility and the emperor himself to strategically located balconies. As the marquês later wrote to Dom Joào, never had Vienna seen such a lavish embassy.

The next day, in accord with the most exacting requirements of court etiquette, Marialva made his formal appearance at court in Hofburg Palace. In the great ballroom Marialva presented Emperor Franz the letter from Dom Joào that formally requested Leopoldina's hand in marriage. Of the gifts Marialva brought to court that evening, the most extravagant was a necklace for Leopoldina. It consisted of a miniature portrait of Dom Pedro, surrounded by large Brazilian diamonds and topped by a tiny gold crown, supported by a chain made entirely of gold and diamonds. A gasp rose from the court as the candlelight was caught by the diamonds. Doubts about the reasons for the Braganzas' peculiar fondness for Brazil vanished on the spot.

Negotiations over Leopoldina's dowry were carried out by Marialva and Metternich, whose favor was assured by a well-timed gift of several ingots of pure Brazilian gold. Her dowry was to be 200,000 florins plus a handsome annual allowance of 80,000 florins. But to Leopoldina the most important part of the transaction was Pedro himself. She knew little about him as yet, only that his portrait showed a handsome young man with large dark eyes, curly hair, high forehead, and fine features. In that attractive face Leopoldina thought she saw the reflection of moral superiority, of goodness and kindliness. To her discrete, even timid, questions about his character, she received the most positive answers; yes, he was good-hearted and loved by his subjects; yes, he was an avid student of the natural sciences; yes, he was not only an accomplished musician and composer but a daring horseman as well. Leopoldina was won by second-hand information and a jeweled portrait.

Soon after the formalities of betrothal, Marialva held a sumptuous ball at his residence and invited the cream of Viennese society. Then, on Dom João's birthday, May 13, 1817, Leopoldina was wed to Pedro by proxy. In celebration of the great event Marialva planned a banquet that would surpass anything the Braganzas' representative had yet shown Vienna. In the Augarten, a large park in the heart of the city, Marialva built a beautiful glass palace, a rotunda with cupola, that would be used only once—in honor of the Hapsburg-Braganza union. On the evening of June 1, two thousand of Austria's highest nobles, the corps of ambassadors to the Hapsburg court, and distinguished officials began to arrive. Greeted by Marialva himself, the guests were treated to sights and sounds that enthralled even the most discerning among them. Thousands of lanterns hung from trees around the glistening palace, and gentle waltzes came from orchestras hidden behind every fragrant hedge.

At nine o'clock the royal family arrived, and Leopoldina, dressed in pure white with Pedro's tiny portrait sparkling at her throat, accepted the first waltz with the marquês. Together they danced to the elegant rhythms so adored by the Viennese while the guests, themselves sparkling with gold, brocades, and gems, looked on. Later, the guests dined on a hundred different dishes from the finest silver, porcelain, and crystal; the royal family ate from plates of solid gold. Marialva stunned Europe when, in the days following the banquet, he ordered the palace converted to an orphanage and the ornaments sold to aid the poor of Vienna. For his unprecedented generosity the people called him king— King Marialva. If young Pedro were anything like his ambassador, Leopoldina was indeed fortunate.

The archduchess might be forgiven if she had come to confuse Pedro, about whom she knew very little, with Marialva, who had showered her with attentions and gifts all during Vienna's lovely spring. Without realizing it, she had come to think of Pedro as a younger Marialva—educated, courtly, considerate. The admiration (some say adoration) she felt for Marialva was magically transferred to the unseen Pedro, but Leopoldina, in her innocence, could not guess the true nature of either man. How could she know that Marialva, a middle-aged bachelor, had for many years been the lover of Queen Carlota Joaquina, Pedro's own mother; and that rumor claimed that Marialva, not Dom

João, was Pedro's real father? Those and other revelations would come later.

When Leopoldina left Vienna on June 12, she was accompanied by her three ladies-in-waiting and a cadre of servants, the countess of Trinburg, and eighty-three-year-old Count Edling, who insisted on going as her chamberlain. Members of a Bavarian scientific mission traveled with her, as did Thomas Ender, the Viennese artist; Dr. Jorge Schäffer, German-born agent and trouble-shooter for the princess; and a librarian to care for her extensive book collection. Accompanied part of the way by Prince Metternich, the entourage journeyed to Livorno and later embarked on the Portuguese frigates *Dom João VI* and the smaller *São Sebastião*.

During the Atlantic crossing, Leopoldina was entertained by an orchestra contracted by merchants of Rio de Janeiro, and she polished her already fluent Portuguese, complaining that the great number of Arabic words in its vocabulary made it difficult to speak correctly. She looked forward with confidence to meeting her husband and his family, as well she might, since she was still unaware of several disagreeable facts about them. Leopoldina did not know of the continual strife between João and his wanton wife Carlota Joaquina, of Crown Prince Pedro's relative ignorance, or of his constant amatory adventures. And of course she knew nothing of the letter Carlota Joaquina had sent to Marialva early in the Vienna courtship: "And don't contract this marriage if the archduchess is very ugly," wrote the queen. "Our Pedro, like you, is crazy about beautiful women, and if he should see an ugly princess, it will be a great misfortune for them both." How well Carlota knew the dangers of a mismatch. Her own marriage to the stolid, obese João was a tragedy, and she knew that hot-blooded Pedro took after his mother to an astonishing degree: both attributed marital fidelity to lack of energy rather than to moral superiority.

The sight that greeted Leopoldina after eighty-two days at sea was breathtaking. Rio de Janeiro stretched sinuously along the curving beaches of Guanabara Bay, its waterfront unscarred by docks, its sand almost pure white. Behind the city, with its narrow streets and white, flatroofed buildings, rose the granite peaks, Sugarloaf and Hunchback, and smaller hills covered with lush green growth.

As a twenty-one-gun salute echoed from the forts around the city, a gilded barge left the hundreds of small craft in the bay and approached the ship carrying the royal family—Dom João, Carlota, Pedro, and his sisters and younger brother Miguel. Leopoldina, on the arm of her protector, the marquês of Castelo Melhor, boarded the barge and fell into a deep curtsy at the feet of the king, her father-in-law. João raised her gently and kissed her as though she were his own daughter, then presented her to Pedro. Murmuring words of greeting, Leopoldina gazed for the first time at her husband. She realized immediately that even a portrait surrounded by diamonds could not do him justice, could not capture the lean and muscular body that gloried in action, the tanned, handsome face, the magnetic maleness of the crown prince. Her heart, in one moment, became his forever.

Leopoldina was to spend one last night on the frigate, since it would have been highly improper for her to disembark before the ceremony of nuptial blessing. The next day, November 6, an honor guard formed on the beach at the Royal Pavilion. At eleven Carlota and the princesses left the palace and proceeded down Rua Direita to the shore, their six coaches followed by a detachment of cavalry. Dom João, Crown Prince Pedro, and his brother arrived soon after, and the entire family was again rowed out to Leopoldina's frigate, where they found the young bride in a gown of white silk embroidered with silver and gold and sparkling with hundreds of brilliants. A fine veil of the lightest white silk fell gracefully over her face and blew in the gentle sea breeze as, after lunch on board ship, they returned together across the bay.

The royal family, Leopoldina, her ladies-in-waiting, and a bevy of important nobles disembarked with great ceremony, entered velvet-draped carriages, and traveled slowly through the carefully sand-carpeted streets between banners emblazoned with the Braganza coat of arms. The air was perfumed by hundreds of flowers and herbs as the procession passed through the three Roman arches built for the occasion by merchants and foreign residents in Rio. At two they reached the Royal Chapel on

Palace Square, where the marriage was blessed before the enthusiastic *vivas* of the people. When Pedro took his princess's hand, cannons boomed their salute from the forts around the bay. In the days following her arrival, receptions, concerts, and even a free opera celebrated the marriage. Only then were Pedro and Leopoldina considered adequately wed, and they settled into the palace of São Cristovào across the marshes north of Rio.

Leopoldina's first night in the arms of her new husband was probably not as dreadful as rumor later described it. Pedro was not the brute that some—such as the chambermaids who eavesdropped at his door—made him seem, and although he had enjoyed the favors of many a Rio beauty, he treated his gentle wife with kindness. Weeks later Leopoldina wrote to her aunt that she had "found in my husband a friend whom I adore for his excellent qualities." She added with satisfaction that the horses in the royal stables were very fast and that the tranquillity of her daily routine allowed for reading, writing, and music. "As my Husband plays almost all the instruments very well, I accompany him on the Piano and in this way I have the satisfaction of being always close to the beloved person." Only the heat of the Brazilian summer and swarms of mosquitoes detracted from Leopoldina's happiness, and no hint of dismay appears in the frank letters she wrote her closest confidante.

Brazil captivated the princess. She found the rich and variegated countryside irresistible and explored its fields, forests, and mountains with all the energy in her sturdy body. Occasionally she came upon a spot that reminded her of home, but she would fight off the wave of nostalgia and continue on her way, remarking to her companions on the beauty of a tropical flower or a brilliant bird. The Austrian princess was no less interested in the exotic human element of Brazil. Almost four million people, half of them black and the rest European and Indian, had intermingled to create a whole new palette of human color.

As Leopoldina observed very soon after her arrival, the institution of slavery was fundamental to Brazilian society. Long since discredited among Europe's more enlightened circles and attacked by Great Britain, Brazil's slavery was both a cause of and an obstacle to its economic development. An elaborate network of laws restricted slaves, mulattoes, and the half million free blacks from advancing in society, as they preserved the privileges of the *reinóis* and the *mazombos*, Portuguese and Brazilian-born whites. Yet those closely guarded privileges were hollow indeed. Whites were freed from hard labor on their plantations, it is true, but there was little they could do to fill long hours of boredom. Wealthy landowners and their families were fed, bathed, and supported by slaves. Urban families sent their slaves out to work as artisans or simple day laborers. Since no man who hoped to rise in society ever engaged in manual labor, and since there were few schools and fewer cultural diversions, the so-called privileged classes were left to stew in a tepid broth of inactivity and ignorance. The only acceptable pastimes for a gentleman were hunting, gambling, and wenching; and gentlewomen were confined to home or church for life.

The Brazilian woman seemed as curious a creature as any of the strange species of fish or fowl Leopoldina found in her new country. No parallel could be found between the industrious housewives or wellborn ladies of Austria and the lethargic, cloistered women of Brazil's middle and upper classes. Carefully chaperoned at all times, their minds protected from the taint of new ideas, the young ladies of Brazil were coaxed into early bloom, married by the age of fifteen, and set to bearing children at once. If they survived the rigors of motherhood, their fragile beauty soon drowned in layers of fat brought on by shockingly poor diets and gross inactivity. With few demands made on them and with servants to maintain the household, nurse the babies, and watch over the children, women had little to do. In fact, some spent their entire lives seated cross-legged on floor cushions, nibbling convent-baked sweetmeats and embroidering endless altar cloths. To the active and healthy Leopoldina, such an existence was unthinkable. On one count, however, she found herself in complete sympathy with her Brazilian sisters, this in the face of considerable criticism. To those who were shocked by the way Brazilian women dressed at home, she pointed out that a light chemise and petticoat, bare legs, and uncorseted bodies were the only sensible attire in a sultry climate. Leopoldina herself wore simple, loose-fitting clothing and refused to cinch in her waist, even though an unnaturally tiny waist was the fashion of the day.

In June following her arrival, Leopoldina told her delighted husband that she was expecting a child. The news was doubly welcome to Pedro, since he had yet to taste the solemn joys of responsible fatherhood. His only other acknowledged child was illegitimate, the product of an affair with the French dancer Noëmi.

The months of Leopoldina's pregnancy passed in cheerful anticipation, and on April 4, 1819, the future queen of Portugal was born. The delivery was surrounded by elaborate protocol. When labor began, the entire government—ministers of state, the king's counselors, the diplomatic corps, and other officials—assembled in the palace of São Cristovão. As soon as the baby was born, even before the umbilical cord had been cut, the highest ranking among them crowded into Leopoldina's chamber to welcome the tiny princess. Shortly thereafter the baby was placed on a large silver platter and presented to those assembled as "the royal princess," to which all answered, "Blessed be the princess."

When the baby had been presented and blessed four times, she was returned to her mother who murmured, "I receive my daughter for the glory of God and the royal house of Braganza." Leopoldina and Pedro disagreed over the baby's name. She would, of course, be named Maria, since the Hapsburg princesses were all Marias themselves. Leopoldina wanted to name her Maria Alba da Glória in honor of Marialva, but Pedro objected— some say strenuously—and so the little girl became simply Maria da Glória.

Leopoldina and Pedro were affectionate parents. They doted on their pretty daughter, and Pedro himself vaccinated her as soon as possible. They found a reliable wetnurse for the baby and assigned a lady-in-waiting to her, but unlike many upper-class parents of the day they did not abandon her entirely to the care of servants. In September 1819, when Maria was almost six months old, Leopoldina wrote to her aunt, "My little daughter is the prettiest and most intelligent child I know; she is already beginning to babble and to stand on her feet, showing an extraordinary strength in her legs. With a pleasure entirely new to me I observe her daily progress and I can proudly say that she knows me and my beloved Husband because, when we are at home, we do nothing but carry her around in our arms by turns."

Although the heat, humidity, and constant rains of spring bothered Leopoldina and made her think longingly of "beautiful Europe," she was still reasonably happy. In the same letter she wrote: "The members of the Portuguese royal family are distinguished by the goodness of their hearts and I can't praise their generosity enough. I enjoy perfect happiness, in my perfect solitude, that pleases me because in this way I have more time to look after my daughter and live only for my Husband and my studies."

Leopoldina quickly resumed her active routine after Maria da Glória was born. Every morning before nine she rode out around the palace of São Cristovão or accompanied Pedro to the barracks at Niteroi where, dressed in a blue dragoon uniform, her blond hair pulled back under a cap, and silver spurs clanking on her boots, she reviewed troops with her handsome prince. She had become a popular figure in Rio. Strange though her habits seemed to the Brazilians, they admired her equestrian skill and respected her intellect. Always at Pedro's side during parades and maneuvers, she appeared often in public and, unlike her shrewish mother-in-law, was friendly with the people.

The frequent trips to Rio and appearances on horseback were halted early in December 1819, when Leopoldina suffered a miscarriage that left her weak and depressed. The following July she was again pregnant, but in October she lost the hoped-for child in the fourth month. Frightened by the miscarriages and the ominous possibility that she would never bear a son, Leopoldina withdrew into a cloistered existence, going out infrequently and dedicating herself to sedentary pastimes. For a time the letters to her aunt ceased as she waited anxiously for another child to be born.

At the time Leopoldina went into seclusion, Pedro was being drawn into a political whirlwind. Since Napoleon's defeats in 1814 and 1815, defenders of European monarchy had waited eagerly for Dom João to return to Portugal. A wave of liberal sentiment was sweeping Europe, and supporters of monarchy begged the king to defend his sovereignty against the double threat of liberal constitutions and parliaments. Although shaken by rebellion in Spain and by alarming news of revolt in Portugal itself, João still hesitated to leave his beloved Brazil. For a time he considered sending Pedro in his place, frightening Leopoldina with the possibility that she might be left behind; but at last Dom João reluctantly consented to return to Lisbon, leaving Crown Prince Pedro to rule Brazil as viceroy and regent.

In the midst of this upset, Leopoldina anticipated the birth of her second child. The long months of expectation were brought to a happy conclusion when on March 6, 1821, Dom João Carlos, heir to the thrones of Brazil and Portugal, was born. Less than two months later, the baby's grandfather boarded the frigate that carried his name, dallied for two days in the hope that something would keep him in Brazil, and finally sailed away, never to return. In his "Instructions for the Guidance of the Prince Royal as Regent" Dom João gave Pedro complete authority over the government and ordered that in the event of the prince's death, "the Regency of the Kingdom of Brazil shall pass directly to the Princess Royal, his wife and my much loved and valued Daughter-in-law." The affection he felt for Leopoldina—for they were similar in temperament and interests—made his departure especially difficult.

Queen Carlota Joaquina had never shared João's love of Brazil. She hated the mixed-blood Brazilians and blamed the tropical climate for her decaying teeth and the hair that grew lushly all over her body. As she boarded ship she threw her slippers into the bay, braying that not even the dust of Brazil would follow her to Lisbon. In the entourage of João and Carlota were the royal prince Miguel, the princesses, and three thousand nobles and ministers of state, most of them Portuguese, who longed to return to their estates in Europe. In the hold of the ship lay chest after chest containing the combined treasure of Brazil and Portugal. Ingots of gold and silver, freshly minted coins, the total assets of Brazil's first and only bank and even that month's deposits by Rio's charitable institutions—a grand total of fifty million *cruzados*—left Brazil with Dom João.

Dom Pedro was left in a tenuous position. His treasury was bare; only paper money and easily counterfeited copper coins were in circulation. A national sense of insecurity filled the vacuum created by João's departure. Exports dropped, business was paralyzed, and credit evaporated. No one knew whether Dom Pedro, armed only with native shrewdness and unbounded energy, was equal to the job of governing. Economic disarray, communication made difficult by the size of his kingdom, and the increasing popularity of constitutional government were problems that confronted the twenty-two-year-old prince.

Dom Pedro's first acts were calculated to save money. The downtown palace was converted to offices for judicial and administrative personnel, and the royal family moved all its possessions to São Cristovão and the plantation of Santa Cruz. Twelve hundred horses had formerly occupied the royal stables; only 156 now remained. In a wise move designed to still criticism, Pedro halved his own allowance before reducing the salaries of government officials.

Leopoldina supported Pedro's economy measures by reorganizing the royal household around slave, rather than paid, labor and by reducing the tremendous costs of the palace kitchen that provided meals to an army of staff and guests. She also refrained from complaining about her own finances, even though by that time, after four years of marriage, it was clear that the generous income promised in her nuptial contract would never be paid. Indeed, the only sum she received had been a gift from the marquês of Marialva while she was still in Vienna. The costs of supporting her personal attendants and of buying books and specimens for her collections had seriously eroded that original sum, and although she spent little on her appearance, she willingly opened her purse to charities and to individuals seeking her help. She had to count on Pedro to refill it, and when his generosity flagged, she found herself absolutely without funds. By September 1821 she wrote to the marquês of Marialva in Paris, promising that she would pay him for the books he had sent as soon as "our pathetic finances are in a state of convalescence." But only by going into debt was she able to pay him back.

Although Pedro claimed to be a republican, he was by training and temperament an absolutist. He was therefore poorly prepared to deal with Brazilian demands for representative government, or with the bickering and strife that accompanied republicanism. Fortunately, Pedro had an able ally in the person of José Bonifácio de Andrada e Silva, a gifted politician who worked diligently to tie São Paulo province to Dom Pedro's government. José Bonifácio had studied in Europe as a youth, and then remained there many years serving Portugal in various official capacities. In 1819 he returned to his native São Paulo. His intelligence and culture recommended him to Leopoldina, and after his success in calming the south, Pedro asked him to be minister of state and foreign affairs. José Bonifácio was called to Rio early in January 1822, and Leopoldina, hearing that he was coming, rode out to persuade him to accept the ministry, a mission in which she was successful.

From the moment of Dom João's departure the previous April, Portugal's increasingly powerful representative assembly, the *Côrtes*, had tried every means to reduce Brazil to its former subservient position. Displeased by Brazil's great advances under the father's loving care, the *Côrtes* was angered by the son's independence of spirit. To each of the *Côrtes's* demeaning orders, Dom Pedro responded with hostility. Knowing his father to be a virtual prisoner of the *Côrtes*, Pedro ignored it and did as much as possible to help the unhappy João.

Lisbon finally realized the hopelessness of controlling Brazil while Dom Pedro ruled from Rio and in December 1821 ordered him to return immediately for the purpose of "completing his education." Leopoldina feared that Pedro would lose Brazil forever if he were to obey the *Côrtes*, and she tried every means to persuade him to stay. Early in January she wrote to her confidant Schäffer, "The Prince is decided, but not so much as I would wish; the ministers will be changed for native-born men who have insight, and the government will be of the kind in the united North American free states. To achieve all this has cost me much—I only wish I could inspire him to greater firmness." The same day she scrawled a second note to Schäffer: "In my hurry I forgot to tell you: that I believe it would be better were the gallant Brazilians to leave my Husband over the government here according to his will; otherwise this small detail might prevent *his staying here.*" By January 9, 1822, the efforts of Leopoldina and José Bonifácio achieved the desired result. Dom Pedro answered the *Côrtes* with the words "Tell the people that I will stay: *Fico.*" Brazil was only a short step away from severing its ties with Portugal.

Clashes between Portuguese troops stationed in Rio and defenders of Brazil's embryonic independence forced Leopoldina, then in her eighth month of pregnancy, and her children to seek safety at Santa Cruz. During the journey little Prince João, not yet a year old, fell seriously ill. As Leopoldina later wrote to her aunt, "The poor little one, who had a weak nervous system, caught some sort of inflammation of the liver and, poorly treated, or rather improperly diagnosed, died after two weeks of continuous suffering and a final epileptic siege that lasted twenty-eight hours. I assure you, dear Aunt, that in my whole life I have never known greater grief and that only my religion and the passage of time will console me."

Little more than a month later, a second princess, Januaria, was born. Although both parents had hoped for another son, Leopoldina found comfort in her new baby and the distraction of arranging for a wetnurse and planning an elaborate baptism. But Leopoldina never completely recovered from her loss. Already sober by nature, inclined to solitary study, the princess found it increasingly difficult to shake off the accumulation of grief, nostalgia for Europe, and loneliness. Circumstance, too, conspired to trap her in melancholy, for as Pedro threw himself increasingly into the swirl of events, Leopoldina was left to her continual pregnancies and domestic worries without the stimulation his company had provided in the tranquil early years of their marriage. Indeed, constantly afraid of miscarriage, Leopoldina became cautious and introspective. Her debts plagued her too, and with Pedro gone so often she despaired of winning his help. Her personal finances had come to such a state that in early August she received a note from a creditor reminding her of a debt that had fallen due the previous week. With no income of her own, she panicked and wrote her friend Schäffer: "My dear Schäffer, I am grievously embarrassed. Read the enclosed letter; the man says he will make a fuss; for the love of God see if you can satisfy him."

Pedro knew nothing of these anxieties, and Leopoldina

sensed that it would be useless to tell him. Seduced on the one hand by the glories of power and on the other by the accessible beauties of Brazil, Pedro became bored with his princess and abandoned her to her stodgy worries. By 1822 Pedro was on the prowl.

During that year events were leading step by step to Brazilian independence. Following José Bonifácio's advice, Pedro traveled from one rebellious province to the next, wooing the people with his vision of an independent Brazil, united in its allegiance to the crown. In May Dom Pedro was proclaimed "Perpetual Defender of the Kingdom of Brazil," and in June he convened an assembly that was to draw up Brazil's new constitution.

Nationalistic fervor, nonexistent before Dom Joào's arrival in Brazil, was now widespread. Dom Pedro was determined to ride that wave of feeling and emerge as the ruler of the new nation. Leopoldina, child of Austrian absolutism, feared that Pedro did not understand the tides he wished to tame. "Everything here is confusion," she wrote her father late in June, adding "my Husband, who unfortunately likes anything new, is enthusiastic, and I'm afraid he will pay dearly for it. As for me, they don't trust me, for which I am thankful because I don't have to give my opinion and thus there are fewer arguments. Don't worry because come what may I won't lack anything, since I have my religion and my Austrian principles." The one consolation Leopoldina found in the midst of the tumult around her was the direction José Bonifácio gave to Pedro's plans. More than any other, José Bonifácio understood both the inevitability of independence and the dangers of setting the large and backward country adrift without a unifying authority.

Disorders in São Paulo called Pedro away from Rio in August 1822. Accompanied by Lieutenant Castro Canto e Melo, his friend Chalaza the court jester, a secretary, and a pair of servants, Pedro traveled southward at his usual breakneck pace. He had been gone only a few days when Leopoldina received word that the Côrtes in Portugal was planning to send a military expedition to punish Brazil for its rebelliousness and to stop all talk of independence. In Bahia a Portuguese garrison still held out against the Brazilians and, hearing that help was on its way, began preparations to attack Dom Pedro's forces. Leopoldina saw that the time had come for Brazil to declare its independence. Clearly she felt that the *Côrtes* had no right to override Dom Pedro, Brazil's legitimate ruler. José Bonifácio concurred, and the Council of State, presided over by the princess regent, declared Brazil's separation from Portugal. Letters were then dispatched to Dom Pedro describing the actions of both the *Côrtes* in Lisbon and the council in Rio.

On September 7 court messengers reached the prince regent. They found him a few hours north of São Paulo at the edge of a small stream called the Iparanga, where he had paused to attend to an upset stomach. After hurriedly reading the letter he strode up the bank to his waiting companions, drew his sword, and shouted, "By the blood that flows in my veins and upon my honor I swear to God to free Brazil." Mounting his horse, he rose in the stirrups with the cry, echoed by his attendants, "Independence or death!"

The Brazilian declaration of independence was not the only notable event of that historic journey. While in São Paulo, Pedro met Domitila de Castro, a twenty-five-year-old beauty whose first glance ensnared the prince in a love affair of fateful consequence. Their first encounter seemed accidental. Yet Domitila's brother was the same Lieutenant Castro Canto e Melo who accompanied Dom Pedro to the south, and it is very likely that their meeting was deliberate and well planned. Armed with a lovely smile, perfect silken skin, and a voluptuous body, Domitila found the prince an easy target. And once she caught him, she held him. This far more difficult feat was accomplished through combining respectful aloofness with an enthusiasm for carnal love that matched his own. By the time he returned to Rio, Domitila's face, body, and voice were engraved on the prince's imagination. The sight of Princess Leopoldina, again pregnant, carelessly dressed, her brow creased with worry, did little to push Domitila's image from his mind.

Early in 1823, some months after Pedro's elaborate coronation as emperor of Brazil, Domitila arrived in Rio de Janeiro. Unfortunately, Pedro was no longer restrained by the presence of Dom João, who loved and supported Leopoldina. Indeed, he seemed unconcerned, or unaware, of the effect that his actions might have on her. Believing that Leopoldina knew nothing of his affair and caring little for what anyone else thought, Pedro went to almost ridiculous lengths to please Domitila.

In February 1823 Leopoldina's third daughter, Paula Mariana, was born. Only eleven months separated Januaria and the new baby, and the strains of constant pregnancy began to take their toll. In June 1823 Leopoldina realized that Pedro's infatuation, already a rich source of gossip all over Rio, was not a brief fling that she could forgive, but a full-blown love affair. She noted his impatience with her, his long absences at night and his moments of preoccupation during the day. News of his escapades reached her, but in public she brushed them aside, preferring to seem ignorant but dignified. To her aunt she wrote the following lines: "I would have many things to tell you and would beg you not to refuse me your advice, but since I am certain that they open all my letters, I must be prudent and remain completely silent about everything that has to do with politics; and there are other matters where the advice of a second mother, which you have been, dear Aunt, would have been indispensable."

It is doubtful that even the duchess of Orléans could have helped Leopoldina cope with those "other matters." Even had she been blessed with brilliant wit, a streak of earthiness, and abundant beauty, Leopoldina would have suffered humiliation sooner or later. By heredity, by temperament, by training, Pedro was inevitably attracted to extramarital adventures. Basic to his concept of maleness was a kind of licentiousness that fed on the inequities of Brazilian society and on the sensuality that had helped populate the vast Brazilian territories. Pedro saw no reason not to indulge his desires. Was not chastity the burden of women whose indiscretions cost them nine months of ponderous expectation? Even priests broke the vows that bound them to life-long celibacy. The emperor, with only the most casual attempt at concealment, enjoyed his infatuation and felt it his due.

For a year Pedro tried half-heartedly to avoid undue scandal. The problem of Brazil's constitution continued to plague him: although he had promised to support a constitution, he and the constituent assembly of 1823 were soon at odds. The assembly, expressing a dominant mood of Brazil, mistrusted Dom Pedro because he was Portuguese by birth. For his part the emperor found it impossible to work with the representative body. Conflict became so acute that even José Bonifácio and his brothers fell away from Dom Pedro. By November they were in exile. In late March 1824 Dom Pedro, in consultation with a few chosen ministers, wrote Brazil's first constitution. The liberal-minded absolutist proved unequal to the rigors of democracy but kept his word to the nation in his own monarchical way.

With some measure of calm restored, Dom Pedro turned to matters nearer his heart. The means he used to hide his affair became more childish, more transparent. In public the royal consorts continued to treat each other with apparent affection, but in private, much to Leopoldina's dismay, they drifted farther apart. Far better than he, the empress realized the cost that obvious estrangement would exact, not only from the Brazilian throne but conceivably from the status of kingship in Europe as well. At that very moment monarchy everywhere was under fire, and the brave experiments in democracy and constitutional government—in the United States, in Great Britain, briefly in Spain—affected nations like a cup of spring wine. Leopoldina knew that the privacy of emperors was afforded no respect by ambassadors from other nations; she knew that the least sign of mortification on her part might very well jeopardize Brazil's prestige abroad. She therefore made no public complaint, permitted herself no dramatic outcry, sent no word to her father. Bound by ties of marriage and duty to the young nation, the empress chose to suffer in silent dignity. Anyway, Pedro's affair was already the talk of European royalty, and nothing was to be gained by adding to the bulging diplomatic mail pouches. Baron von Mareschal, the Austrian minister, wrote to Vienna, "In spite of the fact that he has a favorite mistress, he has never ceased for an instant to show himself a good husband, and takes advantage of every opportunity to praise the virtues of his consort." Others were less charitable. A shocked British visitor wrote simply, "The Brazilians are not at all correct."

During these years the imperial pregnancies continued, now in pairs. In May 1824 Domitila bore her first child by Dom Pedro,

Isabel Maria Brasileira; in the following August, Leopoldina's fourth daughter, Francisca Carolina, was born. If Leopoldina had been careless about her appearance before, her attire now provided what seemed a deliberate contrast to Domitila's fashionable beauty. Her complexion was reddened by the heartless Brazilian sun; her hair was in constant disarray (in spite of the fact that she and Domitila shared the same hairdresser); even her admirers could not forgive the gypsy costume, barely held together by a few big safety pins, that she wore almost every day. Domitila was the empress's opposite. Her beauty regimen lasted for hours daily. Her bosom held aloft by corsets and stays, skin coaxed to a pearly gleam, jewels tucked tastefully about her slender throat, Domitila charmed Dom Pedro anew each day as he peered at her nearby chalet through a spyglass or crept late at night to her terrace door.

Had Dom Pedro been a truly evil man, he could not have been more cruel than he managed to be, with a perverse innocence, during 1825 and 1826. In April 1825 he decided to satisfy Domitila's social ambitions by placing her among the ladies who attended the empress at court. Leopoldina agreed reluctantly to accept the affront, and in gratitude Pedro dedicated a sonnet to her, praising her magnanimity and finding parallels between her and other understanding queens of the past. The sonnet did little to help Leopoldina during Domitila's presentation at court. The sight of her husband's favorite, dressed in an exquisite satin robe frosted with pearls, brought into focus the empress's own sad state.

Humiliated by Pedro, in alarming financial difficulties, again pregnant, Leopoldina nonetheless conducted herself with great dignity. Baron von Mareschal wrote this description of her behavior to her father: "A great sense of prudence, fairness and extreme moderation ... dictated the conduct she would assume in this situation. She not only bowed without hesitation or rancor to the wishes of her husband, but deigned to receive the lady in question with utmost politeness." Emperor Franz sent the baron's report to Metternich with the following comment: "Through the enclosed report of Baron von Mareschal I have learned, alas, how miserable a scoundrel is my son-in-law!"

After the presentation at court, Domitila and her baby came

to live at the palace of São Cristovão. In October Pedro gave her the title of viscountess of Santos, thereby pleasing his mistress and insulting José Bonifácio, whose family had long been the moving force of Santos. It soon became embarrassingly clear that both the empress and the paramour were to give birth early in December. In this, at least, Leopoldina had a tremendous advantage over her rival: her children were born princes and princesses, while Domitila's were, in spite of her title and new position, bastards. On December 2 the long-awaited Prince Imperial, Pedro de Alcântara, was born. A week later Domitila suffered through a difficult labor and delivered a weak male child, Pedro de Alcântara Brasileiro, who lived only a few months.

Early in 1826 Dom Pedro planned a voyage to Bahia and decided to combine work with pleasure by inviting Domitila to go with him. Leopoldina decided to go also, leaving her baby and princesses in the hands of her reliable staff. The week-long voyage was an agony for her, for the pretense at decorum the lovers had maintained in Rio now ceased, and they succumbed to their impulses with astonishing frequency. One particularly awkward blow was dealt by the ship's captain, who mistakenly addressed Domitila as "your majesty." The poor man realized his error and hid in his cabin for the rest of the voyage.

After returning to Rio, Leopoldina insisted that Domitila move out of the palace. Pedro had no choice but to comply. As compensation for her banishment he decided to give Domitila a new title and a new villa. Soon Domitila, now the marquêsa of Santos, moved into an extravagantly refurbished house on the Rua Nova do Imperador opposite the Boa Vista Botanical Gardens. The mansion was a true love nest decorated with wrought iron hearts and elaborate murals and equipped with the only modern plumbing in Brazil—this in a society that chose to believe that ladies do not bathe. It was whispered that Domitila put it to good use by taking a bath every day. Between such rumors and the parties she gave in her new residence, Domitila reached the apex of her prestige.

Although absorbed by his passion, Dom Pedro found time to devote to his children, watching over their education with infinitely more attention than was ever given his own and seeing to it that they received the best care possible. Sincerely fond of all his children, he made no distinction between his legitimate and illegitimate offspring. His heart was touched by the stigma attached to Domitila's little daughter, and he ordered her birth certificate changed from "father unknown" to his own name. So that she might suffer less in comparison with his legitimate children, he bestowed on her the title duchess of Goyás, and made certain the entire court understood that she was to be treated with proper respect, according to strictest protocol. For Leopoldina it was one more in the series of humiliations that had at last become insupportable.

In October 1826, Leopoldina's remarkable forbearance evaporated. Dom Pedro had celebrated his twenty-eighth birthday that month by granting patents of nobility to all of Domitila's family—her father, her brothers, even a distant cousin. To the distraught empress, the court at São Cristovão seemed suddenly filled with people who owed their good fortune to the most despicable of relationships. Deeply worried about the effect of this fact on her innocent children, she asked the Austrian minister to communicate her great unhappiness to Emperor Franz in Vienna; then she confronted Pedro with the demand that he send Domitila far away from Rio.

This Pedro refused to do, and the royal couple quarreled violently. For a brief time after the fight, Dom Pedro tried to be kind to Leopoldina, who was again expecting a child. Then, late in November, he was called away from the capital to Brazil's southern border. Soon after he left, Leopoldina fell ill. On December 2 she suffered a miscarriage and developed a fever that her doctors only knew to treat by bloodletting. For days she lay burning with fever, anxious about the safety of her children and crying out in delirium that Domitila would stop at nothing to kill the little prince. In moments of clarity she begged her servants to prevent Domitila from entering the palace, and after being assured that her rival would not be permitted near her or the children, Leopoldina gained a measure of peace. On December 8, somewhat improved, she dictated a letter to her sister Marie Louise:

*My adored Marie! Reduced to the most deplorable state of health and brought to the last moment of my life amidst great suffering, I also have the misfortune to be unable to explain to you in person all the sentiments that have for so long been inscribed on my soul . . . Hear the cry of a victim who begs of you not vengeance, but pity and help, sprung from your sisterly affection for those innocent children who are now orphans, yet will remain in the power of the same persons who were authors of my misfortunes . . .*

*For almost four years, my adored Mana, as I have written you, for love of a seductive monster I have been reduced to the state of greatest slavery and totally forgotten by my adored Pedro. Lately I have received final proof that he has forgotten me completely, mistreating me in the presence of that very one who is the cause of all my afflictions . . .*

*Ah! My beloved daughters! What will become of you after my death!? . . . Goodbye my beloved sister. May the Supreme Being permit me to write you once more . . .*

Her wish was not granted. Three days later Leopoldina succumbed to puerperal fever.

Pedro remained in Brazil less than five years after Leopoldina's death. Rumor attributed her final illness to him, and his undemocratic ways further undermined his popularity. He and his second wife, Amelia de Leuchtenberg, were forced to leave Brazil in 1833, and two years later Dom Pedro was dead of tuberculosis, the result of a long but successful military campaign to place Maria da Glória on the Portuguese throne.

Of Leopoldina's six children, two died before reaching adulthood and two, Maria II of Portugal and Pedro II of Brazil, ruled a combined total of sixty-six years. Pedro II was barely a year old when his mother died, yet he grew to be like her in many respects. If she looked down from the heaven she so devoutly believed in, Empress Leopoldina would have been justifiably pleased with the way her son guided the sovereign nation that she herself had helped create.

# VII

# Mariana Grajales, 1808-1893

SURVEYING THE RUINS of his American empire in the mid-1820s, Fernando VII could find some consolation in the fact that Cuba, one of his richest possessions, seemed satisfied with its colonial status. Several factors help explain Cuban failure to take up the revolutionary gauntlet with the rest of Spanish America. Throughout the years of fighting, Cuba was the principal staging point for Spanish soldiers on their way to the mainland, and hence was always garrisoned with thousands of troops. Over the entire revolutionary period Cuba experienced an economic boom that extended into the 1860s. Most of this prosperity was based on increased sugar production, which enriched Creole and peninsular landowners and other commercial interests and made them tenacious defenders of the colonial status quo. Burgeoning sugar production brought with it a tremendous influx of African slaves to work the plantations. In that fact lay the final powerful explanation for Cuban conservatism. Between 1800 and 1865 some half million slaves were transported to the island, and by 1817 the combined slave and free black* population surpassed that of the whites. As the number of blacks grew, so too did white fear of slave revolt. The Spanish minister Calatrava could write confidently in 1823, "The fear that the Cubans have of their

*The term "black" is used here and elsewhere to denote mulattoes as well as persons of pure African ancestry. Mariana Grajales was a mulatto.

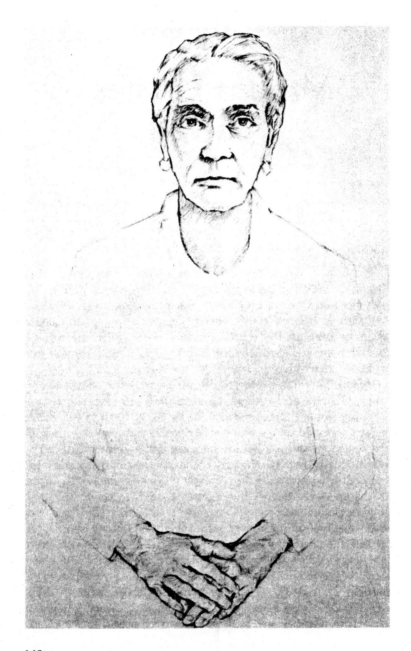

blacks is Spain's greatest security in guaranteeing her domination of the island."

Most troubling to those who profited from sugar and slavery were the free blacks. Less than half as numerous as whites, they formed an intelligent and ambitious group of artisans and small farmers. Directors of colonial fortunes rightly perceived the free blacks as a dangerous anomaly in the society they had created, and over the first half of the nineteenth century tried to hobble them by enacting a series of laws that limited their rights as free Cuban citizens.

When dissatisfaction with Spanish rule touched off the Ten Years War in 1868, many free blacks joined the revolt and assumed positions of leadership in it. They formed one of the more radical contingents in the revolutionary armies, for in addition to political independence they demanded immediate abolition of slavery and an end to the racism that they clearly perceived as harmful to Cuba as a whole. Theirs was a sophisticated nationalism that in time broadened to make them an advance guard of Third World anti-imperialism.

There was no middle ground in the Cuban wars of independence. When men joined the revolt, their families were routinely persecuted by the Spanish authorities. Thus women and children often joined the insurgents and traveled with them for years at a time. Far from burdening the armies, they staffed hospitals, operated kitchens, and offered field support that otherwise might not have existed. The best known among these *soldaderas* of the Cuban wars of independence was Mariana Grajales, an iron-willed free black to whom the Spanish referred shudderingly as "the mother of the terrible Maceos."

Santiago de Cuba maintained a prison for runaway slaves not far from the neighborhood where Mariana Grajales grew up. As a child she often walked down streets lined with two- and three-room houses until she caught sight of the jail. On days when the Cuban sun poured down on the city as though through a tropical magnifying glass, Mariana watched as the runaway slaves, the *cimarrones*, gathered around the windows of their cells to catch a breath of fresh air. Their faces represented almost every

shade on the human palette, from the mahogany of recently arrived Africans to the tan of those whose genes had mingled with
those of whites over two or more generations. Many bore scars
from the overseer's whip or showed signs of rough treatment at
the time of their recapture. Others, their bodies gaunt from fever
and poor food, had put up little resistance when they were found
and now waited patiently for their masters to claim them. Those
faces of despair peering through the bars became for Mariana living symbols of the slave system she grew to hate.

Of all the races to come to Cuba, the African's lot was
harshest, as the *cimarrones* could attest. *Bozales*, newly arrived
slaves, were a common sight in Santiago de Cuba, and it was not
until 1820, when Mariana Grajales was twelve, that town fathers
protested the custom of leading slaves naked through the
streets—a protest lodged not out of concern for the dignity of
slaves, but in the interests of protecting the free population from
so uncivilized a sight. Cuba was almost as inhospitable to the Chi-
nese laborers who came as indentured servants, only to find
themselves treated as slaves. At the other end of the color spec-
trum were white landowners whose wealth came from plantations worked by slaves. Mariana saw them in downtown Santiago de Cuba and caught glimpses of their wives and daughters as
they drove by in two-wheeled carriages, fans held gracefully in
their hands, dainty feet encased in satin slippers.

Mariana herself was a free mulatto whose parents fled to
Cuba in order to escape race-related turmoil in Santo Domingo.
They lived modestly in Santiago, worked hard, and managed to
live decently. Because Spanish colonial laws limited education for
blacks, both slave and free, Mariana never attended school, and
no one knows whether she learned to read and write. In spite of
the handicaps of race and poverty, she grew into a proud young
woman who was sure of her own worth in a society that did its
best to undervalue it.

When she was twenty-three, Mariana left her father's house
to marry Fructuoso Regüeyferos. Marriage to a man of similar
background and sentiments was by far the best option available to
her. Free union between people of her group was at least as common as marriage, and although women entering such arrange-

ments had few guarantees of support from their men, they were better off than those who fell into the trap of concubinage to wealthy Creoles. Marriage between persons of different racial backgrounds was prohibited by law, yet the large number of children of mixed parentage proved that the races did indeed intermingle. The seeming availability of women who, unlike the cloistered white ladies of Cuba, were visible in the market and in the streets encouraged men to seek liaisons in classes other than their own. And the fact that there were fewer white women than men—only ten to every twelve or thirteen men—added another motive for cross-class dalliance. Mariana neatly avoided the pitfalls of seduction and established instead a legally constituted home for her children.

Four sons were born to Mariana and her husband—Justo, Felipe, Manuel, and Fermín. After scarcely nine years of marriage, Fructuoso died and Mariana became a widow and the sole support for her little boys at age thirty-two. There was nowhere to go but home, and in 1840 she moved back to her parents' house.

Mariana Grajales did not long remain single after Fructuoso's death. She was, after all, an attractive and respectable widow in the prime of life, and her sons were of an age to begin helping with family chores. Soon after the period of mourning was over, Mariana met a Venezuelan immigrant named Marcos Maceo, a friend of her father's who was a relatively successful small businessman and farmer. Like Mariana, Marcos was a mulatto and a widower, the father of six children. In 1843, Mariana left her parents' house and moved to Marcos's farm in San Luis, near Santiago de Cuba. Friends and relatives saw the wisdom of the match and approved of it, though it was not sanctified by a formal marriage. Still, the home they established was as solid as any household begun with greater pomp and ritual.

Mariana was thirty-five and Marcos some years older when they met. The little girl who stared at *cimarrones* in the prison of Santiago de Cuba had grown into a stalwart opponent of slavery in all its forms. Her feelings were natural for one of her position and experience, for abolitionist sentiment prevailed among free blacks and mulattoes, many of whom were former slaves or descended from slaves who had bought their freedom through exceptional effort. The line between slave and free was not always clear, and free mulattoes like Mariana often maintained social contacts with urban slaves through the godparent relationship and other friendships.

Mariana's fierce beliefs were not at first shared by Marcos. He had tried to stay aloof from involvements since his arrival in Cuba in the 1820s. The wars of independence in Venezuela, where he had fought valiantly for the Spanish king against the armies of Bolívar, early soured him on war and political strife. Although his brother remained in the king's service in Cuba, Marcos devoted himself to commerce and agriculture. Las Delicias, his farm in the Majaguabo region of San Luis, produced enough sugar cane, sweet potatoes, and fruit to satisfy his large family, plenty of corn husks and stalks to feed his mules, and tobacco for the cash market. In Santiago de Cuba, he owned a three-room house, stuccoed with lime and sand, that had an ample patio with fruit trees growing in back.

Events of 1843 forced Marcos to reconsider his apolitical stance. During that year slaves on plantations in Matanzas province rebelled against their masters. In groups ranging from a few to two hundred or more, the rebel slaves fought to free themselves and escape to *palenques*, settlements of runaway slaves, deep in the mountains. Most of the rebellions were brutally suppressed, and executions and deaths by flogging were meted out with a liberal hand. Slave revolts had occurred at regular intervals for decades. Now, however, the slavocracy began to see abolitionist conspiracies at every turn. Captain-General Leopoldo O'Donnell, gripped by panic, tried to quell the unrest. Early in 1844 he seized on rumors as proof of a widespread conspiracy led by abolitionists, some of them white, some free blacks. He ordered the supposed leaders of the plot executed, among them a well-known poet, a highly educated dentist, a musician, and a land-owner—all middle-class mulattoes and blacks.

Not content with that perversion of justice, O'Donnell set up a military commission to persecute the nonwhite population of Cuba. In all, seventy-eight alleged participants of the "Conspiracy of the Staircase," so called for the stairway-like scaffold on which "conspirators" were flogged to death, were executed outright. Hundreds of others died of torture, mistreatment, and disease, and a thousand more were imprisoned on the flimsiest of evidence. Only twenty whites were punished; all other victims were free blacks and, in lesser numbers, slaves. The consequences of the "Conspiracy of the Staircase" were not lost on Marcos and Mariana. The group of which they were a part had been singled out for persecution, and although the Maceos escaped personal loss, their rights of citizenship were jeopardized.

Beginning in 1844 Captain-General O'Donnell enforced a series of measures designed to prevent free blacks from influencing slaves. He gave slaveowners broad powers to keep them from making contact with plantation slaves. Meetings of free blacks were strictly supervised; "disrespect" of whites became a punishable crime. Slaves freed after May 1844 were to be exiled from Cuba, and free blacks who, like Marcos Maceo, had moved to the island from another country were ordered to emigrate. To protect himself from deportation, Marcos persuaded a friendly bureaucrat to declare him a native of Santiago de Cuba. Spanish officials' handling of the "Conspiracy of the Staircase" alienated many Creoles and free blacks, who saw it as one more example of Spain's repressive, arbitrary policies. Those who opposed slavery were forced to conclude that abolition would occur only after Cuba won its independence from Spain.

In spring of 1845, Mariana left the farm in Majaguabo and traveled to Marcos's house on Providencia Street in Santiago to await the birth of a child. Antonio de la Caridad Maceo y Grajales was born on June 14. His baptism took place late in August and was followed by a lavish party hosted by the baby's parents and his godparents, Don Ascencio de Asencio and his wife Salomé. Don Ascencio was a wealthy Creole lawyer of some standing in the city, a dutiful godfather and over the years a true friend of Marcos and Mariana. On Antonio's baptismal certificate, not outstanding for its accuracy, the baby was described as the "legitimate son" of Marcos Maceo, "a native of this city."

Mariana celebrated her thirty-seventh birthday shortly after Antonio was born. Eight more children followed—Baldomera, José, Rafael, Miguel, Julio, Dominga, Tomás, and Marcos, each separated from the next by a year or two. On July 6, 1851,

Mariana and Marcos were married in San Luis, an act that merely reaffirmed the bond between them. Over a period of fifteen years she bore Marcos's children with a strength that belied her increasing age. In 1857 two children were born—Dominga in the spring, Tomás scarcely eight months later—and in 1860, their last child appeared several months after Mariana's fifty-second birthday. Of all Mariana's children, only one, Manuel Regüeyferos, died before reaching adulthood.

Throughout the 1850s and 1860s Mariana watched over her family from the ample, rough stone house at Las Delicias. Her kitchen garden boasted an abundance of herbs—mint and lemon balm for tea, thyme and coriander for soups, medicinal plants like bright orange and yellow calendula blossoms for salves and remedies. Plantain and banana trees grew so close to her kitchen that she picked the fruits only minutes before they were to be prepared, and orchards lay beyond the tobacco shed, stable, and other outbuildings. Over all towered the trees of Majaguabo, casting shade on the wide veranda of the house and the patio outside. When Mariana went to Santiago de Cuba, she carried large sacks woven of *majagua* twine and filled with provisions to restock the storeroom of the house on Providencia Street.

The family grew and prospered as though protected by some magic charm. Mariana and Marcos, through careful planning and frugality, bought a second farm in Majaguabo and called it La Esperanza, Hope. Even before they grew their first moustaches, the sons were a formidable work force, helping with chores on the family farms and driving the mule team that Marcos hired out to carry produce and tobacco from farms in Majaguabo to market in Santiago de Cuba. Mariana controlled her tribe by enforcing a few basic rules—respect for parents, a reasonable curfew, and above all strict attention to duty.

All was not work, however, and in spite of the curfew, the younger Maceos became the central attraction of Majaguabo's social life. Broad-chested and handsome, the older boys enjoyed the attentions of young ladies and the approval of other young men who admired their skill with horse and machete. It was said that the Maceos never missed a dance, never lost a race. When they were old enough, the boys went to school in Santiago de Cuba.

Spanish law prevented them from progressing beyond elementary studies, so after a few years they were back in Majaguabo to work full time on the farm.

In 1862 Antonio, the oldest of Marcos's sons, joined his older half-brother Justo Regüeyferos in managing their father's mule train. Business often carried them into Santiago, and they kept abreast of the news of the day. It was Antonio and Justo who brought word of the independence of Santo Domingo and stories about the war to end slavery in the United States. So it was that news of the wider world penetrated the back country of colonial Cuba.

Of all the regions of Cuba, resentment against colonialism was strongest in Oriente province. During the mid-1860s support for independence spread through a network of Masonic lodges in major towns of eastern Cuba. The Grand Lodge of Colón was founded in Santiago in 1859, and shortly thereafter Vicente Aguilera, Carlos Manuel de Céspedes, and others founded Redemption Lodge in Bayamo. In August 1867 Aguilera and other wealthy Creoles set in motion the mechanisms of revolt. Creoles in major cities and towns formed revolutionary juntas to search out potential leaders for the struggle against Spain. Communication between towns was set up, supporters identified, military supplies stockpiled, and plots hatched. Cuba thus geared for rebellion four decades after the rest of Latin America had seized its independence from the crumbling Spanish empire.

Thanks to Don Ascencio, Antonio was part of that effort. Don Ascencio had long recognized special qualities in the Maceos' firstborn, and although he feared Antonio's race would prove a handicap, Don Ascencio was an unflagging supporter of the young man. When Antonio married María Cabrales of Majaguabo in 1866, his godfather acted as his sponsor. Two years later he sponsored him again, this time when Antonio was initiated into Santiago's Grand Lodge.

Well into 1868 secrecy shrouded the Masonic conspiracy, for Creole revolutionaries feared Spanish retaliation should suspicions be aroused. As leaders emerged from the various lodges and as territorial responsibilities were assigned, more and more Cubans, both black and white, entered the plot, the Maceos

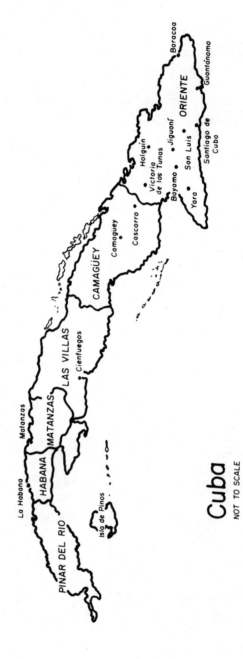

GULF OF MEXICO

CARIBBEAN SEA

PINAR DEL RIO

La Habana
Matanzas
HABANA
MATANZAS
Isla de Pinos
LAS VILLAS
Cienfuegos
CAMAGÜEY
Camaguey
Cascorro
Holguin
Victoria
de las Tunas
Bayamo
Yara
Jiguaní
San Luis
Santiago de
Cuba
Guantánamo
Baracoa
ORIENTE

Cuba
NOT TO SCALE

156

among them. Still, leaders disagreed on the proper moment to un-
leash the forces of revolution. The more cautious among them
urged that they wait until the following spring after the sugar
harvest, when food and cash would be most abundant. Others
worried that the cover of secrecy might soon evaporate and that
the juntas might be arrested before a shot had been fired.

By September 1868 word to prepare for revolution reached
the countryside. During a trip to Santiago that month, Marcos
agreed to organize Majaguabo for the approaching conflict. He
knew without a doubt that the revolution was imminent, yet
conflicting emotions assailed him as he returned to the farm.
What would Mariana say? They were no longer young; what
would happen to her once the revolution began? What if she
didn't want him to fight? Silent and sad, Marcos entered the
house early in the afternoon before any of his sons had returned
from the day's work. As he slowly described to Mariana all that
he, Ascencio, and the others had been planning for so many
months, her happiness was evident. At age sixty she saw at last
the end of Cuba's enslavement by Spain, of black enslavement by
whites, and she had no reservations about sacrificing all they had
to rid Cuba of the Spanish or, failing that, "to die in the attempt."

In the month that followed the Maceos fanned out through
Majaguabo district to enlist their friends and neighbors in the
coming struggle. María Cabrales, who had been living with her
husband Antonio at La Esperanza, was sent to join Mariana and
the other women at Las Delicias, and the isolated farm was
turned into a military depot and encampment. Early in October,
Mariana traveled to Santiago on family business. Don Ascencio
contacted her there and told her that he needed to see Marcos as
soon as possible. Realizing that the matter was urgent, she hurried back to Las Delicias with the message. When Marcos reached
the home of his friend, Ascencio told him that the revolution
would break out at any moment. The small army that the Maceos
had raised over the past weeks would be contacted by an officer
of the revolutionary command as soon as the time for action
arrived.

A few days later, in a move that surprised even some of his
fellow conspirators, Carlos Manuel de Céspedes, wealthy Creole,

Mason, and revolutionary, declared Cuban independence. Spanish Captain-General Lersundi received the news with some skepticism. Cuba was well garrisoned with loyalist soldiers and volunteer militiamen, many of them veterans of the wars in Santo Domingo. Doubting that Creole forces could even begin to challenge such an army, he nevertheless ordered a general alert and prepared to meet the rebels on the battlefield. Throughout eastern Cuba, Creole landowners, lawyers, and merchants sympathetic to the revolution transformed themselves into officers and soldiers.

News was slow to reach Majaguabo, however, and the Maceos grew increasingly uneasy as days passed with no word from the revolutionary command. To increase their uncertainty, the Spanish spread rumors that bands of outlaws were loose in Oriente and that no one in the countryside was safe. The women—Mariana, Dominga, Baldomera, and María Cabrales—worried that they might be attacked while their men sat waiting at La Esperanza. Finally Marcos sent sixteen-year-old Miguel to a nearby country store to find out what was happening beyond the borders of Majaguabo. There he met Captain Juan Bautista Rondón, a friend of the Maceos who was in command of some four hundred rebel troops, their first contact with the revolutionary army. In a matter of hours Rondón joined Marcos, Antonio, and the others at La Esperanza. While the Majaguabo volunteers hurried off to say last farewells at home, the Maceos and Rondón's company left for Las Delicias.

Mariana and the other women were startled by the shout that called them to the door, but when they recognized the voice as that of Marcos, they stepped outside to see him standing with a handful of men. "Do you know this gentleman?" boomed Marcos, pointing to Rondón. Mariana's only answer was a gasp, for at his signal Rondón's four hundred armed men moved out of the shadows and formed a great semicircle behind them. "These," laughed Marcos, "are the highwaymen you were so worried about! The Revolution has begun!"

Recounting the scene nearly thirty years later, María Cabrales described "la vieja Mariana" as immensely pleased that there were so many men determined to fight for their country.

"Overflowing with happiness" she went into the house, took the crucifix from her room, and returned to the veranda. "On your knees, fathers and sons," she cried, "before Christ who was the first Liberal to come into the world. Let us swear to free our country or to die for her!" Antonio, José, Justo, Felipe, Julio, and Fermín, the oldest of Mariana's sons, rode off to war that night. With them went the Majaguabo recruits, who swelled Rondón's company to almost eight hundred men.

From the first, the conflict included civilians as well as soldiers. The Spanish command treated families of rebels as rebels themselves, and many old people, women, and children took refuge in the mountainous jungles, the *manigua,* of Oriente. For several days Marcos stayed with Mariana, their daughters, daughters-in-law, and the two youngest boys—Tomás, eleven, and Marcos, eight—while they packed and moved to El Piloto, a secluded farm not far from Majaguabo. They left none too soon, for a Spanish sympathizer denounced the Maceos to authorities in San Luis, and troops rode out to Las Delicias to arrest them. Eighteen-year-old Rafael Maceo had stayed behind to guard the farm when his family left for the mountains. He was seized by Spanish soldiers who burned every building to the ground, then carried him off to prison.

When Marcos heard of his son's capture, he rode to San Luis to offer himself in exchange for Rafael's freedom. Spanish officials jailed Marcos, but did not free Rafael. Several days passed before two friends of Marcos, both Spaniards, secured his release; Rafael later escaped, thanks to the inattentiveness of his guards. Both men, father and son, joined Antonio and the others. Of the older children, only Miguel remained with Mariana in hiding, but when she sent him to Antonio's encampment with a supply of clothing, he decided to stay on there and fight. By early November nine Maceos were fighting for Cuban independence.

High spirits, excitement, and illusions of an early victory were fueled by early rebel successes. Revolutionary forces wrested control of Bayamo and Jiguaní from the Spanish. Many who had waited to see if the movement was viable now joined patriot ranks. Veterans of Santo Domingo's war for independence—Luis Marcano, Máximo Gómez, Modesto Díaz—assumed command of the army and taught Cubans the basics of war in that most effective of classrooms, the battlefield.

Antonio's progress through the ranks was spectacular, a source of pride for his mother and his young wife. All the Maceos were exceptionally good fighters, but Antonio combined that quality with a seeming inability to lose a battle. He rose overnight from soldier to sergeant on the strength of his leadership of the Majaguabo volunteers. Other promotions followed quickly. When he visited Mariana in November, he was already a lieutenant. In December he was promoted to captain, in January to commander, and scarcely ten days later he earned the insignia of lieutenant colonel. To those who fought with him, he seemed most comfortable with machete in hand, astride one of his magnificent horses, plunging after a platoon of Spanish soldiers.

After a few initial victories, the revolutionary forces found further success elusive. Spanish troops, well armed and experienced, poured into the field where they posed a striking contrast to the undersupplied rebels. Céspedes, president of Cuba's new republican government, had failed utterly in persuading the United States and Great Britain—seemingly natural allies of Free Cuba—to recognize the revolution. Arms, supplies, and ammunition, so desperately needed to bring the war to a speedy and successful close, were not forthcoming from either nation. Only small shipments of supplies managed to reach Free Cuba, and those were far from enough.

A few Cuban generals proved able to fight under such conditions, most notably Máximo Gómez, the wily guerrilla fighter from Santo Domingo; his best pupil in matters of war was Antonio Maceo. Suffering from constant shortages and threatened by far superior forces, Máximo Gómez divided his command into mobile guerrilla units that spread out through Oriente toward Guantánamo, at Cuba's eastern tip. From their forest encampment, Gómez's commanders planned attacks on sugar plantations, on Spanish garrisons, and occasionally on towns and villages held by the Spanish. Their most important weapons besides the machete were surprise and well-planned retreats into the wilderness.

Antonio Maceo excelled in guerrilla warfare, never leaving a single detail of the attacks to chance and ensuring that each fallen enemy soldier contributed his supplies to Maceo's men. So successful was he that as the months and years of war dragged on, his men were well clothed and reasonably well armed and fed at a time when many of Free Cuba's soldiers were half-naked and hungry.

During the first year of the war, the Maceo family suffered a series of painful losses. The revolution was scarcely a month old when Captain Justo Regüeyferos was captured and shot while visiting his wife near San Luis. In mid-May Antonio, commanding a company that included his own father and brothers, attacked the Spanish garrison San Agustín. During the bloody encounter, Marcos Maceo fell from his horse, mortally wounded. He died in Antonio's arms with the words, "I've kept my promise to Mariana." Six days later Antonio was shot in the thigh, his first wound. His men carried him on a makeshift cot to the old *palenque*—the runaway slave settlement—where Mariana, María Cabrales, and the families of other rebels lived.

Deep in the *manigua*, in a crude jungle hospital, Antonio's wound healed rapidly. Mariana was deeply grieved by the death of her faithful Marcos only days earlier, but she displayed the fortitude that would carry her through difficult days to come. Like a civilian general whose army was made up of old people, women, and children, she enforced certain rules that applied to all who nursed the wounded rebels, the *Mambí* soldiers. They were to bear death, defeat, and the discomfort of life in the *manigua* without complaint. When Mariana approached her son's hammock, she chided him for letting so insignificant a scratch slow him down. "That'll heal in a minute," she said, "and then you can go get a real wound, something to worry about!"

In June 1869, before Antonio was fully recovered, tragedy struck three times in quick succession. Antonio and María's first and only children, a boy and a girl, died within days of each other. Then word came from Santiago that sixteen citizens, Masons involved in the revolutionary conspiracy, had been carried off to a remote farm and executed with machetes, their bodies robbed and mutilated. Among them was Don Ascencio, Antonio's godfather.

Mariana was in her sixties when the war cut her off from the past and thrust her into an uncertain future. The shady veranda and cool rooms of the house at Las Delicias had gone up in smoke; the house on Providencia Street was useless to her as long as the Spanish controlled Santiago de Cuba. She put the familiar routines, expectations, possessions of a lifetime behind her without regret. From the circle of huts in the *manigua* she watched over the families of soldiers, nursed the wounded, and grieved silently for the dead. If the heavy rains that seeped through flimsy roofs made her old bones ache, no one ever heard her complain. If at night she lay awake remembering her beloved dead or worrying about the seven sons whose lives were in constant danger, no one ever saw her serene face creased with anxiety. She was "the woman who doesn't cry," who cared for her sons, her family, and spoke at all times of her uncompromising support for the war and an independent Cuba.

As Spanish reinforcements poured into Cuba, the count of Valmaseda, commander of counterinsurgency forces based in Bayamo, issued a proclamation that showed how far the Spanish were prepared to go in order to put down the uprising. "He who is not with me is against me," announced Valmaseda, "and so that my soldiers may recognize the enemy, I issue the following general order: Every man, fifteen years or older, found outside his farm, and who cannot justify his motives, will be executed. All uninhabited dwellings will be burned. All dwellings not flying a white flag as a sign that its occupants desire peace will be reduced to ashes. All women who are not living in their own homes or with relatives will be concentrated in the towns of Jiguaní and Bayamo, where they will be maintained. Those who do not present themselves voluntarily will be taken by force."

Soon after this declaration of war on civilians, the Spanish began methodically executing all rebel soldiers taken in battle. In response, the revolutionary forces formed a brotherhood called "El Silencio," complete with rites of initiation and secret ceremonies. Each soldier swore to risk his own life to keep his wounded fellows from falling into Spanish hands. So well did the system work that wounded rebels were dragged to safety even under heaviest gunfire. Tales abounded of men whose arms were broken and whose mangled limbs were torn off as they were dragged over rough terrain. Brutal though such treatment seemed, many of the wounded lived to fight again, and the Spanish were deprived of whatever satisfaction the executions might have given them.

One reverse after another threatened the revolution with total collapse in the early 1870s. The coasts and cities of Oriente swarmed with Spanish troops and, as if that weren't enough, cholera afflicted the island as well. In Santiago de Cuba, gravediggers abandoned the congested cemeteries and citizens piled their dead into long ditches that served as common graves. Out in the once-productive countryside, fertile farms lay idle and abandoned, the rural population severely reduced by the double onslaught of war and epidemic.

Cholera reached finally into revolutionary encampments and *Mambí* settlements of the *manigua*. With the plague came redoubled Spanish efforts to crush the rebels. Loyalist troops pursued the *Mambís* into the mountains and succeeded in cutting off the trickle of supplies that had reached Free Cuba. Whole platoons fell because the rebels lacked ammunition with which to answer the attacks, and even Antonio Maceo's men, well provisioned compared to others in the Cuban army, fell back before Spanish advances. At one point Antonio's company withdrew to the settlement where Mariana and the other women maintained a field hospital. Spanish troops surprised them there, and for over an hour Mariana was trapped in a ditch as the battle raged around her.

Gradually, against all odds, the Cuban army overcame the setbacks of the early seventies. The cholera epidemic subsided, and the opposing armies reached a kind of equilibrium. Revolutionaries throughout Oriente adopted Maceo's method of ambushing enemy columns for supplies and taking food from abandoned farms. Each unit became self-sufficient, although none was so well supplied that it could mount frontal assaults on Spanish positions. The rebels carried out ambushes and skirmishes while the Spanish stayed close to fortified positions.

Máximo Gómez realized that, failing decisive action, the revolution was stalemated. As long as rebel-held territory remained within the borders of Oriente and Camagüey, the Spanish military command was free to concentrate large numbers of troops in those regions. The rich sugar cane plantations in the west continued operations as though the war did not exist, providing the Spanish with vital food supplies and revenue. Efforts to draw western Creoles into the war were met with obstinate opposition. Wealthy landowners supported many goals of the revolution, but they were not eager to see their slaves freed or their canefields turned into a battleground. Efforts to carry the war into the west were further complicated by regionalism. When Máximo Gómez led his men into Camagüey, he found that revolutionary commanders there consistently placed personal ambitions and regional jealousies above the welfare of Free Cuba. In the case of Antonio Maceo, those jealousies took the form of racial prejudice. Creole officers of Las Villas who found themselves under Maceo's command refused to fight under a mulatto and complained bitterly to the government. In a few months Antonio returned to Oriente, frustrated by the prejudices and divisiveness he saw in the west.

By 1874, the midpoint of the war, Mariana had lost four more sons: Fermín and Felipe Regüeyferos, Julio and Miguel Maceo. The death of Miguel after the Battle of Cascorro was an especially tragic one. Twenty years old when he was fatally wounded, Miguel had already shown an aptitude for battle challenging that of his famous brothers Antonio and José. When word arrived at camp that Miguel was dead, Mariana turned to fourteen-year-old Marcos, her youngest son, and commanded, "And you, stand up straight. It's time you fought for your country!" Mariana believed that one son should replace another, so she sent them, one by one, to battle until none was left.

After his brief excursion into Camagüey province, Antonio returned home and continued his harassment of the Spanish. Still the specter of racism followed him, for on February 1, 1876, Modesto Díaz was named commander of Oriente after the previous commander's capture by the enemy. The post should have gone to Antonio Maceo, but the revolutionary government followed a policy of giving Creole officers preference over a black or mulatto. Old Mariana's hopes that the revolution would be color-blind were betrayed, and her son found himself on the defensive in spite of his complete devotion to Free Cuba.

Throughout 1876 and the first half of 1877, Antonio and his men ranged almost at will over the province, destroying military posts, burning canefields and liberating slaves. Then, on August 7, 1877, Antonio rode his big mare Concha into a wooded glen called Mangos de Mejía where a Spanish company lay in wait. For once his luck abandoned him and enemy bullets knocked him from his horse. His brother Tomás placed him on a stretcher made of saplings and vines and carried him to Félix Figueredo, a medical doctor attached to their unit. Only the blood trickling from his mouth and nose gave Tomás hope that his brother still lived. When that limp and bloodied body reached the settlement at Los Indios where Mariana was camped, the women gathered weeping and wailing around her hut. Mariana shooed them away, shouting "Out of here, skirts, out of here! There's no time for tears!" With water and rags she washed the blood from Antonio's broad back and shattered right hand, then stepped back as Colonel Figueredo and Máximo Gómez came to inspect the wounds.

No one who saw the extent of Antonio's injuries believed he could recover. Five bullets had pierced his back, two penetrating the chest cavity and a lung; three had struck his hand; and the palm was studded with bits of metal from his own revolver. From the first day he burned with fever as his body fought the wounds. Signs of gangrene began to appear in his hand. Figueredo had few medicines and could only pray that the two bullets in his chest, one very close to the spine, had not damaged a vital organ.

Some days later Máximo Gómez left to take command of Antonio's troops, depending on José Maceo and twelve skilled riflemen to protect the fallen officer. Spanish forces, some two-hundred strong, pursued Maceo to finish the work begun at Mangos de Mejía, as Antonio moved from one hiding place to another to elude capture. Although José and his sharpshooters slowed the Spanish with deadly rifle fire, still the enemy pursued so closely that Antonio was forced to move into the region controlled by *Mambí* Lieutenant Colonel Rodríguez. This time he went on foot, stumbling rather than walking, led by Mariana and followed by María. As the Spanish came within rifle range, he called for his horse and, incredibly, mounted and rode away to safety. Late in September Félix Figueredo wrote these lines to Máximo Gómez: "This General Maceo, like all good insurgents, heals better with water, iron and fire than with balms and ointments; while his doctor takes notes so that, should the patient save himself from Death's clutches and survive, he can ask the wise men of the Academies and medical Professors if it is possible that in this land of tetanus and malaria, a man prostrate on a rough bed of twigs . . .; his lungs pierced with the lead slugs of a Remington . . . can get up amidst the seriousness of his wounds, walk miles on foot, eat nothing, sleep not a wink in three days, ford rivers, ride off on horseback and say at the end of such violent fatigues, that he feels much better." After two weeks of unrelenting pursuit, the Spanish brigadier had only Maceo's abandoned cot to show for his costly efforts.

Once fully healed, Antonio vowed to collect with interest the debt owed him by the Spanish. During the last months of 1877 and into the first weeks of February 1878, he attacked Spanish commander Martínez Campos's troops, wiping out entire columns and moving freely in the area north of Santiago de Cuba.

One week after his remarkable string of victories, a small party of Cuban officers led by Máximo Gómez made its way to the *Mambí* camp. Gómez had come to say goodbye to Mariana and to relay some bitter news to her son. Even as Maceo and his men were performing brilliantly in Oriente, revolutionary leaders had signed a pact destined to end the war. The Pact of Zanjón was the result of several factors, among them dissension within Cuban ranks, the conciliatory policy initiated by Captain General Martínez Campos months before, and, most of all, a profound weariness on both sides of the conflict. But the pact did not free Cuba of either Spanish rule or slavery. Two weeks later, with his vow to free Cuba ringing in his ears, Antonio met Martínez Campos at a place near Santiago called Baraguá and categorically rejected the Pact of Zanjón. Although hostilities broke out anew on March 23, Martínez Campos ordered Spanish troops to respect the ceasefire at all costs. Even Antonio could not fight against soldiers who answered his fire with white flags and shouts of "Viva Cuba!" The war was at an end.

Under the Pact of Zanjón, Martínez Campos provided safe passage for members of the Maceo family who wished to go into exile. Mariana, María, the Maceo daughters and their families, Tomás, and Marcos left their beloved Cuba in April 1878 and went into exile in Kingston, Jamaica. Antonio, José, and Rafael stayed behind, hoping they could fight on. Both sides—loyalist and revolutionary—conspired to remove Antonio from Cuba so that the peace agreed to by a majority of antagonists could settle over that exhausted island. In May, Antonio agreed to leave Cuba in search of financial support for the war in Jamaica and New York. Whether he truly believed that he could stop the drift toward peace is doubtful, although he later claimed that he had been "deceived" by both his friends and his enemies into accepting a voluntary exile. Only José and Rafael stayed in Cuba. They returned to the house on Providencia Street in Santiago for a short time but soon became embroiled in a hopeless "Little War." At the end of that conflict they fell into Spanish hands and, with their families and friends, were sent to prison, first in North Africa and later in Spain, where Rafael died.

Mariana, depressed by a penurious exile in Kingston, began to feel the terrible weight of old age, hopelessness, and grief. A decade of bloody struggle and the sacrifice of her husband and six sons seemed to have accomplished nothing. What was worse, Rafael had died far from home and José languished in a Spanish prison, while Antonio wandered about the Caribbean in a fruitless attempt to find support for a second rebellion. In that state of discouragement Mariana received a letter from José, who described the sad state of his affairs and expressed the fear that he would not live to see her again. Never before had Mariana asked a Spaniard for a favor, but the mother who proudly sent her sons to war could not bear to let another one die miserably in prison. She visited the Spanish consul in Kingston to beg for José's freedom. In his dispatch to Madrid of September 3, Consul Francisco E. Gómez wrote with some astonishment that he had received the "mother of the terrible Cuban chieftains Antonio and José Maceo," and that she assured him of her sons' desire to live in peace with Spain.

Shortly after Mariana's visit to the Spanish consul, José escaped and made his way through North Africa to France and then to the United States, finally arriving in Kingston in January 1885. Soon thereafter the chagrined Spanish once again received word of plotting by the "terrible Maceos."

Mariana did not live to see Cuba become independent in 1902 or to see Antonio and José renew the battle, fulfilling with their deaths in 1896 the vow they had made to her nearly thirty years before. But she had always known that Cuba would some-day be free, whether by her sons' hands or by those of younger men like José Martí, who visited her in 1891 and shortly before her death in 1893. "She caressed my face and looked on me like a son," wrote Marti, whose talk of liberating Cuba brought a spar-kle to her dim eyes. He sat with the old woman and watched her wrinkled face grow animated as she reminisced on a particularly outstanding lance thrust by one of her sons, or of the time an-other, "bleeding from every part of his body, lifted himself and with ten men drove off two hundred of the enemy." Marti sensed the power that Mariana exercised over all who came into contact with her, and it was he who wrote the epitaph that catches the essence of her contribution to Cuban independence: "And if one trembled when he came face to face with the enemy of his coun-try, he saw the mother of Maceo, white kerchief on her head, and he ceased trembling."

# VIII

# Gabriela Mistral, 1889-1957

RICHNESS AND DIVERSITY characterize Latin America's contribution to world literature. From the colorful, pictographic codices of anonymous Mayan and Aztec masters to the jewel-like fantasies crafted by Jorge Luis Borges in our own time, countless memorable works have been produced by Latin American writers of poetry and prose. Some of the brightest lights among these *littérateurs* appear in the field of poetry. Sor Juana Inés de la Cruz, the seventeenth-century *savante*, has already been discussed. Later centuries saw Rubén Darío, founder of the modernist school, and Nobel Prize winners Miguel Ángel Asturias and Pablo Neruda continuing the tradition of great poetry in Latin America.

Such writing has never been the sole property of a literary elite, but rather a part of the public domain. The people of Latin America love words—seem almost intoxicated by them. Their Romance languages and temperament lend themselves to poetic endeavor. What lovesick adolescent has not poured out his or her emotions in verse, and what visitor spending any time in a Latin country has not been awakened in the night by verse set to the music of the serenade?

This widespread appreciation of the written word and of individuals skilled in the use of written language has had its practical applications. Many a gifted writer or poet has achieved

170

prominence solely on the strength of his mastery of the idiom. One of the most outstanding of these is Marco Fidel Suárez. The illegitimate son of a mulatto washerwoman, Suárez became an accepted and honored member of the hidebound Colombian elite and was ultimately elected national president. One so humbly born could never have entered Colombian *haute politique* without having first won renown in his youth as a grammarian and essayist. Latin Americans prominent in nonliterary fields have also excelled in the writing of poetry and prose. The names of Bartolomé Mitre, Domingo F. Sarmiento, Andrés Bello, and José Martí are but a few of the many that could be cited.

The story of Gabriela Mistral illustrates these generalizations about the writers of literature and their place in Latin American culture. She began her career as a schoolteacher in rural Chile—a station befitting an impoverished, rather homely country girl. But the provincial teacher felt a need to express her innermost feelings through the poetry that over a period of years earned her international fame. She was lionized in her own country, becoming as much a national resource as the forests, mountains, and rivers of the countryside she wrote about.

Gabriela Mistral was both an introspective person and one of the vocal and unselfish humanists of her day. Her first calling was teaching, and a great deal of her poetry was written to be read and enjoyed by children. She was acutely attuned to the needs of women and children, particularly those who were innocent victims of the European conflagration of the 1930s and 1940s. The imagery she employed was so powerful, yet so unique, that she has had no imitators. Neither did she follow any preexisting school of poetry.

Although she had a strong personality and an open face and flashing smile that impressed all who met her, Gabriela Mistral was at heart an introvert—perhaps even a misanthrope at the end of her life. Like many gifted persons, she had an uneasy existence. Late in life she sought consolation in a personal, almost Franciscan, kind of Catholicism, but her constant travels and an innate pessimism deprived her of any real peace. Gabriela Mistral was much like the poetry she wrote—simple and unadorned, yet hiding an intensity and meaning disturbing in their implications.

Gabriela Mistral claimed, almost sixty years later, that her only sweet memories were of the years before her tenth birthday. In the village of Montegrande on the banks of Chile's Elqui River, she—then little Lucila Godoy Alcayaga—breathed the country air and gazed at the Andean *cordillera* that opened like gigantic jaws around the river valley. Her education during those years was left to nature. She learned to distinguish one place from another using only her sense of smell, to tell one season from the next not by the calendar but by the fields and sky, to decipher the alphabet of country sounds before that of written language. "I was happy until I left Montegrande; and after that I was never happy again," she wrote, remarkably forgiving of the small disasters and poverty of those years. Her father Jerónimo Godoy was as fond of Chilean wine as he was of his freedom, and he drifted away from home when Lucila was three. Petronila, his wife, welcomed him back without comment when, every few years, chance brought him to the Elqui valley. He never stayed long, however, and Petronila and Emelina, her daughter by a previous marriage, had to manage the family without him. Lucila never resented her footloose father; neither did she forget the hardships suffered by the little family, brought on by his failings.

Yet pleasure far outweighed pain during her years in Montegrande. The stern Andes printed their image on her mind's eye and the fertile earth of the valley lent its perfume to her waking hours. Those shapes and smells never deserted her, even when she left for Vicuña, her birthplace, to begin her formal education at age nine. She attended school for just three years, hardly enough to qualify her as an educated person. In fact, in later years she included herself among the company of the self-taught. Emelina, her elder half-sister, was a warm and devoted teacher who directed Lucila's education for several years after her formal schooling ceased.

Brief though it was, Lucila's educational career was important. She came into contact with popular poets and wrote her own first poems, dedicating them to her best friend and copying them carefully into a school notebook. To lighten the financial burden of her education, Lucila acted as a guide to the director, Doña Adelaida Olivares, who was blind and needed help getting to and from school. On more than one occasion she performed other duties as well. In 1902 Doña Adelaida entrusted thirteen-year-old Lucila with a quantity of notebooks to be distributed among her classmates as needed over a month's time. Somehow she ran out too soon, and Doña Adelaida accused her of stealing them. Lucila, acutely shy in the best of circumstances, was unable to speak a word in her own defense even when the director denounced her publicly before the entire student body. Lucila was overwhelmed by the accusation and sank to the floor unconscious. Hours later, as she crept home from school, a small band of girls met her in the plaza and chased after her with taunts of *ladrona*—thief. Even though her innocence was later proven, Lucila Godoy never returned to school, nor, characteristically, did she ever forget the incident.

The rankling memory of her unjustified disgrace was less damaging to Lucila than was the more subtle injustice of racial prejudice. During her first days in Vicuña, and perhaps before, she became aware that she was perceived with subtle disapproval as a country girl of undistinguished lineage, whose green eyes, dark heavy brow, and downturned mouth testified to the mingling of Chile's two major races in her ancestry. Lucila soon came to believe the racist notions popular in Chile (and in the rest of the Western world at that time), even as she absorbed the more positive love of sunlight, trees, and rural quiet from her Montegrande home. "I belong to the group of unlucky people who were born without a patriarchal age and without a Middle Ages," she wrote many years after she had achieved worldwide fame. "I am one of those whose insides, face and expression are uneasy and irregular, because of the graft; I consider myself to be among the children of that twisted thing that is called a racial experience, or better, a racial *violence*." On one hand she was her own most acid critic, referring to herself at times as *mestiza de vasca*—Indian and Basque half-breed—and attributing her failings to racial mixture. However, she bridled at any personal affront, attributing it to that same prejudice with which she was herself afflicted.

By the time she was thirteen, the timid Lucila Godoy considered herself an outcast. As a defensive reaction she began to cultivate a sense of tragic separateness. This carefully nurtured spiritual isolation accounted for the feeling of desolation that accompanied her.

Economic necessity intruded early and forced Lucila to choose a profession. Her sister and father were teachers, and it was decided that she too would teach. Her education proceeded at home under Emelina's direction, and both mother and sister saved and borrowed enough to pay her way through the teacher training school in La Serena. In 1904 she passed the examinations required for entrance and prepared to begin her course of study. Unexpectedly, and at the last moment, she was turned away. No official explanation was ever given, but Lucila's impassioned, somewhat socialistic poems that had begun to appear in the local press undoubtedly prejudiced school authorities against her. Lacking the protection of a powerful or wealthy sponsor, Lucila Godoy had no choice but to continue her education privately under Emelina's gentle tutoring and to enter teaching through an alternate route. The following year, at age sixteen, she was named assistant to the primary schoolteacher in a small town a few miles from La Serena, and in 1906 she moved to La Cantera, where she occupied a similar position.

A young railroad employee, not yet twenty-five years old, first noticed Lucila when she visited the Cantera train station to pick up her mail. Soon he began to visit her boardinghouse, and the two established a bond of affectionate regard. He was Romelio Ureta, an intense young man given to wearing peculiar patent leather shoes with elongated toes and waxing the ends of his rather sparse moustache. They shared an interest in poetry and read aloud the florid, grandiloquent verses of Vargas Vila and other popular poets of the day. After a time Romelio began to visit her less regularly. Lucila saw him in the company of another girl, suffered from the rejection, and poured her distress into verse.

Several years passed, and no one came to take Romelio's place in her affections. She became involved in Santiago's theosophical society, studied Oriental philosophy, especially the writings of Rabindranath Tagore. She mused on reincarnation, pantheism, and other beliefs foreign to her Catholic background but congenial to her temperament. Her poems and prose writings continued to appear in local newspapers—*The Voice of Elqui, El Coquimbo,* and *Reforma*—and she discovered a passion for letter-writing that would last a lifetime. Slowly her name spread beyond the immediate borders of the region. In spite of the adolescent tone of some of those early works, Lucila Godoy already showed signs of remarkable power and sensitivity.

Then in November 1909 Romelio Ureta committed suicide. Only one item was found on his body: a postcard he had received some time before from Lucila Godoy. Although his death had nothing to do with Lucila, she was nonetheless deeply moved by it and by the inexplicable fact that he had remembered her shortly before taking his life. In the weeks following she wrote six, perhaps more, sonnets of such intense importance to her that she put them away and kept them from public scrutiny for several years.

The "Sonnets of Death," as they were called when Lucila Godoy entered them in a national contest five years later, were far different from her earliest poems. Those immature works, written when she was fourteen and fifteen years old and under the baneful influence of Vargas Vila, caused her some embarrassment later, and she wrote that she would "never forgive those who published my first babblings with great fanfare, misspellings and horrible taste."

By 1909, however, the breadth of her experience was greatly increased. Rubén Darío, the great modernist poet, and Amado Nervo, a popular Mexican poet, as well as the Nobel Prize–winning poet Tagore, had earned her admiration and studious attention; the years of contact with the Bible, a thousand poems in itself, strengthened her style so that it could more easily carry the weight of her stringent, passionate honesty. The "Sonnets of Death" revealed for the first time that Lucila was a gifted poet. The impetus that drove her to express her deepest feelings in words—written, structured, rhymed—and to send those pieces of herself off to be published, set her apart from the mass of humanity who seek expression in unheeded tears, complaints, or confidences. Yet she sought an audience for her work hesitatingly, torn by her shyness on one hand and the conviction, on the other, that the poet is a pathfinder, a seer whose words point men and women the way to greatness of spirit. Only the profound be-

lief in her own poetic vocation could in the end persuade her to
reveal the innermost thoughts and feelings of Lucila Godoy.

A year after the "Sonnets of Death" were composed, after
four years as a teacher's aide and school clerk, Lucila went to a
Santiago normal school to take examinations in a broad range of
subjects, hoping to earn a teacher's equivalency diploma. Her
work was brilliant, the product of many lonely hours of study,
and she was thereafter permitted to teach in secondary school.
During the next two years she taught at high schools in Traiguén
and Antofagasta. Then in 1912 she was assigned to the secondary
school in Los Andes, not far from Santiago. There Lucila found an
environment well suited to her needs and tastes. Accustomed to
being criticized for her verses, she found herself the object of sympathetic interest in Los Andes, and her work in poetry and prose
was published in an increasingly broad selection of periodicals in
Chile as well as in Rubén Darío's journal *Elegancia* in Paris. Her
contacts were extensive. Among them was Pedro Aguirre Cerda,
a politician who occupied a score of important positions in
Chile—including the presidency—and who was instrumental in
helping her throughout her career. Through her letters and
through frequent trips into Santiago she established more and
more connections with Santiago's literary elite.

Early in her stay in Los Andes, Lucila Godoy chose a
pseudonym, not the juvenile kind she had used earlier, like
"Soul," "Solitude," or "Someone," but a well-modeled one inspired in part by a French Provençal poet whose work she admired. From the archangel of good news and comfort she chose
her first name; and from Frédéric Mistral—or perhaps from the
Mediterranean wind that blows across southern France—she
took a new last name. "Gabriela Mistral" fitted her new self far
better than the old, fitted the persona she had created as carefully
as her poems. As she wrote to Amado Nervo, "This soul of mine
today is far different from the one I had at birth." Indeed, by the
time she reached her twenties, Gabriela Mistral scarcely re-
sembled little Lucila Godoy, paralyzed by shyness, hardly able to
speak in the presence of adults. In her new incarnation, that
timidity was transformed into a stately reserve, a serenity that
belied her relative youth. Convinced of her homeliness, she

dressed plainly, in dull colors, wore flatheeled shoes (perhaps to compensate for her height), and strode about Los Andes bareheaded in outright defiance of the fashion of the day. Any effort at self-adornment would have seemed ridiculous to her, rather like gilding a mud pie. But to those who sought her out, she was by no means unattractive. Rather, she seemed imposing and distant until suddenly she broke into a broad grin that showed her pure white teeth, a smile that changed her face so completely that she seemed a different, much younger person. Gabriela Mistral continually charmed her admirers by these sudden contradictions: the green eyes and open smile in that dark face; the streak of whimsy hidden in a mantle of prim intensity; and her voice, measured and deep, that retained the rough country cadences of her native valley. Those who met her rarely, if ever, forgot her.

In 1914 a panel of three judges named her the winner of a national poetry contest, the *Juegos Florales.* She had submitted three "Sonnets of Death" to the competition and won by a vote of two to one. The award ceremony took place in Santiago Theater on December 22, 1914. In was an elaborate program of speeches, recitations, music, and even the selection of a queen in honor of the event. The only element missing was the award-winning poet herself. Claiming to be unable to attend, Gabriela came in disguise and watched from the balcony as her verses were read by another poet. One account of that peculiar occasion noted that she could not afford to buy a new dress, but it is far more likely that her own reticence made it impossible for her to appear.

In the aftermath of the *Juegos Florales,* Gabriela Mistral began to feel the effects of her increasing fame. Her poems were in demand for anthologies and literature texts throughout Latin America. Yet disillusionment followed on the heels of her success. In a letter probably written in 1915, she complained vigorously about "undesirable people, by which I mean *literary* ones" in Santiago. She was repelled by the two-faced characters she met through the *Juegos Florales:* "That's why I told you that the J. F. was the most hateful thing in the world," she wrote; "I came to know firsthand several *luminous* cerebral types whose hearts are rotten and who don't know what loyalty is; I was placed among them and every time I'm with them, I wish I had never been anything more than Lucila Godoy." Her first experience with that common human tendency to praise and flatter, then criticize out of earshot, disgusted Gabriela. "I don't know if I have already told you this," she added in the same letter, "but nothing in the world is worth as much to me as a good man, a person whose heart is fresh and fragrant and doesn't spout green juice of ill-will." Gabriela demanded absolute loyalty from her friends and was prepared to return it; but infighting and criticism, endemic in Santiago's literary circles, revolted her and she became less tolerant of it as the years passed.

In that throng of false friends, Gabriela did find a few true and faithful ones. Doña Fidelia Valdés Pereira, director of the Los Andes secondary school, consistently gave Gabriela support and encouragement. As would be characteristic of her through life, she had a handful of intimate female friends. Perhaps her most influential supporter was Pedro Aguirre Cerda. Years later, at the height of her fame, she wrote of Aguirre, "I owe everything to him; he was the only Chilean who had faith in me"—a comment that demonstrates, among other things, how demanding she was of her friends. It was he, as Chile's minister of justice and education, who named her director of the Punta Arenas secondary school for girls in 1918. With no formal education, the former clerk of a rural primary school now found herself in sole charge of a high school far away from her native Elqui valley. Punta Arenas was, in fact, far from almost everything. Located at Chile's extreme south, the small city was a port on the Straits of Magellan, a provincial capital where wind-blown clouds brought rain squalls, almost without warning, to torment sailors and city folk alike. That harsh region, where in summer the sun sets only reluctantly and winter nights last too long, affected Gabriela strongly, and she wrote a series of poems, "Patagonian Landscapes," about the austere south of Chile.

On her first night in Punta Arenas, she wrote the poem she considered to be her best, "Poem of the Son," and dedicated it to Alfonsina Storni, the Argentine poet. The poem recounted the powerful longing she had felt for a child and then, with the passing years, her bitter satisfaction that such a child had never been born.

Gabriela Mistral knew that she was never to have the most fundamental and most natural human experience: love that culminates in the birth of a child. By 1918, however, her sense of loss seemed on its way to a kind of healing. With no children of her own to care for, she would love and care for any and all children. While still in Los Andes, she wrote in a letter to a friend, "I'm not going to Santiago this month, I'm very tired and need to regain strength for my work, my only reason for living. I have given myself to the children and only for them do I guard my health and spirits. I'm an old maid in love with other people's children." Teaching, already her profession, became, with poetry, her vocation.

For a number of years Gabriela Mistral had searched for a way to merge her two vocations, poetry and teaching. Aware of the scarcity of literature for children, she had often written verses for school occasions, many of which had found their way into print, but she continued to lament the dearth of good children's poetry, suitable for school. As early as 1915 she hoped to publish a book of her school verses. "I have wanted to write a new kind of school poetry," she wrote in that year, "because the poetry now in vogue doesn't satisfy me; school poetry shouldn't stop being poetry because it's for school use, it should be more so, more delicate than any other, deeper, full of things of the heart: quivering with the breath of the soul."

With the passing of time the gentle sermons of "Hymn to the Tree," "Guardian Angel," and "Prayer for the Nest" were joined by a series of genres on similar themes: cradle songs, *rondas* (rounds or choruses in verse), and prose poems, among others. Her ideal, the model she followed and wished to equal, was the body of Spanish popular verse, whose supple simplicity came from constant use over many years. *Mestiza* America had had little time to create its own popular poetry, and Gabriela confessed that her own efforts to write children's poetry had, with a few exceptions, failed. Years later she described her children's poems as a "stiff plaster mold, beside the elastic flesh of popular [verse]." Speaking of her "Cradle Songs" in particular, she continued, "They were born, poor things, showing their crippled feet, to induce some musician to set them walking, and I wrote them half out of love for the 'lullabies' of my infancy and half to serve other women's emotions—the poet is an untier of knots, and love without words is a knot, and it drowns."

In 1919 Gabriela Mistral received word that she was to be transferred from Punta Arenas to Temuco. A photograph survives of the ceremony of farewell—the *despedida*—given by the students of her school. It shows the entire student body assembled in the school's auditorium, the youngest girls carefully arranged on tiers in front and the older ones spilling onto the stage in a crowded jumble. In the center stands Gabriela Mistral, thick and tall in a long, dark, shapeless dress, hands clasped soberly in front of her, her face expressionless.

Gabriela was director of the Temuco girls' secondary school for only a short time, but she lived there long enough to meet a teen-age boy, then named Neftalí Reyes, who approached her timidly, hoping to be allowed to use her library. She was happy to share her books, and the friendship between Gabriela Mistral and Pablo Neruda, Chile's two great poets, dates from that encounter. Another encounter, less direct, took place in Temuco as well. As she later described it, she was walking through a poor neighborhood when she saw a pregnant woman resting uncomfortably in a doorway, obviously close to giving birth. While Gabriela watched, a man passed and made a crude remark causing the woman to blush with embarrassment. Out of a sense of empathy inspired by the belief that maternity is of all conditions the most sacred, Gabriela wrote a series of prose "Poems for Mothers" expressing the powerful hopes and fears of women.

At the same time that Gabriela Mistral was writing with profound sympathy about women and children, she was becoming less and less like them. Virtually without family, in a literal sense she had no home. From time to time she did visit her aging mother and sister in the Elqui valley, but the frequent moves from one school to the next kept her from putting down roots anywhere. In 1915 she hinted at her bizarre lifestyle while answering a friend who had invited her to stay in his home. "I always stay in boardinghouses," she explained, thanking him for the invitation. "I am such an odious guest. I don't eat meat and I spend all day in the street ... Only in boardinghouses do they tolerate all that." Her only permanent dwelling was her school, where, surrounded by students, she worked, taught, and slept or, since sleep was an increasingly elusive luxury, wrote the letters, essays, and poems that never ceased to flow from her pen. But this relative homelessness, the constant transfers and the brevity of each stay bothered her very little. From her father she had inherited a love of travel; she was like him, *patiloca*, footloose: "I'm a vagabond and I don't deny it. The world is beautiful to see and perhaps when I'm dead I won't be able to roam about as much as I like."

Gabriela Mistral's plans for publication of her school verses were never carried out, and although her work was well known outside Chile, no book bearing her name had yet been published. That initiative was reserved for a Spanish literary critic living in the United States, Federico de Onís. In February 1921 Onís delivered a lecture on Gabriela to students and teachers of Spanish at Columbia University. When he explained that no volume of her verses was available, that her poems were scattered far and wide throughout the Spanish-speaking world, they volunteered to help underwrite the costs of publication. On behalf of the North American Spanish Teachers, Onís wrote to Gabriela requesting her consent in the undertaking. After some hesitation she agreed and forwarded to him a collection of poems that were published in 1922 under the title *Desolación.* The volume was an immediate success. A second edition was published in Santiago the following year, and an anthology of selected poems appeared soon thereafter in Spain.

In May 1921 Gabriela became the first director of the newly inaugurated Sixth School *(Liceo)* for Girls in Santiago, a large, impressive building with a faculty of thirty teachers. Some months after moving to Santiago she met the Mexican José Vasconcelos—philosopher, poet, writer of short stories and memoirs—who was at that time his country's minister of public education. Impressed by his interview with Gabriela, he returned to Mexico determined to secure her help in reforming Mexico's educational system. In the name of his government he invited her and her friend Laura Rodig to spend six months in Mexico at that nation's expense. Gabriela accepted the invitation and arranged with the Chilean government to carry out a study of Mexico's extensive reforms during her stay.

The invitation, a gesture of great friendship between the two nations, did not bring unqualified happiness. The failure of a Senate measure that would have provided her with some financial support from home, and the suspicion that Chile did not perhaps share Mexico's high opinion of her, were disappointing. Still, the excitement of leaving on her first international voyage buoyed her. Accompanied by Laura Rodig and another friend, Gabriela boarded the ship *Aconcagua*. They passed through the Panama Canal and traveled first to Cuba, then to Mexico, where Gabriela was received with great warmth and enthusiasm.

The six months stretched into almost two years. Everything possible was done to make her stay fruitful. Gabriela was given a comfortable house, and Palma Guillén, a bright young university teacher, became her secretary. She received an ample salary that was paid even after she left Mexico for several months' travel in Europe and the United States. During her stay, she worked to establish a series of practical schools for women, the *Escuelas-Hogar* bearing her name. She traveled about the country helping organize educational programs in rural areas and overseeing new mobile libraries. Convinced that even the most humble citizen can and should appreciate first-class literature, she edited an anthology of poetry and prose that included many of her own pieces. Entitled *Readings for Women*, the volume was published by the Mexican government in 1923.

Gabriela Mistral fell in love with Mexico as did Mexico with her. As she described it, the most powerful impression she felt during the first days in Mexico was that of peace: "I arrived at the house they have for me in the country. I went up to the roof. The horizon is immense and I felt embraced by light from the sky and by the silence of the fields all around me. For the first time in eighteen years I know I can work in peace, without the sound of the hourly school bell, without money worries that perennially trouble my life."

Laura Rodig, her faithful companion, described an incident that shows the depth of Gabriela's attachment to Mexico. A Congress of *Campesinos* (peasants and farmers) was to be held in the great auditorium of the University of Mexico. Gabriela decided to attend after being assured that she could go unofficially. But someone among the thousand persons in attendance recognized her, and she reluctantly agreed to appear on the stage with the other dignitaries. During the enthusiastic applause from the audience, a *campesino* in the balcony shouted above the noise, "I'd like to give that pretty lady a hug." It was almost by accident that he was heard at all, but Gabriela acknowledged him and with a gesture invited him to the speakers' platform. The audience responded to the novel event with shouts of encouragement and great hilarity. Sombreros sailed into the air as the young man made his way to the front. The trip seemed to take forever, and Gabriela and the directors of the congress felt increasingly uncomfortable. Finally he arrived, but on coming face to face with Gabriela, his courage suddenly deserted him and he stood transfixed with fright. A tense, expectant hush fell over the audience. Sympathetic to his plight, Gabriela moved closer to him and, taking his hands—hands brown and hardened from manual labor—in hers, in a symbolic gesture that escaped no one present, gently kissed them.

While Gabriela was still in Mexico, her friend José Vasconcelos had occasion to travel to Chile on official business. At one point he sent her a cablegram, its meaning quite mysterious at the time, saying "More than ever convinced that the best of Chile is in Mexico." Only after his return did Vasconcelos explain: during his visit a Chilean dignitary had asked him why the Mexicans had invited "la Mistral" when there were so many more interesting women than she in Chile. Vasconcelos's response was in the cable.

Gabriela Mistral, the *patiloca*, found travel so much to her liking that after 1924 she never returned home for more than an occasional visit. Leaving behind at least one statue of herself and numerous schools, avenues, and libraries bearing her name, she departed Mexico for the United States and Europe. During that first trip abroad, *Ternura (Tenderness)*, a collection of poems for children, many of them drawn from *Desolación*, was published in Madrid.

In barely three years she had published five books, establishing herself as one of the brightest stars in the world's literary firmament. If in 1912 she changed from Lucila Godoy into her own literary creation, the teacher-poet Gabriela Mistral, in 1924 she changed once again from persona to personage. Her every move was watched by admirers and critics, her comments dutifully recorded and reported, her travels punctuated by meetings with other well-known literary figures, by public appearances, by speeches and fanfare. Her fame made it impossible for her to fit back into the niche she had left behind in Santiago, so in 1925 at age thirty-six she retired on a small teacher's pension and began a kind of odyssey through the Americas and Europe as Chile's representative to one international organization after another: the League of Nations, the Institute of Intellectual Cooperation, the Congress of Educators in Switzerland, the International Federation of Universities in Madrid, the Institute of Educational Cinema in Rome, and so on.

During the late 1920s a military government came to power in Chile. Appreciating Gabriela's renown throughout Latin America, it offered her an ambassadorship to all Central America, a post she brusquely refused by speaking out against the government itself. In retaliation her pension was suspended, leaving her virtually nothing to live on. Once word of her dilemma was made public, Eduardo Santos, editor of the Bogotá daily *El Tiempo* and future president of Colombia, offered her a sum equal to her pension in exchange for a monthly newspaper article. Similar arrangements were made with newspapers in Buenos Aires, Mexico, Costa Rica, and Madrid, so by dint of hard work Gabriela was able to support herself, her mother, and her sister.

Until 1930 Gabriela lived in France in rented houses near Paris, and later in southern France where she could enjoy both the sun and a less expensive way of life. During the late twenties, possibly in 1928, she adopted a nephew named Juan Miguel Godoy, the child of a half-brother on her father's side. The little boy was just an infant when she brought him to Europe, and she gave him a nickname "Yin-Yin" in tribute to the light and joy he brought into her life. He later baptized her "Buddha" and inspired her to write for children with naturalness and spontaneity, free from didactic ends as she sought only to amuse her little Yin.

Gabriela and Juan Miguel roamed the Western Hemisphere early in the 1930s. She taught courses at Barnard College, Middlebury College, and the University of Puerto Rico, and visited Central America and the West Indies. When the government of Chile returned to civilian rule, her pension was restored, and she was named honorary consul to Madrid in 1933. The post brought her no salary but carried with it certain social benefits. All was well until 1935, when a letter she had written to an old friend in Chile found its way into print. In the letter she criticized the Spanish character and ended by exclaiming "I don't know what I'm doing in Spain!" It took a week or so for the bomb to explode. When it did, Gabriela left for Portugal, where she tried to discover who was to blame for her disgrace. She believed that someone wishing to cause her harm had brought that Santiago newspaper article to the attention of the Spanish public with predictable results. Gabriela's estrangement from Spain never healed. She distrusted the Spanish, feeling herself—a *mestiza*, a *campesina*—at a disadvantage among them.

In 1935 a group of outstanding European writers who admired Gabriela's work petitioned Chilean President Alessandri to find a place for her as a paid consul. On September 17, with the president's encouragement, the Chilean Senate named Gabriela Mistral a consul for life. From then on she would be free to live anywhere in the Americas or Europe on a salary sufficient to her needs, and only by an act of Congress could her position be suspended or modified.

Gabriela did not take the honor lightly. During her lifetime abroad she represented her nation and her Americas well, trying to dispel misconceptions about Latin America and speaking out for humble people—women, children, Indians, *mestizos*, and *campesinos*. She pleaded their case in poetry, prose poems, and articles that appeared in periodicals throughout the Spanish-speaking world. The plight of women was especially important to her. She knew the trials of women whose men are destroyed by alcoholism, and she knew the subtle as well as overt discrimination suffered by women who leave traditional ways of life for careers in education and the arts. From the very first she had been aware of the discouraging treatment given women writers. Either they were not criticized sternly enough—implying that no woman could be judged by the same criteria that men apply to each other—or their work was dismissed as hopelessly feminine.

After several years in Lisbon and Oporto, Gabriela went to

Guatemala as general consul and *chargée d'affaires*. From there, in 1938, she traveled down the Atlantic coast of South America, first to Rio de Janeiro, then to Montevideo, where she took part in an historic public meeting with Alfonsina Storni of Argentina and the Uruguayan Juana de Ibarbourou. The three women poets read autobiographies in verse to an enthralled audience, little suspecting that in a few months the tormented Alfonsina would commit suicide. Later, in Buenos Aires, Gabriela met with Victoria Ocampo, for many years director of the Argentine literary magazine *Sur* and the publishing house of the same name.

Out of that meeting came the decision to publish a volume of Gabriela's poems written since the appearance of *Desolación* and *Ternura*. Ocampo offered to underwrite the costs of publication herself; and Gabriela responded by giving the proceeds of its sale to Basque children who were victims of Spain's civil war. *Tala*, variously translated as *Havoc* or *Felling*, was Gabriela's personal favorite among the books of verse published under her name even though it was not greeted with the enthusiasm her earlier works had enjoyed. Collected in that volume, and dedicated to her friend and former secretary Palma Guillén, were the poems written after her mother's death in 1929, a series of verses about the American landscape, the disillusionment of middle age, and her feelings of rootlessness, of being forever in a foreign land.

Her already eventful journey was crowned by her reception in Chile. After an absence of thirteen years, however, she found herself a foreigner in her own country. Everywhere she went in Santiago during that visit, she was treated with glorious warmth by Chileans—and the smile that shines from photographs taken during the visit are proof of the pleasure she felt. But Chile was no longer home. She was more in touch with the Chile of her multi-colored memories than with the nation that welcomed her in 1938.

Gabriela returned to Europe and established a Chilean consulate in Nice on France's Mediterranean coast. When war broke out the following year, she moved to Brazil, settling first in Niteroi and, in 1941, in Petropolis. But the tentacles of war stretched across the Atlantic and followed her to her haven. To the south in Argentina Juan Domingo Perón supported the Nazis and Italian fascists; to the north, the United States entered the war on the Allied side; and in cities and towns throughout the Americas people took sides with varying degrees of vehemence. Gabriela was antifascist by temperament and philosophy and had opposed Franco's regime in Spain as she had Chile's military government of the late 1920s. In Petropolis she and her son Juan Miguel favored the Allies, the French in particular.

Years of residence in France had given her adopted son, now in his teens, a decidedly French manner, and his schoolmates ridiculed him for being different. Gabriela worried about him, but when she counseled him to leave school, he refused. By 1943, at age seventeen, Juan Miguel became enamoured of a young girl, German by descent, and was subjected even more to the taunts and teasing of other young men who laughed at his slight hunchback and tried to convince him that the girl mocked him in his absence.

"Yin" was visibly upset by such treatment but seemed able to put the attachment behind him. With Gabriela he made plans to continue his studies, paid annual dues to various organizations, and even rearranged his room. Then suddenly he was dead of arsenic poisoning. Gabriela sat at his bedside through the endless hours preceding his death, suffering an agony of the spirit that equaled his physical pain. In the days following his death she was unable to walk, unable to think, only aware of the horrible loss. Her son, her "Yin," was dead. It was impossible for her to believe that he had committed suicide. Someone must have driven him to it, or drugged him, or perhaps he was actually murdered by a band of evil youths. The rest of the world might believe that he took his own life, but she could not. Even so, it was difficult for her to understand the catastrophe: "Ah, but I have to return to my old heresy and believe in Karma from past lives in order to understand what phenomenal, what terribly high crime of mine was punished by my Juan Miguel's night of agony in a hospital, so frightening in spite of the incredible stoicism with which he bore the hot coals of arsenic in his poor, beloved body." In her dreams she saw him alive again; she felt him near during hours of sleeplessness. Dangerously suspended between reality and her grief, she reached out to the dead youth, the companion of her years of travel, the arm she had leaned on in the strange streets of Europe. Juan Miguel had been her only blood tie to the future, and now she was alone, trapped in her own mortality. Among all the people who had known her, who had sought her out, she counted only six as friends. When Palma Guillén, one of that number, arrived in Petropolis shortly after the tragedy, she found Gabriela alone, locked in her big house, in a dreadful state of isolation. Her bitterness spread out in waves, threatening to drown her in its venom.

For two years she languished in Brazil, her heart already weak, now doubly burdened with diabetes. Then on November 15, 1945, she received word that she had been awarded the Nobel Prize for Literature, the first Latin American poet and one of very few women so honored. Her comment on hearing the news: "Perhaps it was because I represent the women and children." Three days later she boarded ship and sailed for Stockholm.

The Nobel Prize enthroned Gabriela Mistral, crowned her queen of Latin America's literary kingdom. At the award ceremony Sweden's King Gustave, elderly and white-haired, presented the award. Tall and straight, draped in a black velvet gown, the former schoolteacher and *campesina* faced the king and in the serene dignity of her manner rivaled him in majesty. In short words of thanks, Gabriela accepted the prize humbly, not for herself, but for Latin America and for the "poets of my race."

Like all "coronations," this one was preceded by years of political maneuvering. An Ecuadorian writer, Adela de Velasco, first suggested that Chile place her name in nomination while Gabriela's friend of many years, Pedro Aguirre Cerda, occupied the Chilean presidency. He wholeheartedly supported the idea and instructed Chile's diplomatic corps in Europe to promote her candidacy, a task that fell to another friend, Chile's ambassador to France, who was from Gabriela's native province. Excellent French and Swedish translations of her verses were prepared. Rumors swirled about her before the awards in 1944; they came to nothing. In 1945, similar rumors spread through Latin America, this time with glorious success, and Gabriela Mistral underwent the final transformation into queen of her aesthetic kingdom.

Not all queens are happy, however. Gabriela, honored by the

world, yet consumed by grief and her inborn melancholy, left Stockholm, toured Europe briefly, embarked for the United States, and finally came to rest in California where she bought a house with her prize money. She who had brought unequaled honor to Chile rejected the warmth that her country could have offered in return and chose a foreign country as her abode. Far from her own people, trusting only a handful of friends, Gabriela withdrew from the world and in solitude mourned her dead. She wrote a series of poems on grief and loss during those bleak years and later, in 1954, saw them published in her last volume of verse entitled *Lagar (Wine Press)*.

Gabriela, alone with her fame, her poetry, and memories of things too painful to tell, fell into the hands of a companion who was unworthy of her trust. *"Nací distraída,"* she said of herself, "I was born absent-minded." That unconcern for the daily details of life made her easy prey for the unscrupulous person who kept her sedated while visitors were turned away at the door. A young North American named Doris Dana, scholar and linguist, daughter of a wealthy New York family, learned that the famous poet lived in California. Appearing at Gabriela's house, she pushed aside the unprincipled housekeeper, entered, and found Gabriela, almost blind from diabetes, drugged and unaware that she had signed away her ownership of the house. Recognizing her desperate need, Doris Dana rescued Gabriela from that purgatory and cared for her like a daughter, with patience and love, until the end of her days.

By 1948 Gabriela's health was very poor. On arriving in Mexico she suffered a collapse, and only the constant care of a physician saved her life. For a time, as Chile's consul in Veracruz, she remained in the land of so many warm memories, where school children by the thousands recited her *rondas*. Because she was forbidden by her doctors to travel to the capital city, Mexico's literary elite traveled to her and paid homage to the queen of poetry. In 1950 she began her travels once again: first to Washington, then to Naples and the little Italian town of Rapallo, where she established her consulate.

Age and fame did not bring Gabriela tranquillity; if she felt pleasure over the honors and tributes paid her, it did not show.

Even her most fervent supporters knew of *su memoria enemiga,* her hostile memory that seemed to cherish the bad and forget the good things of her life. She was a misanthrope, expecting the worst, seeing the worst, and recounting with barely controlled passion the injuries and tragedies accumulated over many years. She fought with Federico de Onís, the original publisher of *Desolación,* and complained that she never earned more than a hundred dollars from that popular book. She was never reconciled with the Spanish people and until her last days spoke of the hatred she imagined Spain harbored toward her. The Chilean literary critic Raúl Silva Castro became her archenemy in 1935 when he published a study of *Desolación* and *Ternura.* Silva Castro wrote that her work was overvalued, that her poetry suffered from imperfections in rhyme and meter, and that her poetic vocabulary was often coarse and masculine. No matter that dozens of other critics praised her verses, recognizing that Gabriela's primeval spirit could never be contained in perfect poetic forms, that the words of *mestiza* America were as valid artistically as the vocabulary of Spain. Gabriela felt the wounds of criticism far more sharply than the balm of praise.

Most incomprehensible was her distrust of Chile. In the last decade of her life, she chose to believe that a minister of education had forced her to leave Chile in the 1920s by naming her delegate to an international institute in Paris—as though she were not happy to receive the post. She continued to believe that her short visit to Chile in 1938 had been marred by hostile glances cast toward her in the streets. She believed against all evidence that she could never return to Chile to live peacefully among her own people. Friends wrote constantly about the ceremonies in her honor throughout the country, about invitations from one organization after another. Gabriela remained skeptical. Even when a group of friends persuaded the Chilean government to award her an extraordinary prize of a half million pesos, Gabriela continued to doubt Chile's love for her.

Finally, after years of hesitation and excuses, she was persuaded to return home in 1954. Palma Guillén, by then a member of Mexico's diplomatic corps in Rome, helped her embark at Genoa. Accompanied first by Margaret Bates, then by Doris Dana, she wound her way through the Americas, from New York to La Habana and finally to Chile. Wrapped as securely in her incredible fame as she was in the smoke from her everpresent cigarettes, the stately, melancholy queen moved from one mass reception to the next. Her stay in Chile was a triumph. Dressed in her long, shapeless coat, her face creased by fatigue and illness, she was decorated, applauded, honored by the Chilean nation, and then, in the care of Doris Dana, she left home once again.

Her life ebbed and finally slipped away under an onslaught of physical ills on January 10, 1957. When she died in a hospital on Long Island, New York, she weighed scarcely ninety pounds. Gabriela Mistral's final journey took her from New York to Santiago, and finally to a small hilltop in Montegrande. Her gift to the world, an inheritance in poetry and prose, remains behind in four collections of verse and a multitude of prose pieces, some gathered into anthologies and many still buried in newspapers and magazines. Original, unique, Gabriela Mistral left behind no crowd of young poets to follow in her footsteps, founded no new school of poetry. Her verse, intense, chiseled by pain and comprehension, belongs not to the literary elite, but to the children who sing her *rondas*, to the mothers who nurse their babes in poor huts of the Andean *cordillera*, and to Latin Americans who look not to Europe but to their own land for sustenance. Gabriela was teacher, poet, queen—an enigma wreathed in smoke who touched the deepest strains of human feeling as few have ever done.

# IX

# Eva Perón, 1919-1952

TWO REVOLUTIONS ROCKED the twentieth century: one was made by people and the other by machines. The first was attended by great human strife. In Mexico in 1910, in Russia seven years later, and yet later in other parts of the world, ordinary people undertook a violent and usually bloody reshaping of their destiny. The second revolution began when inventions brought the earth's millions face to face with their history and thrust them into the middle of it. Radio signals reached even the most remote mountain valley, informing people of events taking place in London, Paris, Tokyo, and their own great cities. Roads penetrated the hinterlands, unleashing a swelling flood of humanity that crowded into urban areas.

In this context of human revolution and rapid technological development, the beautiful Eva Duarte de Perón found her place. A product of the revolutionary age and a shrewd manipulator of the forces shaping twentieth-century society, she symbolized the irresistible human and technological change that has left nothing unaltered in modern times.

Eva Perón appeared in Argentine history in the mid-1930s, a time of great uncertainty the world over. Severe economic problems were tumbling civil governments, giving rise to military dictatorships in many countries. Argentina, too, witnessed such a change. Between 1930 and 1943 a transition to military rule was

completed, bringing Colonel Juan Domingo Perón to national prominence. Soon thereafter Perón and radio personality Eva Duarte formed the alliance that would reshape the foundations of Argentine political power.

Juan and Eva could not have been better suited for the roles they chose to play. They were an attractive, exciting couple; but more important, they were of the people. They appealed to the millions of poor and disinherited Argentines as two of their own who had achieved success. Not only that, they held the hated oligarchs in the palms of their hands and manipulated them like puppets. The relationship between Juan and Evita Perón and the masses was an organic one. The couple played on the theme of paternal concern for their people, their "shirtless ones," with consummate skill. And they used radio and other forms of mass communication with a flair that rivaled and in ways surpassed contemporaries such as Franklin Roosevelt and Benito Mussolini.

Of the two Argentine leaders, Evita is by far the more difficult to judge objectively. She was literally worshiped by the masses who wanted to have her canonized even before her untimely death. So virulent was the hatred of her wealthy enemies that they cursed her even as she lay dying of cancer. The passage of time has made it no easier to assess Eva Perón. For millions she was a saint—the incarnation of truth and hope. For others she was crude, avaricious, and corrupt. It is perhaps the better part of wisdom to accept the historical Eva as a tangle of dissonant perceptions. Yet she was no less paradoxical than the age that produced her.

Juana Ibarguren smoothed the skirt of her black dress and turned to see that her five children, bundled against the cold July winds that swept across central Argentina, were huddled behind her, cowed as much by the weather as by the cold stares they were about to face. Juana was determined to pay her last respects to the man who had fathered her children and looked after them faithfully for twelve years. But Juan Duarte's wife and legitimate children were so strongly opposed to the appearance of his "other" family that it was only by order of the provincial governor, a friend of Juana's, that she and her children were permitted to attend their father's wake. Quietly the six black-clad figures entered the Duartes' large house and filed past the open coffin. Terrified by the disapproval evident all around them, the children said not a word and barely looked at the familiar face that lay so still among long white candles and floral wreaths.

As soon as the wake was over, Juana left the house in the little town of Chivilcoy and led her unhappy brood back to their home in nearby Los Toldos. The determination that had taken her to Juan Duarte's funeral suddenly deserted her, and she began to wonder how she and the children would manage without Juan's protection and wealth. She could look for a job, of course, but in a small town like Los Toldos almost no decent jobs were available to an uneducated woman. It wasn't that the region was poor; it was in fact one of the richest agricultural zones in the world. But the land was owned by a few wealthy families who scarcely acknowledged the existence of the landless poor of the town. Their attention was fixed on sophisticated Buenos Aires, the great city to which provincial wealth flowed. As everything of value passed from the provinces to the capital, the countryside supported only a small middle class and a large lower class. Women like Juana were trapped on the lowest rung of Argentina's social ladder.

Juana and her children stayed in Los Toldos for three years after Juan Duarte's death. Then in 1929 they packed their possessions and moved to Junín, where the family was soon established over the restaurant of a friend, an Italian immigrant. Just how Juana managed to provide for her family is not clear. Some say that she opened a boardinghouse; others, less charitably, that she began receiving male visitors on a regular basis. Be that as it may, Juana's children were successful in finding places for themselves in the rural middle class. By that time Elisa Duarte, Juana's oldest daughter, had a job as postal clerk, and Blanca was enrolled in normal school studying to be a teacher. But her third daughter was something of a problem. By the time she reached her teens María Eva Duarte could only be described as stage-struck. Magazines and radio programs that reached Junín from Buenos Aires seemed to feed Evita's dislike for the provincial town and cramped apartment where the family lived, and her impatience to leave home and seek her fortune soon overcame all other considerations. Her school work, never more than mediocre, ceased altogether as she dreamed of life as a movie star or theater actress.

In 1934, when Evita was fifteen years old, a famous singer came to Junín on tour from Buenos Aires. Eva was not timid about meeting him. After winning his sympathies with a heavy dose of flattery, she confessed her driving ambition to enter the world of acting and begged him to take her to the capital. Such pleas from the worshipful yet self-confident girl were persuasive, but the seasoned performer hesitated, foreseeing the difficult life Evita would find there. Juana herself pleaded with him to let Evita try her luck. Perhaps she was as convinced as Eva that the future lay in Buenos Aires and in the public eye. In any case, mother and daughter finally persuaded him to take her to Buenos Aires.

Buenos Aires in the 1930s was a kind of Argentine mecca for thousands of immigrants from the interior provinces. Rural communities, as Juana Ibarguren knew well, were split into two rigid classes, one extremely wealthy, the other barely able to get along. It was from the latter group that the steady stream of job-hunting immigrants came. They settled in droves in south Buenos Aires neighborhoods like Avellaneda, Nueva Chicago, Barracas, and many others. In 1936 alone more than eighty thousand people descended on the city, most of them poorly educated, penniless, and armed only with hope and, like Evita, the ambition to make their fortunes. Remarkably, 75 percent of those immigrants were women.

Evita traveled the 150 miles from Junín to Buenos Aires early in January 1935. She was fifteen, virtually uneducated, yet pretty in an adolescent way and full of great hopes. Her health had always been rather poor, and it suffered as she struggled to win minor parts on the stage and in radio. For four years she lived precariously on income from bit parts and radio work that paid at best thirty-five dollars a month. Yet the determination she had inherited from her mother stood her in good stead. She eagerly cultivated the friendship of powerful men who were able to help advance her career. In 1939 she won her first worthwhile part in radio and soon persuaded a wealthy soap manufacturer to become her sponsor. By 1942 Jabón Radical, another soap manufacturing company, agreed to sponsor her radio drama series.

Evita was suddenly secure. After seven long years of constant struggle, her radio career was firmly established. For the first time she indulged her taste for luxury by renting a comfortable apartment on Calle Posadas near the Radio Belgrano station where she worked. Her style of dress gradually became less adolescent and more elegant, and she underwent a happy transformation from brunette to blond. As her own wealth increased, Evita, aware of the responsibilities that money brings, searched for ways to help her family back in Junín. Never shy about using influence, she approached her new sponsor, and her older brother Juan Duarte was soon offered a position at Jabón Radical.

As Evita was establishing herself comfortably as a radio actress, a group of army officers, unhappy with the weak conservative regimes that had ruled since 1930 and strongly influenced by fascist dictators Mussolini in Italy and Hitler in Germany, sought to seize the reins of power in Argentina. In June 1934 the military revolution became a reality, and the last vestiges of civilian rule disappeared.

Evita was well equipped to ride the wave of transition to military rule. Using an irresistible combination of flattery and personal beauty, she became friendly with several officers of the new government. A special friend was Lieutenant Colonel Aníbal Francisco Imbert, the new director of posts and telegraph. With his help Eva found it quite easy to secure a license for her new radio program, a series of dramatic biographies of famous women that began late in 1943.

The new government had been in power only six months when a natural disaster struck. The province of San Juan, located far west of Buenos Aires at the foot of the Andes, was almost destroyed by earthquake. In the capital a great charity performance was planned to raise money for victims of the quake. The entire acting community would attend and so would the highest-ranking officials of the new government. On January 22, 1944, the night of the performance, Evita and Lieutenant Colonel

Imbert were already in their seats when a tall, amiable-looking colonel came in surrounded by a bevy of attractive actresses. Before the evening was over, Eva and the colonel, Juan Domingo Perón, were acquainted and well on the way to becoming the most astonishing couple in Argentine history.

The details of this meeting are obscured by clouds of propaganda sent up by Peronist mythmakers. It seems safe to say, however, that within a relatively short period, Perón moved to an adjoining apartment on Calle Posadas, where he and Eva settled into an ordinary kind of domestic life. The match was instantly successful. Perón at forty-eight was tall, handsome, and blessed with a charming smile. Evita, now twenty-five, was petite, blond, and expensively dressed, a perfect ornament for the ambitious widower. Perón had power and prestige, but his political ambitions were not yet satisfied. In Evita he recognized a talent for publicity that would be useful to him and an ambition that equaled his own. The two shared similar backgrounds as well: both were products of the illicit union of wealthy men and women of the lowest social stratum. And above all, Evita knew how to bind Perón to her with tireless outpourings of adulation, gratitude, and praise. In later years she would compare him to Alexander the Great, to Napoleon, to José de San Martín, and even to God in an apparently successful attempt to win his trust and undying love.

A month after the San Juan earthquake, the military regime named Perón vice president in General Edelmiro J. Farrell's new government. The vice presidency, although certainly an important position, was less valuable to Perón than two positions he had held since early in the military regime. As minister of war, Perón boasted in 1944 that he had on file undated retirement applications from 90 percent of all military officers. Anyone who displeased him was subject to immediate "retirement." As secretary of labor and welfare his control over employers and trade unions was less absolute; yet he had made great progress in replacing union leaders with his own men—such as Cipriano Reyes of the meatpackers union—and in urging employers to grant workers more benefits and higher wages. The successes Perón had won for labor were reflected by a leap in union membership, from 350,000 in 1943 to a million two years later. Many of the newest union members felt a personal sense of gratitude to Perón, who appeared to be an authentic advocate of the working class.

The gleam of Perón's power illuminated Evita as well. Never one to accept a free ride, however, she began a new radio series, "Toward a Better Future," soon after they met. Twice a week she delivered short speeches on topics like patriotism, the family, self-sacrifice—all essentially propaganda for Perón and his work at the Secretariat of Labor and Welfare. Her talent for emotional, dramatic speechmaking was clearly apparent in this series. Anti-Peronists have hinted that Perón himself used to stop work at 7 o'clock each Wednesday and Friday evening to listen to Eva's impassioned praise of him over the radio. It is certain that thousands of workers not only listened but believed her when she described Perón as a patriot and defender of the great Argentine working class.

During this period, Evita received her initiation into politics and union organization. She became president of the actors' union established in 1944, and as time went on she began to participate more and more freely in the political strategy sessions that often took place in Perón's Calle Posadas apartment.

As her political education progressed, so did her wealth. Eva's critics claim that aside from her radio career and her work in the actors' union, she became increasingly skillful at the age-old profession of graft. For a fee she would secure scarce merchandise such as unexposed film and automobile tires for eager buyers. By 1945 Eva claimed an estate of more than a million pesos, in addition to a residence some ten minutes from downtown Buenos Aires and an abundance of fine clothes and jewels. The girl from Los Toldos was suddenly a wealthy woman. But even though she thought nothing of buying magnificent gifts for her friends, she still carefully examined every bill to be sure no one dared try to cheat her.

By 1945 several of Perón's military associates began to complain that it wasn't proper for Perón to be "chasing after the actress Eva Duarte," as they phrased it. Perón, secure in his power, answered, "Well, what do you expect me to chase, actors?" The remark seems to have closed the subject. Vice President Perón's relationship with Eva did not go unnoticed by her employers at Radio Belgrano. By 1945 she was earning more than $6,000 a month, a salary related more to her association with Perón than to her talent as an actress.

By early spring of 1945 Perón had become so powerful a threat to groups within the military government that General Farrell asked for Perón's resignation from his posts as vice president, minister of war, and secretary of labor and welfare. Under increasing pressure, Perón yielded to the demand and on October 9 submitted his resignation. Almost immediately Evita was fired by Radio Belgrano. Their luck seemed to have deserted them. Middle-class and professional groups staged anti-Perón rallies outside the officers' club in Buenos Aires. Convinced that the course of wisdom lay in flight, Perón and Eva packed up their money and slipped away from the capital. Before long they were detained by Buenos Aires police, who imprisoned Perón on an island in River de la Plata. Eva was allowed to return to Calle Posadas, where for four frantic days she tried to free Perón. Five years later in *La razón de mi vida (My Mission in Life)* she wrote the official version of those days of anxiety when she "rushed into the streets looking for friends who might still be able to do something for him." False friends in positions of power refused to help her; but, she wrote, the workers of the city opened their hearts to Perón in his hour of need. The result was the triumphant Peronist "Day of Days," October 17, 1945, when a huge day-long strike and demonstration brought the capital to a standstill. A crowd of thousands of Argentines gathered in the plaza outside the presidential palace and, armed with banners and pictures of Perón, demanded his immediate release.

Whether or not the demonstration was a spontaneous response to Evita's desperate pleas, or whether it was prudently planned in advance, the Peronist Day of Days was something the military government could not ignore. Perón was brought quickly to the presidential residence, the Casa Rosada. As he stepped out on the balcony he was greeted by a roar of delight from thousands of meatpackers, railway employees, and textile and garment workers, many of whom were women. All of them were convinced that Perón was their savior. President Farrell embraced him on the spot, and Perón turned to the crowd with his arms outstretched. In the warmest, most fatherly terms, Perón thanked them for supporting him in his hour of need. In answer to shouts from demonstrators asking where he had been, Perón claimed already to have forgotten. A man who cannot forget bad memories does not deserve the respect of his fellows, he said, and he wanted to be loved by those gathered together that day. For did he not love and understand them because they had suffered as his old mother had suffered? Longing only to be one of them, he announced his resignation from the army and melodramatically handed over his sword and sheath to General Farrell. Then, cautioning them to disperse quietly because there were ladies in the crowd, he begged them to stand before him just a moment longer so that he might feast his eyes on them.

Perón's great success on that day was due in large part to Evita's faithful efforts in his behalf. In gratitude, Perón took her back to Junín, where they were married in a secret civil ceremony witnessed only by Colonel Domingo Mercante, a loyal supporter from the Secretariat of Labor and Welfare, and Eva's mother and brother. Almost immediately Perón announced that he would run for president, and with Eva at his side he plunged into the campaign.

The campaign was a violent battle between candidates of the National Democratic Union party and Juan Domingo Perón. Mass media were used constantly, but Perón, with Eva at the microphones of Radio Belgrano, was easily more effective than the Democratic Union–controlled newspapers. Eva and Perón traveled by rail throughout Argentina, appealing to nationalist and class sentiments, distributing small gifts and pictures, and arousing the admiration of rural as well as urban workers. Emphasizing their own humble backgrounds at every opportunity, Eva, dressed in extravagantly expensive clothes and jewelry, and the genial Perón spoke to working-class Argentines in terms that appealed strongly to a group long ignored by national institutions. Traditional government had looked to wealthy landowners and industrialists—the oligarchs—for support and had treated powerless segments of society with contempt, if at all. Trade unions established before Perón's rise appealed mainly to European immigrants who understood their socialist, syndicalist appeals. The new wave of migrants from Argentina's own rural provinces were left largely alone, to sink or swim as they might. Evita and Perón, however, not only recognized the existence of these new classes, but seized on the old disdainful names privileged Argentines had given them—terms like *cabecitas negras* (little black-haired people) and *descamisados* (shirtless ones)—and turned them into symbols of unity. Perón spent long hours being photographed in his shirtsleeves, and Eva with her beautiful clothes came to represent a *descamisada* who made good.

About halfway through the campaign, the United States government published a "blue book" that was highly critical of the fascist military regime in power since 1943. Although it was probably intended as a warning to Argentines, it had exactly the opposite effect. Perón increased his nationalistic appeals, and Argentines, offended by United States interference in their affairs, rose to his defense.

The election took place on February 24, 1946, and, most observers agree, was relatively fair. Perón won over 52 percent of the nearly three million votes cast. In the Chamber of Deputies Peronists won two out of every three seats, and in the Senate there was virtually no opposition. One of the Congress's first acts was to impeach every member of the conservative Supreme Court, so that by the end of his first year as President, Perón had complete control over all three branches of government.

Perón's inauguration on June 4, 1946, was in many ways indicative of things to come. Eva, especially, seemed to enjoy flaunting long-established custom by behaving in ways no president's wife had ever done before. During the ceremony her friends the Doderos occupied a place of honor close to Perón himself, even though Alberto Dodero was an industrialist with no official connection to Argentina's new government. In a gesture that was almost insulting to staid members of Argentine society, Eva chose to wear a gown so low-cut that Cardinal Archbishop Copello, seated next to her during the banquet, was literally afraid to look at her.

Evita's unusual behavior left wealthy Argentina aghast. The president's wife was traditionally offered a place of honor in highest social circles. But the wealthy matrons of Buenos Aires were horrified at the thought of receiving Madame Perón in their homes. To them Eva was a person of shady reputation who had come from the depths of society. Her wealth and power were won by the most questionable means and certainly could not make up for her lack of breeding, education, and family connections.

As soon as Perón became president, war broke out between Evita and the ladies of the oligarchy. The first battle was waged over the presidency of the Beneficencia, a social service organization that had received high-society support for many years. Custom dictated that the president's wife should preside over the Beneficencia, but Eva's wealthy enemies refused to offer her the position. When she demanded to know why, they responded that she, at twenty-seven, was alas too young. At that Eva kindly offered the services of her mother, Juana Ibarguren, who was, if possible, less acceptable than Evita herself.

Her rejection by Argentina's social circles appears to have hurt Eva deeply. Although she reacted to the experience with outward scorn, she took every opportunity to humiliate the women who had humiliated her. On one occasion when a group of well-born ladies gathered to protest her opposition to the Beneficencia, she ordered their arrest and had them carried off weeping in police vans. After days of imprisonment along with prostitutes and petty thieves, she finally permitted their release. On other occasions elderly matrons were forced to receive her in their homes in exchange for special favors that only the president could grant.

In *My Mission in Life* Eva later claimed that it was she who rejected Argentine society, not vice versa. "The oligarchy has never been hostile to anyone who could be useful to it," she wrote. "Power and money were never bad antecedents to a genuine oligarch." Yet her later vindictiveness toward those same oligarchs is compelling evidence that she was in fact wounded by them. Perhaps for that reason she dressed defensively, extravagantly, during the early years of Perón's presidency. Her hair, her jewels, her clothes all betrayed a deep insecurity as well as the desire to seem wealthier than the wealthiest aristocrat.

Yet Evita's actions during her six short years of glory cannot be fully explained in terms of vengeance or mere ambition. In her book she claimed that she could never have been satisfied with the passive role usually played by the president's wife. This is undeniably true. Coupled with energy and vitality that seemed at odds with her physical frailty was a body of ideas, simplistic perhaps, but founded in personal experience, that led her to choose a path of action no Argentine woman had followed before. Principal among those ideas was the view of society as composed of two groups—the privileged rich and the downtrodden poor. The former class was proud, cold, and, in a word, bad; the latter, from which she herself had come, was good. The evil committed by the wealthy and the suffering of the poor could only be stopped by reversing the balance of power, seizing wealth by cunning and force, if need be, so that the workers and rural poor could gain benefits they had never before enjoyed.

The methods Evita chose to use in her campaign for the Peronist brand of "social justice" were highly personal, arbitrary, and haphazard. Soon after Perón was inaugurated, she set up an office at the Ministry of Labor and Welfare, where she quickly overshadowed the minister himself. From her office she also organized and directed the Social Aid Foundation, a successor to the more traditional Beneficencia. From her double position of power she forced employers to grant benefits and salary increases to trade unions while at the same time she demanded, and received, huge donations from all sectors of Argentine society. The moneys were then distributed almost at random to the poor and needy. Evita's position gave her a rare opportunity to exercise unchecked power. No laws had been written to govern the activities of a president's wife, so Eva found herself in a kind of legal vacuum. Only Perón could have controlled her, and he chose not to try. So she forged ahead with her grandiose social welfare plans and with her largely successful attempt to convert the labor unions into her devoted followers.

At its height the Social Aid Foundation annually took in fifty million dollars—some say one hundred million—from donations, wage deductions, and "voluntary" contributions. None of this money was taxable, because the foundation was considered a government agency. At the same time, however, it was free from external control so that no accounting of funds was ever required. Hospitals, schools, and children's homes were built by Eva's foundation, and help was made available to any disaster victims who caught her eye. Under the blotter on her desk was a stack of hundred-peso notes that Evita gave out one by one to the thousands of people who came to her for aid.

Critics claim that the public facilities she built were hollow shells used for propaganda purposes rather than for the benefit of the needy. The large hospital named after President Perón was found to be immaculate but empty. The Children's City in Belgrano and the Working Girls' Home were expensively furnished but hardly used. Some even suspected that Eva's welfare work was largely mythical, a kind of private fantasy designed to please her alone. Operations of the foundation were so well protected from the public eye that no one really knows what goals it achieved.

In one area, however, Evita's activities were highly visible. The movement for women's rights had long existed in Argentina. Yet at the same time Eva was wielding power as de facto minister of labor, women were still denied the right to vote. Married women occupied much the same legal position as children under Argentine law, and female workers, numbering almost one million in 1944, were paid an average of 40 to 60 percent less than men performing the same job. Unlike most military officers, and in direct opposition to the fascist concept of women's proper role, Perón was sympathetic to the feminist movement. Soon after his inauguration, he and Evita established a "right to vote" association and began a forceful campaign for female suffrage. These efforts were rewarded with success in September 1947, when the largely Peronist Congress granted Argentine women the right to active citizenship. Eva was not satisfied with this victory alone. Through the newly formed Peronist Women's Party, she campaigned for equal pay for equal work, divorce, and civil equality, all basic feminist goals. In 1949 women in the textile industry won equal pay, and a minimum wage law granted women salaries only 20 percent less than those earned by men.

Eva's successes in the feminist movement rested on her

ability to make women's rights palatable to most Argentines. Unlike the upper-middle-class feminists of preceding decades, Eva was able to persuade the great mass of her countrymen that the time had come to grant women equal rights. Yet her arguments were curiously conservative and traditionalist. She argued that women are basically different from men, moved by emotion and intuition rather than intellect. For that reason, they would have a positive, gentling effect on national politics. Those who claim that women should not be paid the same wage as men are wrong, she said, because a woman who is paid less has an unfair advantage in getting jobs. And because the family as an institution is so important, she proposed that mothers and housewives receive wages paid by the workers of the nation in recognition of their valuable contribution to society.

Through the Peronist Women's Party she organized *unidades básicas* (basic units), small women's clubs located throughout Buenos Aires and the provinces. In addition to instilling loyalty to Perón in their members, the clubs urged women to become aware of their need for economic and political independence from men. The positive contribution women can make to society was emphasized, as when Eva said, "I should rather say that the world at the moment suffers from a lack of women. Everything, absolutely everything in this world, has been conducted on men's terms." Eva's feminism conceived of women in their traditional roles as wives and mothers, yet within that framework she supported programs that went far beyond anything Argentina had seen before.

While occupied in her work at the Ministry of Labor, the Social Aid Foundation, and the Peronist Women's Party, Eva maintained a daily work schedule that stretched from eight in the morning to midnight and placed her under constant pressure. Nothing in her background had prepared her to deal effectively with the labor disputes and social problems she tried to settle, and her intervention was often shallow and capricious. Businessmen who claimed that they would go bankrupt if employees were granted wage increases were forced to raise salaries anyway. Poor children from the country were brought to Buenos Aires, lodged in the best hotels, and treated like royalty for several weeks, only to be sent back home to the same hard existence. On many occasions Evita prescribed medicines for persons who came to her for help, unconcerned by her lack of any medical training. Worrisome as her activities were to others in Perón's government, to the thousands of men, women, and children who came to her for help, she was nothing less than a good fairy, a kind of Argentine Virgin Mary who answered the prayers of the Peronist faithful.

Evita, involved as she was in social welfare and union affairs, continued to cultivate power, both economic and political. With Perón and her shrewd businessman friend Miguel Miranda, Eva accumulated vast sums of money through questionable import deals. Soon after he became president, Perón established the Banco Central, which controlled most banking operations in the nation, and the Argentine Institute for the Promotion of Trade. Both agencies were directed by Miguel Miranda, who sought to bargain with foreign buyers so that Argentina's raw materials, meat, and grain would bring higher prices than in the past. In this he was exceedingly successful during the post–World War II years, when Western nations, their agricultural production diminished by war, were desperate for food at any price. It was rightly claimed, however, that the benefits of higher international prices did not reach Argentina's ranchers. As a result cattle production declined, and with it the nation's economy.

In fall of 1947, from April to early June, when Argentina's beef and grain were in greatest demand in Western Europe, Evita left Buenos Aires and began a semiofficial tour of Spain, Italy, Switzerland, and France. For two and a half months she, with a large entourage that included her friends the Doderos, was fêted, decorated, wined, and dined. In Spain, Generalisimo Francisco Franco awarded her the Great Cross of Isabel the Catholic as Evita, dressed in a long mink coat, stood perspiring in the summer heat of Madrid. Along the way, she delivered radio addresses to the women of each nation she visited. After the Pope failed to decorate her for her welfare work and instead sent warm greetings to the ladies of the Beneficencia, Evita showed her disappointment by delivering a rather acid speech to Italian women. In France she was received graciously and accorded the attention the French traditionally give beautiful women. One Parisian commentator was heard to remark, however, that "beautiful as Madame Perón is, she would be more welcome dressed as a frozen side of beef." But the lure of Argentine food was not enough to persuade Great Britain to receive her with the honors Eva demanded. After negotiating with Buckingham Palace from Paris, Evita decided to skip England altogether and sail for Brazil and Argentina.

While she was gone, forces within the military tried to persuade Perón to curtail Eva's activities. He refused, but Evita became more determined than ever to consolidate her political power. Anyone who posed a threat to her control quickly disappeared, either exiled to Uruguay or imprisoned. Cipriano Reyes, Perón's supporter in the meatpackers union, was accused of plotting to assassinate the Peróns and suffered immediate imprisonment. Colonel Domingo Mercante, witness at the Peróns' wedding, went into exile when his vice presidential ambitions became known. Juan Atilio Bramuglia, a loyal Peronist, was exiled when he won international acclaim as Argentina's delegate to the United Nations. Even Miguel Miranda, the Peróns' financial adviser, had to flee secretly to Uruguay when a remark he made at a party aroused Eva's anger.

At the same time Evita was busy banishing officials who seemed either too successful or disloyal, she surrounded Perón with people whose allegiance to her was absolute. Her mother's friend from Junín was named director of posts and telegraph, giving Eva almost complete control over all radio licensing in the country. Juancito Duarte, Eva's brother, left his job as a soap salesman to become the president's private secretary. Each of her brothers-in-law was given a position in government. Blanca's husband, a lawyer, was appointed governor of Buenos Aires province and later named to the Supreme Court. Elisa's husband Major Arrieta was elected to the Senate. And Herminda's husband, a former elevator operator, became director of customs.

By 1951 Peronist control over Argentina's communications system was complete. In 1947 Eva had bought *La Democracia*, a daily newspaper published in Buenos Aires, and began writing a regular political column. Soon after, she acquired Radio Belgrano, the station where she had once worked for thirty-five dollars a month. Independent newspapers like *La Nación* and *La Prensa*, owned by wealthy Argentines who were highly critical of the Peróns, were muzzled through government control of newsprint. *La Prensa* was gradually reduced from thirty-two to twelve pages a day. In the wake of labor disputes that closed the paper down early in January 1951, Perón bought *La Prensa* for 5 percent of its real worth. In October *La Prensa*, once an outspoken enemy of Peronism, became the official voice of Eva's national labor federation.

Evita's power peaked sometime in 1950. From then on forces far beyond her reach, forces that she was powerless to control, began to be felt. By July 1950 her lush beauty had faded somewhat, replaced by a pale, tired look that was reinforced by dark, tailored suits and blonde hair that she wore pulled back tightly in a bun. At about that time, she decided to run for the vice presidency. Reasoning that women had won equal citizenship and that she already functioned as an unofficial vice president, Eva persuaded Perón to support her candidacy. The movement steadily gathered momentum, and on August 22, 1951, the Perón and Perón ticket was officially announced. Eva was so confident of her nomination that she planned a huge demonstration in Buenos Aires to span four days in late August. She boasted that two million people would come to cheer her. But in spite of the free transportation, food, lodging, and entertainment promised by the government, the rally was a disaster. Scarcely a quarter million people came and the demonstration was abruptly cancelled after the first day.

Opposition to Eva's vice presidential ambitions was as widespread as it was unexpected. Argentina's military establishment was especially horrified at the thought that in the case of Perón's death, the commander in chief would be not only a woman but Evita. Under irresistible pressure from high-ranking officers, Perón persuaded her to withdraw her candidacy. On August 31, Eva delivered an emotional radio address to the nation claiming that because she was only twenty-eight, she could not legally run for the vice presidency. At that time she was thirty-two, as most Argentines knew. Soon after the broadcast she suffered a severe emotional and physical collapse from which she never recovered.

A dismal parallel can be drawn between Evita's health and that of Argentina's economy. The years of Peronist extravagance plus a run of ill fortune had as devastating an effect on Eva's frail body as it had on national finances. Through gross mismanagement, widespread graft, and two years of drought, Argentina's cattle production had dropped and its financial reserves disappeared. More and more money was printed to cover governmental expenses—including huge outlays for Peronist propaganda—and the resulting inflation wiped out many of the workers' wage increases. Food that had always been abundant and cheap was suddenly scarce. Another symptom of Argentina's economic ill health was the drop in the value of the peso. In the postwar flush of prosperity the peso was valued at 4.8 to the dollar. Two years later, in December 1949, it dropped to almost sixteen pesos to the dollar, and by 1951 it plunged to twenty.

Shortly before the November 1951 presidential election, Eva was discovered to be suffering from cancer. She underwent surgery in early November, and very shortly thereafter Perón was reelected by a 62 percent majority. Almost two million women voted for the first time in an atmosphere of extreme emotionalism. Prayer vigils were organized outside Eva's hospital, and throughout the nation open-air Masses were said for her recovery. During the campaign, Eva's picture and name appeared as often as Perón's even though she was no longer politically active.

The course of the disease was not long delayed by the November operation. During her last months Eva received every honor Perón could bestow on her, among them the titles of "Spiritual Leader of the Nation" and *"Capitana Evita."* In December 1951 *La razón de mi vida* appeared and became a best seller, as well as required reading for all school and university students. On May 1, 1952, she made her last speech, and in June Eva stood in an open limousine and traveled the distance from the Capitol to the Casa Rosada, where Perón was to be inaugurated for the second time. The experience so taxed her strength that she collapsed during the ceremony. Less than two months later, on the evening of July 26, 1952, Evita died.

Outpourings of grief were spontaneous and overwhelming.

Her embalmed body lay in state for the three years that Perón managed to stay in power without her. By 1955 economic stagnation and opposition from the church brought Juan Domingo Perón's downfall. Such was the power of Evita's memory that her body was secretly moved during the anti-Peronist revolution, only to reappear years later when Comrade Evita had become a symbol of leftist militance.

During her few years in power Eva was an important force for change. She recognized broad-based groups in society— women, workers, lower-middle-class families—that had never been considered important by traditional governments. Her impassioned advocacy of the rights of Argentina's disadvantaged was genuine, for it sprang from her own experience as a woman who grew up without benefit of money or prestige in a society ruled largely by and for men.

It is only partially ironic that leftist groups active twenty years after her death chose Eva as their symbol. Her devotion to power and lust for wealth at almost any cost seriously diminish her reputation as a selfless advocate of the poor and downtrodden. Yet in her few years on the national political stage, she was able to express the kind of antiaristocratic militance echoed by those who wish to take power from established groups. In a speech delivered nine months before her death she said: "I have wanted and I want nothing for myself. My glory is and always will be the shield of Perón and the banner of my people, and even if I leave shreds of my life on the wayside I know that you will gather them up in my name and carry them like a flag to victory." Her name has indeed become a flag, not so much to victory as to battle, in the long and still unresolved struggle between tradition and change in Argentina.

# X

# Tania, 1937-1967

EVENTS TAKING PLACE in Cuba after Fidel Castro's dramatic takeover of the island in 1959 thrilled socialists the world over. Moving uncertainly at first, then with dispatch, Castro turned his government into the first thoroughly Marxist-Leninist one in the Americas. His success in restructuring Cuban society along collectivist lines almost overnight seemed to prove what revolutionaries had always believed: that bourgeois capitalism is a perverse stage of social development that will in time be destroyed and replaced by more humane state socialism. And how appropriate that the political movement already successful in the East should make inroads in the West—particularly in Latin America, a showplace of all the worst in capitalist economies. There wealthy minorities owned most of the land, resources, and means of production, while the masses suffered varying degrees of privation.

During the 1960s there was scarcely a Latin American country that did not have its little band of Castroite guerrillas searching for the grand strategy that would draw peasants into their ranks as a first step in the triumphant march on the national capital. What follows is the story of one such effort to bring about revolution in Bolivia, and of the woman whose life-long belief in the revolutionary way to social justice led her to an untimely death in the jungles of eastern Bolivia. Tamara Bunke, "Tania" to

214

her comrades, and her Comandante "Che" Guevara are the principals in one of the most remarkable of the failed guerrilla campaigns sparked by Cuba's success. The Bolivian fiasco was a brief, tragicomic saga of highly trained revolutionaries who committed every conceivable error on their way to ignominious destruction. But hindsight suggests that even had its military aspect been flawless, the Bolivian adventure was doomed from the start. Few of the revolutionaries were Bolivians. They were a motley group of foreigners speaking Spanish with accents strange to the ears of farmers in the countryside, and they were led by a man whose white skin stirred ancient prejudices among the largely Indian Bolivians. Whereas Fidel Castro had an extensive network of sympathizers in Cuba's urban population, Tania and Che had no such support. Cuban revolutionaries built on the revolutionary mistique of José Martí and the Maceos to topple a hated dictator, while those in Bolivia fought against a national president supported by a people largely content with their own Bolivian Revolution of 1952.

What the story of Tania seems to show most clearly is that movements for social reform in Latin American countries must originate in the citizenry of those countries. And the repeated rejection of Marxism by the ordinary Latin American suggests that Latin peoples must search out their own paths to social justice rather than adopt economic and political theories incompatible with their unique cultural personalities.

Braulio, the guerrilla scout, had already reached the opposite bank when Tania, next to last in line, rolled up her pants legs and stepped into the cold waters of Río Grande. Knapsack hunched high on her shoulders, her M-1 rifle aloft, she stepped gingerly along behind the other guerrillas who were soon strung out from one bank to the other. Too late Braulio realized their danger. He had scarcely glimpsed the soldiers hidden in ambush when they opened fire, defiling the calm of late afternoon. Tania, dressed in a faded green and white shirt, was one of the first to fall, like a target in a shooting gallery, into the swiftly flowing water, Streaks of blood spread out downstream, gory paths her body followed as it floated away from the ambush site.

Seven days later Tania's corpse was found three kilometers away, badly decomposed, with the knapsack still on her back. Among the articles inside, Bolivian soldiers found a sky-blue nail file and face powder, a few photographs, documents, an address book, a tape recording of indigenous music of eastern Bolivia, and one hundred U.S. dollars carefully tucked away in a film cannister. An army helicopter carried her body to Vallegrande, where it was placed in a coffin and given Catholic burial. Of all the guerrillas who were killed that day and in the next six weeks, only Tania received a proper burial. Perhaps more interesting to the world at large, she was the only woman in the entire guerrilla force.

The life that ended in Río Grande's waters on August 31, 1967, began almost thirty years earlier when Haydée Tamara Bunke Bider was born in Buenos Aires. Her parents were Europeans living in Argentina. Erich Bunke, her German father, a communist since 1928, and Nadja, her Russian-Jewish mother, emigrated from Nazi Germany to escape the great net of persecution that threatened them with extinction in 1935. Although they would have preferred to take refuge in Russia, the mecca of many European communists, the way to Buenos Aires was quicker and safer. A nucleus of Argentine communists had settled there; Nadja's sister and a large population of Germans—some, like the Bunkes, refugees from Hitler's fascism—already lived in the capital city. With their first child, Olaf, not yet a year old, the Bunkes arrived in Buenos Aires in late 1935. By the time Tamara was born two years later, her parents were stalwart members of the local communist party organization, and her father, a physical education instructor, presided over an antifascist sports club.

Tamara and Olaf were raised to believe in communism as other children learn to accept the religion of their parents. From the time they began to talk, the children knew not to tell anyone about the clandestine meetings that took place regularly at home because, as Nadja put it, "the police might take Mommy and Daddy away." Even as a small child, Tamara carried secret messages to her parents' friends and distributed tracts and underground newspapers in the streets of Buenos Aires. The Bunkes took every opportunity to teach their children the doctrines of

Marxism even as they involved them in the day-to-day chores of the political underground. Tamara and Olaf learned to see society in terms of classes and to cast the blame for social contrasts and injustices on capitalism, imperialism, and bourgeois exploitation. The "catechism" of communism that Tamara absorbed in those early days was doubly persuasive, its idealism untainted by too close an association with power and its practice all the more exciting because it was fraught with danger. That combination of elements—idealism and danger—was to be present in Tamara's orthodoxy throughout her life, even during the years when her beliefs were shared by society at large.

Apart from the beliefs held by Tamara's family, her life was much like that of any other child. She had a doll named Cuca, rode horseback, swam, danced, attended school, and took music lessons. Her parents doted on her, encouraged and praised her. Much more outgoing than Olaf, she had her special friends, a boyfriend or two, and spoke perfect Spanish with a recognizably *porteño* (Buenos Aires) accent. At home Erich and Nadja required the children to speak only German, at times refusing to answer them if they spoke in Spanish. The Bunkes never relaxed their efforts to teach the children German, for they knew that sooner or later they would leave Argentina.

Sixteen and a half years went by before the Bunke family left for Germany. Much had happened during their absence. A war had been fought and won against Hitler and his Nazi minions; six million Jews had been murdered; and Germany, almost destroyed by war, found itself split into two nations, one capitalist, one communist. The Bunkes traveled to East Germany in July 1952. Tamara was loath to leave her home and friends behind, and left determined to return one day. In the meantime she faced the awesome task of adapting, at age fourteen, to a completely new life in a nation half her own age and covered with the rubble of war.

In the first weeks after her arrival, Tamara was sent to a small town near Potsdam to stay with friends of her parents until the Bunkes could be assigned jobs and living quarters somewhere in East Germany. Far from the pleasant city of her childhood, far even from her parents who awaited word on jobs and housing in

East Berlin, Tamara struggled with German, endured the jokes about her Spanish accent, and began, slowly, to adapt. Five or six weeks later the Bunkes moved to Eisenhuttenstadt, a city so newly founded that there were virtually no living quarters, only a huge, new steel plant surrounded by half-built schools and apartment buildings. When Tamara joined her parents there, she found them camped out in a small, unfinished apartment that they shared with three other teachers. Erich and Nadja taught classes, he in physical education, she in Russian language, in a school that was still under construction. Tamara had occasion to remember those pioneer days a decade later and found inspiration in the stoicism with which her parents faced scarcity and deprivation for the sake of the new nation.

Olaf and Tamara began school in October 1952 at "Clara Zetkin," a preuniversity secondary school located two and a half kilometers from home. Tamara was drawn into several communist youth organizations like Free German Youth, a premilitary training society, and the German-Soviet Friendship Society. She soon excelled in a broad range of activities, among them gymnastics, marksmanship, music, and dance. Compared to other children her age, who had lived under communism for less than a decade, she excelled in enthusiasm as well. The lessons taught by her parents during the years in Argentina were well learned, and Tamara grew into a model communist youth, already a candidate for party membership at age eighteen, untiringly dedicated to the socialist cause.

She never forgot Latin America, however, and although she spoke German well and studied Russian in school, Spanish remained her native tongue. Scarcely two years after settling in Germany, Tamara began working as an interpreter, first for various youth organizations, and later for the Ministry of International Affairs. In 1957 she traveled to Moscow for the VI Youth Festival and helped organize the seventh biennial festival to be held in Vienna. Back in East Germany she entered Humboldt University, where she sought out Latin American students who came there to study. A one-woman welcoming committee, she helped newly arrived students settle into the strange environment and, in exchange, begged for news of Latin America. Those who met her during those years remember her as outgoing and lively, yet obsessed by the need for contact with the continent she had left behind.

In a statement written when she became a full party member in 1958, Tamara described her deepest ambition: "I was educated and learned to think and act as a Marxist-Leninist in the Democratic Republic of Germany. For that reason it is very natural for me to struggle all my life, in one country or in another, and under any circumstances, in the files of our party. . . . My greatest desire is to return to my country, Argentina, and offer all my energies to the party there." Slowly, under the press of exciting developments in Latin America, her longing to return to the continent of her birth and the deeply instilled dedication to communism led Tamara toward a new and overpowering interest: Cuba.

When it became apparent in 1960 that Castro's Cuba was being transformed into a communist state, Tamara, and indeed all of East Germany, reacted with great excitement. Here, after all, was a Latin American country revolutionized by a pitifully small band of guerrillas—a few armed, bearded men who invaded Oriente and overthrew a venal dictatorship against what appeared to be tremendous odds. The details of Fidel's revolution enthralled Tamara. It did not matter that Cuba's integration into the Soviet-dominated bloc of nations occurred after Castro came to power. Nor was Tamara concerned that dictates of economic necessity forced Castro and his lieutenants to turn away from the native socialism of José Martí, their original inspiration. In Tamara's eyes, Cuba was the scene of the newest, most successful communist revolution in the world. Her thirst for information about Cuba could not be quenched.

Early in 1960 Tamara received a copy of the anthem of Castro's Twenty-sixth of July movement. She translated it into German and watched with satisfaction as the anthem was performed throughout East Germany. At the same time she began visiting the offices of an international women's federation located across from Humboldt University. Hortensia Gómez, a Cuban official of the federation, provided Tamara with news of Cuba and fed the fires of her obsession. By then her decision was made:

somehow she must go to Cuba to work personally for the revolution.

As Cuba joined the communist bloc, it began to establish cultural and economic ties with sister nations like East Germany. Tamara was in demand as an interpreter for the delegations and missions that arrived with increasing frequency. In December 1960, as a representative of Free German Youth, she attended a reception for the commercial delegation from Cuba that had come to sign trade agreements between the two countries. Ernesto "Che" Guevara, director of the National Bank of Cuba and soon to be named minister of industry, led the group. Tamara first met him at the reception, although she already knew much about him through stories of his revolutionary exploits. When she traveled with him to Leipzig to act as his interpreter, her reaction to Che was predictable. Handsome, charismatic, like Tamara Argentine-born, a revolutionary who had struggled and fought with Castro in the Sierra Maestra, Che inspired in her admiration, devotion, and the determination to follow him to Cuba as soon as possible.

The opportunity to leave East Germany came soon, for that same month Tamara became interpreter for Cuba's National Ballet during its tour of East Germany. In response to her obvious desire to live in Cuba, an invitation was sent to her in April 1961, possibly on the initiative of Che himself. The East German government gave her permission to travel, and when the ballet troupe returned home in May, she went with them.

Tamara arrived in Havana less than a month after the famed Bay of Pigs fiasco, the attempted invasion of Cuba by United States–sponsored Cuban exiles. The invasion was a complete failure, and from it Castro's government emerged in a greatly strengthened position. Tamara was swept up in the general excitement as Cubans closed ranks and vowed to defend the revolution from outside aggression. The experience was inspiring, and she threw herself into the life of postrevolutionary Cuba with vigor.

For a time she stayed at a hotel in Havana. Everything, as she carefully noted in letters home, was provided by the government; she lacked nothing and was "extremely happy." She went to work in the Ministry of Education as a foreign translator, at first as a virtual volunteer, later for a modest salary. Eager to become a part of the revolution, she joined the militia that stood guard in shifts at the Ministry, and wore its blue uniform with pride. The massive literacy campaign that was launched in mid-1961 claimed her attention, and she spent much of her free time tutoring illiterates.

For a time her work in the Ministry, the militia, and various committees absorbed all her attention. Tamara's co-workers during those first years in Havana described her as energetic, enthusiastic, hard-working, a model communist. She was pretty, too, in a quiet way—blue eyes, light brown hair, slender, very feminine and graceful, but strong and athletic as well. Certain phrases or slogans appeared often in her conversation and in letters home, homilies like "He who can't do little things will never achieve great things" and "Every revolutionary should behave as such wherever he may be" and the ubiquitous "Country or death; we shall conquer."

Late in 1961 Tamara met Che Guevara again. As a member of one of two volunteer brigades, she spent a day doing construction work on a school for the International Student Union in Havana. One brigade was made up of women; the other included the minister of industry himself, Che Guevara. Almost immediately the brigades challenged each other to a contest to see which could work faster. Good-natured heckling followed, but when Che's team began to win, he switched sides and the game ended in a tie. After the workday was over, Tamara entertained her fellow workers on the guitar, teasing with a smile, "I'll bet you can't beat me at this, *comandante*."

Her duties as translator and interpreter placed Tamara in increasing contact with upper-echelon officials of Castro's government. She often translated for East European delegations during their meetings with Che and Raúl Castro. As she had done in the past, she made contact with visitors from other parts of Latin America whenever possible. From Argentine visitors to Havana she got packages of *yerba mate*, the robust tea of the pampas, to give to Che, whom she saw with some frequency after 1961.

In early 1962 Tamara began to tire of constant translation. This was not the kind of revolutionary work she had aspired to when she left East Germany. The plodding labors of a bureaucrat could not long hold her imagination, for she felt called to fight against the bourgeois regimes of Latin America, to free oppressed peoples of the continent. Armed struggle, guerrilla training, the role of women in the revolution were topics that played on her mind even as she labored in the Ministry of Education or sat through interminable meetings of her local Committee for the Defense of the Revolution. In a letter to her parents dated April 7, 1962, Tamara wrote: "Our comrades in the different Latin American countries need to understand that they must abandon their offices and libraries and employ every means to begin the armed struggle." She quoted Fidel Castro's statement that only two or three countries could undergo a peaceful revolution. All the others must prepare for armed revolt, a fight to the death.

Gradually Tamara spent less time in the Ministry, the militia, and the volunteer work brigades. Secretly she began a study of Argentina to determine the practicality of beginning a revolution in that country. The letters home ceased for a time as the study absorbed all her attention. Then in September 1962 she sent a blistering letter home: "A few days ago a cable was delivered to me at the Ministry. Contents: 'Family of Tamara Bunke without news of her . . .' With all frankness I must tell you that this has displeased me very much. Just because you haven't heard from me for a few months, now you're making a big fuss." She warned them never to write to the Ministry again and begged them to understand that "the revolution demands much." Tamara went on to say: "And if the time comes when the Party should give me a difficult assignment? How wonderful it would be if I could say: my parents would be proud if they knew about this mission; perhaps it's hard on them, but if they were in my place they would do the same! This may happen very soon. . . ."

But the mission Tamara longed for did not materialize for some time. Long months of training had to pass before she became a technically skilled underground agent. As late as October 1962, during the missile crisis that threatened yet another invasion from the United States, Tamara could write home with bubbly enthusiasm, "There's nothing finer than to be in the middle of a critical situation, where the revolutionary struggle is the hardest ... To live well, with every comfort—I could have done that in Berlin, where I had everything. The Latin American revolution is coming into the foreground, and I have the good luck to be able to participate in it!"

Later letters were far less spontaneous as she learned the habits of secrecy and reserve demanded of an intelligence agent. The door of her apartment, once open to friends and neighbors, was kept locked, and Tamara became aloof, deliberately misinforming co-workers about her activities. By late 1963 she confessed to her parents, "It's getting so hard to write about oneself." There was, after all, very little she was at liberty to say, since most of her waking hours were spent deciphering codes, writing invisible messages, using radio transmitters, and learning to lead a double life. Still, in the same letter, she added a passage that revealed the innocent, almost childlike obsession that governed her life. Complaining that the heat had taken away her appetite, Tamara related how she forced herself to eat, as her mother might have, by saying "One spoonful for mother, another for daddy, one for Lenin, another for Fidel." The young woman, weaned on dogma, addicted to uniforms and slogans, yet playful, pretty, and personable, gradually transformed herself into that loneliest, most precarious of all creatures—an international spy, an undercover agent who hoped to pave the way to continental revolution.

In March 1964, after more than a year of training, Tamara met with Che Guevara in his Ministry office. Until that moment she had only guessed at her ultimate mission. Now, at last, she knew that her destination was Bolivia. After establishing a new identity, Tamara would enter that land-locked nation to prepare the ground for armed revolt. She would make contacts within the Bolivian government and armed forces, travel throughout the interior, and study the situation of miners, peasants, workers. Her next instructions would be sent directly from Havana. Above all, she was to reveal her true identity and mission to no one. Vigilance would be her only security.

At the moment Tamara began her journey to Bolivia, Che Guevara's position in Cuba was ambiguous. Since 1960 he and Fidel Castro had supported the idea that the Cuban revolution had to be repeated throughout South and Central America. As the only socialist country in all of Latin America, isolated by the United States economic blockade, Cuba could not hope to establish normal trade relations with any neighboring state. Instead, the island was forced to rely on Soviet benevolence and trade with already industrialized nations of the communist bloc. Che's dream of rapid industrialization of the island could not succeed as long as Cuba lacked economic ties with other developing nations in the Americas. Without a community of sympathetic nations in its own hemisphere, Cuba would remain economically dependent on countries more interested in sugar than in its industrial development.

Shortly before his March meeting with Tamara, in a speech to the World Conference on Trade and Development in Geneva, Che signaled the dangers of foreign investment in developing nations. This theme was a constant one in his speeches and public statements. Without industrialization, he claimed, Cuba would be locked into poverty and a weak position in the world. But international forces were arrayed against Cuban progress. The USSR, like the imperialist United States, wanted to exploit Cuba for her own benefit, he said. Only when a community of socialist nations, forged by revolution, appeared in Latin America would this situation change.

His tarring of the Soviet Union with the brush of imperialism had unfortunate consequences for Che. The public statements embarrassed Castro, who recognized the USSR as Cuba's principal defense against the United States. Castro saw that Che was rapidly becoming a liability. It was impossible simply to dismiss Che from his high office—he was far too popular in Cuba and with Latin America's militant left to dispose of so easily. Then, too, the beleaguered Guevara was innocent of disloyalty to Castro. The differences between the two men were ideological, the products of natural disagreements between idealist and pragmatic politician. Still, somehow, Che would have to be silenced.

After March 1964, while Che's position deteriorated within Cuba, Tamara cautiously began her career as advance agent of the revolution. After leaving Havana, she traveled to Europe, where in six months she established a new identity, a seamless cover to hide her socialist sympathies, her connections with Havana, even her family background. Every detail of Laura Gutiérrez Bauer's personality was carefully worked out, coinciding where necessary with Tamara's own past, differing with it where possible. During the months in Europe, Tamara adopted a modest disguise—a black wig that kept her from being recognized even when she passed within blocks of her family's apartment. In September she made friends with a young Parisian named Alice, whose letters later served as a cover for messages from Havana. Then with an Argentine passport provided by Havana, she flew to Peru and made her way to Bolivia in late 1964.

Laura Gutiérrez spent her first weeks in Bolivia visiting museums and making contacts with people who might help her settle into her new life. At the archeological museum in La Paz, she met the painter Moisés Barrientos, a relative of Bolivian president General René Barrientos. Her cover worked beautifully, and she was easily accepted as an ordinary Argentine girl who was interested in Bolivian archeology and ethnology. The painter offered to introduce her to the director of folkloric studies in the Ministry of Education, and almost immediately Laura found herself on its volunteer staff as an investigator of Bolivian folklore, recommended to the Ministry more by the tape recorder she owned than by the letter of introduction she obtained from the Argentine consul. For a time, Laura was drawn into the social life of the La Paz embassies, meeting government officials and on one occasion President Barrientos himself. No one who met Laura guessed that every move she made, every contact, was dutifully recorded and sent to Havana.

After establishing herself in La Paz, Laura began searching for documents that would permit her to live and work in Bolivia indefinitely. The Argentine passport she carried did not show her own fingerprints, and it soon proved a serious liability in her quest for papers. Through a network of friendships, however, she met a right-wing journalist who provided her with the work certificate required by Bolivian immigration regulations. Next, a well-placed lawyer, who believed Laura to be a close friend of a Peruvian colleague, offered to help out when she told him that she had lost her passport. He advised her to follow the time-honored expedient of bribery, and within a half hour of paying La Paz police a healthy sum, she received the all-important identity card.

By early 1965 Laura was ready to set herself up as a German tutor to eight private students. Although she received money from Havana and made every effort to live frugally, she needed an obvious source of income to avoid arousing suspicion. She tutored her students for several hours every day and spent the rest of her time studying ceramics at a craft shop in La Paz. As a researcher with the Ministry of Education she traveled throughout highland Bolivia, taping folk music and learning as much as possible about the country.

By far the most useful of all Laura's contacts in La Paz was Gonzalo López Muñoz, a highly placed governmental official who, as chief of information, worked within the National Palace itself. Laura recognized his potential usefulness and carefully cultivated his trust by tutoring his children in German and visiting his home often. In return, he employed her as a commercial agent for a weekly magazine.

By late 1965 Laura was well established in Bolivia. She had complete freedom of movement throughout the country, her tape recorder and position with the Folklore Commission justifying trips to even the most remote areas. Friendships and acquaintances reached into cultural and intellectual circles of La Paz and even into the President's offices. Only the Bolivian passport eluded her. To secure it she turned to an unbeatable ploy: marriage. A young engineering student named Mario Antonio Martínez who lived in her boardinghouse conveniently proposed to Laura in mid-1965. Mariucho, as she called him, never suspected Laura's real identity. Because his parents never would have allowed him to marry, he was easily persuaded to give her complete freedom in exchange for keeping the marriage a secret. Early in 1967, after achieving Bolivian citizenship, Tamara divorced her perplexed husband against his will. Mariucho had unknowingly served to establish Tamara in Bolivia and, his usefulness at an end, found himself discarded.

By early 1966 Laura had done her job so skillfully that no one among her new friends suspected the least duplicity. With unrelenting care she avoided political involvement, associated with Bolivians who were somewhat right of center, and played her role as an ethnologist perfectly. Still the long months of acting, the isolation from friends, family, and an environment congenial to her beliefs took their toll. Her first direct contact with Havana through an agent code-named Mercy did not come until more than a year after her arrival in La Paz, almost two years after she left Cuba. Mercy spent two months with Tamara, first in La Paz, then briefly in Cochabamba, and finally for a month-long refresher course in espionage techniques in São Paulo, Brazil.

Tamara's reaction to Mercy was evidence, perhaps, of the emotional stress she endured as Laura Gutiérrez Bauer. In his company Tamara was as volatile as Laura was even-tempered, given to fits of pique, periods of irritability and emotionalism. She wept when she read Fidel's latest speech and the letters from her parents, who now wrote to her in Spanish to facilitate Havana's handling of their correspondence. The two "comrades" argued constantly—about Tamara's compulsive thrift, her hot temper and imagined insults. But interspersed with their quarrels, they managed to devote many hours to perfecting Tamara's espionage skills, and Mercy reported to Havana that she showed great powers of assimilation in spite of her nervous state. After Mercy's return to Havana, Tamara traveled to Buenos Aires, where she awaited a new Argentine passport, this one with her own fingerprints. Although she had no immediate need for the document, Havana provided it for that future date when, her work completed, she would renounce Bolivian citizenship and leave the country.

But events already taking place insured that Tamara would never use her new Argentine passport. Curiously, those events began in March 1965 and dealt not with Tamara but with Comandante Che Guevara. On March 15 Che returned to Havana after a four-month tour of Africa, the USSR, and Peking. At every opportunity along the way he had criticized the Soviet Union for its imperialist attitude toward the developing nations of the world and had spoken vividly of a tricontinental, third-world revolution that would free nations like Cuba from dependence on the superpowers. As he stepped off the plane in Havana, haggard and depressed, Che entertained no illusions about Fidel's probable reaction to his performance. Castro was, in fact, sorely embarrassed. Cuba could no longer afford a minister of industry who criticized his country's greatest benefactor at every turn. The next day Che Guevara, the second most popular man in Cuba, dropped totally out of sight. Even his wife and terminally ill mother could not find out where he was. In April, in answer to intense questioning by foreign journalists, Castro replied enigmatically: "Major Ernesto Che Guevara will be found where he is most useful to the revolution." Much of the world assumed he was dead.

Che Guevara was very much alive. In July 1965 he left Cuba in disguise to join an unsuccessful guerrilla movement in the African Congo. Almost nine months later he and his soldiers were back on the island plotting a new military operation. Fatefully, they selected Bolivia as the site for the next "war of national liberation." Che himself would lead the campaign.

By May 1966 Tamara/Laura had a new name: Tania, the code name by which she was known in secret communiqués between La Paz and Havana. From that month on, Cuban guerrilla fighters trickled into Bolivia, some overland, others by air from Europe to La Paz. First to arrive was Tania's old friend Papi, who had trained with her in Cuba and had taken over her apartment when she left in 1964. As others arrived, Tania helped them find living quarters, food, and clothing, occasionally cooking for them and searching for apartments and houses to rent for other arrivals. Tania was not told who would lead the movement, but she probably guessed that Che was involved. She recognized the recent arrivals as men of importance in Cuba—army majors, highly placed officials, all of them trusted Guevara supporters.

The advance contingent had two important jobs to accomplish before their leader "Ramón" arrived. First, they were to contact Bolivians who sympathized with the guerrilla movement, men like Jorge Kolle Cueto and Mario Monje of Bolivia's Moscow-leaning communist party; Moisés Guevara, a Bolivian communist of the Peking school; and the Peruvian guerrilla leader Juan Pablo Chang Navarro. Second, they were to choose a zone of guerrilla operations somewhere in eastern Bolivia. Coco Peredo, one of the first Bolivians to join the movement, explored the Santa Cruz area and in July bought a farm on the Ñancahuazú River, near Camiri. On the property they found a farmhouse with a zinc roof, the "Calamine House" that became the guerrillas' first camp. Gradually men and supplies—hammocks, radio receivers, arms and ammunition, medicines and foodstuffs— were collected at Ñancahuazú, and by October a clearing for the base camp had been hacked out of the jungle in a canyon some distance from Calamine House. Within easy reach of the new camp were freshly dug storage caves, a large but primitive kitchen with an earth oven, gardens, a few head of cattle, and an admirable system of field latrines.

Early in November a middle-aged, balding man named Adolfo Mena González flew into La Paz. Visas on his Uruguayan passport showed that the peripatetic Mena González had been in La Paz several times in October. This time, however, he came to stay, for the ordinary-looking traveler was none other than Che Guevara, ready to launch the first stage of the continental revolution.

Bolivia's national chief of information, Tania's good friend Gonzalo López Muñoz, provided her with papers that proved invaluable during the early stages of the movement. How she persuaded him to give her sheets of blank, official stationery with his signature at the bottom can only be guessed. But when Che arrived in La Paz, Tania gave him a letter of introduction written on stationery from the National Palace and signed by López Muñoz, Barrientos's own aide. The document identified Mena González as an anthropologist and called on government leaders to cooperate with him during his stay in Bolivia. Such hospitality caused López Muñoz considerable trouble a year later when his unknowing cooperation with the guerrillas was discovered.

A few days after his arrival, Che and a number of aides drove to Ñancahuazú, leaving Tania behind to watch over new arrivals and maintain contact with the small group of supporters in the capital. Their first days in camp were marked by enthusiastic optimism. Che enjoyed the reaction of the men who penetrated his disguise. One young Bolivian was so shocked to find himself in the presence of the legendary Che that he drove his jeep off the road and into a ditch. Once in camp, Che announced that he had come to establish a nucleus of revolt. If all went well, he would move on to Peru to establish a second front there. If things went against them, he promised to stick with them to the end. In any case, he planned to make Bolivia a second Vietnam and was confident that the guerrillas, flexible and mobile, could outwit the combined military forces of Bolivia and the United States, if necessary, in the war of liberation. So great was Che Guevara's prestige that the handful of men gathered in the jungle clearing readily believed he would lead them to victory, even against the overwhelming odds confronting them.

Tania stayed in La Paz during November and December, coping with problems of communication and watching for recruits. Title to one of the two jeeps was transferred to her so that she could travel more easily between La Paz and Santa Cruz. Che still conceived of her role as a nonmilitary one. Recognizing the importance of her connections with the cultural and governmental elite of Bolivia, he counted on her for information from the outside and to act as courier on special missions to communist leaders in neighboring countries. With this in mind, Che called her to Ñancahuazú late in December. With her went her friend Papi, soon to become the guerrilla Ricardo, and Mario Monje, first secretary of the Bolivian Communist Party. Che welcomed her warmly and outlined her mission in talks that lasted late into the night.

Her few days at the encampment were unusually festive. The guerrillas enjoyed good food and drink and listened to music that Tania had taped from Radio Havana. The occasion was recorded on film. Tania took pictures of everyone, using a flash at night, and later developed the film in La Paz. No one there seemed to think their need for secrecy would be compromised by the existence of so many snapshots. In fact, picture-taking was epidemic, beginning as soon as Che arrived at Ñancahuazú and continuing throughout the campaign. On the afternoon of January 1, 1967, Tania listened to Fidel's New Year's speech broadcast from Havana, then left for La Paz with the Bolivian Coco and another comrade. On January 21, in accord with Che's instructions, she flew to Buenos Aires, where she contacted two Argentine communists whom Che referred to as Mauricio and Jozami. In his end-of-the-month analysis recorded in his diary, Che wrote, "Tania left but the Argentines have shown no signs of life, nor has she."

Tania was only partly successful in carrying out her mission to Argentina. Ciro Roberto Bustos, the artist and communist sympathizer first code-named Mauricio, later Carlos, agreed to accompany her to Bolivia, although he later claimed that she had merely invited him to a "political meeting." Jozami, a leftist journalist, was unable to leave for Bolivia immediately, and his later attempts to make contact proved fruitless. Tania gave Bustos the necessary travel documents, and on February 28 they flew to La Paz. They planned to make the trip to Ñancahuazú with Régis Debray, a young French Marxist, professor of philosophy in Havana, and author of a book on guerrilla strategies.

Back at the base camp Che divided his men into three groups—a small vanguard under Marcos, a rear guard under Joaquín, and the center column under his own command—and on February 1 set out on a training march to the unreconnoitered region north of Río Grande. Although it was intended to last only a month, the journey stretched into a grueling test of endurance lasting well into March. Several of the men, including Che, who suffered acute attacks of asthma, fell ill soon after the march began, slowing the pace of the entire band. Lacking a guide, they lost their way time and again and had to depend on *campesinos* to orient them. The farmers themselves were another disappointment. They collaborated only in very limited ways with the guerrillas, and none seemed willing to throw in their lot with them. Hunger began to dog their steps, and after food supplies ran out early in March, the men subsisted on small birds and palmetto hearts. To climax their miseries, two Bolivian recruits lost their lives in the river. Che Guevara called these losses "our baptism of death in an absurd manner."

While Che's men struggled to find their way back to the camp at Ñancahuazú, Tania supplied Debray and Bustos with letters of introduction on the unwitting López Muñoz's stationery. Leaving La Paz early in March, they drove four hundred arduous

# Tania in Bolivia

NOT TO SCALE

miles to Camiri, parked Tania's jeep there, then continued on to Calamine House and the base camp. They were surprised to find Che out on the training march, but settled in to await his return. In so doing, through some incredible lapse of judgment, Tania disobeyed Che's specific instructions to protect her independence of movement. Perhaps she hoped for new instructions or expected to be asked to take Debray back to La Paz. Or perhaps the old lure of armed conflict, the romance of sacrificing everything to the cause of revolution, caused the blunder. At any rate, Tania did not leave camp, and the days of waiting slowly stretched into weeks. When Che finally returned on March 20, he found Tania still waiting, trying to forget the horrible fact that her jeep, full of incriminating documents, was parked in Camiri.

Tania's fears were fully justified, and had events not already caused serious damage to the guerrillas, she alone would have borne responsibility for the ensuing disasters. But by the time police examined the contents of her jeep, two deserters had already talked to authorities, and errors committed by two of Che's most trusted lieutenants had alerted the army to the guerrilla presence at Calamine House. Rumors that had circulated in La Paz for weeks found confirmation: something was indeed afoot in eastern Bolivia.

By the time the exhausted, half-starved men straggled back to the base camp, such chaos reigned that Che at first hardly noticed Tania's grave error. His rage was directed against those who had destroyed the secrecy so vital to early stages of guerrilla warfare. Che could no longer pretend to control events. On March 23 he himself compounded those errors when he permitted his men to ambush an army platoon downriver from the camp. Seven soldiers died in the clash; the guerrillas took fourteen prisoners, four of them wounded. Che talked to the soldiers, saw to it that the wounded received treatment, then released them. The next day army planes bombarded the guerrilla zone, and up in La Paz, Barrientos called on the American Central Intelligence Agency for help in combating the guerrillas of Ñancahuazú.

Che's band, numbering forty-seven combatants and visitors, was placed on the defensive at once. Everything that could have gone wrong did so with unbelievable speed. On March 27 news gleaned from radio reports convinced Che that Tania's cover had been blown. "Everything appears to indicate that Tania is spotted," he wrote, "whereby two years of good and patient work is lost." His deduction was correct. Tania's jeep contained two suitcases full of clothing and an address book that led them straight to Laura Gutiérrez Bauer's apartment in La Paz. CIA operatives listened to her recordings of indigenous music for several days before deciding that they contained nothing on the mysterious anthropologist. Although "Laura" was hopelessly compromised by the investigation, Tania the guerrilla emerged not from evidence found in the jeep but from the testimony of two deserters who saw her at the base camp. They reported that a young woman, who seemed to be in charge of a number of recruits, wore jungle fatigues, carried a submachine gun, and stood guard with the others by turns. The connection between Laura and Tania and the existence of Tamara Bunke were not established until much later.

The incident of Tania and her jeep raises more questions than it answers. Those who recalled Tania's early connections with East Germany and the fact that she was the only member of Che's entourage who belonged to a Moscow-leaning communist party wondered, not unreasonably, if she might not have been working as a double agent for both Che and Soviet intelligence. Some have even concluded that Tania deliberately sabotaged Che's guerrilla movement, although had that been her objective she could easily have caused him considerable harm without implicating herself. The puzzle of the abandoned jeep is perhaps best handled by placing it in the context of all the other problems besetting the guerrillas. Everyone made mistakes; there was an epidemic of blunders. The magic generated by Che's presence in that isolated camp inspired his followers with revolutionary zeal, but it in no way protected them from constant slip-ups. By late March, Che himself had committed a series of errors. He had failed to present his movement in terms Bolivian farmers and miners could accept, and as a result no new recruits joined his group. Just as serious, he revealed his presence long before the guerrillas were prepared to face the Bolivian army.

When Tania found herself trapped in the jungles of Ñancahuazú, the severity of these problems was still not apparent. A man named Pombo, one of only three survivors of the expedition, later remembered that she seemed eager to become a guerrilla fighter. She probably enjoyed her first weeks at the camp, for after two years of being immersed in what she scornfully called the "bourgeois society" of La Paz, it was a relief to take off her wig and begin life as a revolutionary in the company of old friends and, of course, Che Guevara.

As napalm bombs fell on the area of Calamine House and two thousand Bolivian troops encircled the so-called Red Zone, Che prepared to move his men and supplies to a new camp. Contrary to his own concept of guerrilla mobility, he lingered in the zone for eleven days after the March 23 ambush, giving the army ample time to pinpoint his position. Although the men spent a full day hiding the supplies they had accumulated at base camp, soldiers discovered a wealth of other evidence when they searched the farm several days later. Medical supplies, billing receipts, and even a photograph of Che lay scattered about to be seized by the startled Bolivians as proof that Guevara himself commanded the guerrillas. That was all the Bolivians needed to bring in the United States CIA and Green Berets in full force. Arms, ammunition, transport vehicles, and counterrevolutionary experts soon flooded into the country.

Che's first concern after leaving Ñancahuazú was to escort Bustos and Debray out of the combat zone. Each had his assignment: Bustos was to return to Argentina as an advance agent of the revolution; Debray would go straight to France to secure supplies and other assistance for the revolutionary movement. On April 14 Che wrote in his diary: "It is not clear how the operation is to be effected, but it would appear to me that it would be best for everybody to go out and operate around this area of Muyupampa but later draw back into the woods. If it is possible, Danton [Debray] and Carlos [Bustos] should continue toward Sucre-Cochabamba, depending on the circumstances."

The next day Joaquín's rear guard absorbed several men, among them the *"resacas"*—four Bolivian recruits so untrustworthy that Che called them "dregs." On the sixteenth Tania and the guerrilla Alejandro, both suffering from high fevers, proved unable to keep up with the vanguard; the next day Che assigned them to Joaquín's column as well, along with Negro, the Peruvian doctor, and two other sick men. Free from the slowest members of the group, Che decided after much hesitation to take the vanguard and center, some twenty-seven men, to the outskirts of Muyupampa. From there Bustos and Debray would set out on their own. Before leaving Joaquín's unit, now composed of sixteen men and Tania, Che instructed them to wait near camp for three days, then to move around within the same area until his return.

Both groups followed the plan: Che delivered Bustos and Debray to Muyupampa, and Joaquín waited quietly at the camp. Both actions met with disaster. Bustos and Debray were arrested as they walked down the street, and the rear guard never saw Che and his men again.

Several days passed before Joaquín suspected that they were in trouble. Every day army planes and helicopters flew overhead, and neither Joaquín's scouts nor the pair of guerrillas Che sent to search for the rear guard were able to make contact because Bolivian soldiers blocked the way. Pressure from the army forced the column to stay in virtual hiding—maintaining silence, cooking at night behind crude shelters, and lying low during the day—at the very time it needed to be most visible. The lost column wandered furtively about the Ñancahuazú area for two months hoping that Che would somehow find them.

The strongest man in the rear guard was Braulio, a black Cuban and a former lieutenant in Castro's army. Not as subject to the fatigues that beset many of the others, absolutely trustworthy, Braulio acted as a scout, foraging for food and when necessary chopping through the thick jungle growth to clear a path for the rest. Joaquín, the rear guard commander, was a Cuban as well and boasted considerable experience in guerrilla campaigns. Marcos ranked as high as Joaquín and had commanded the vanguard until Che demoted him in late March. At the other end of the scale were the four dregs: Paco, Pepe, Chingolo, and Eusebio. And somewhere in between were six Bolivians, Negro, the physician, and his three patients.

Tania recovered from her fever and a hurt leg during the

days of waiting. She made every effort to fulfill the duties that all shared by turns—guard duty, cooking, collecting firewood. But her enthusiasm for guerrilla life waned after early April. In various ways, subtle at first, she came to feel that many in the rear guard blamed her for their misfortunes. In a sense, that was correct. Che perhaps acted from an exaggerated concern for the only female member when he left her—and sixteen others—behind. Then too the harshness of life on the run was greater than she had imagined. The romance of armed conflict became lost in a welter of mistakes and misjudgments, poor food, illness, unproductive tension, dirt, and fear. Gradually Tania withdrew into herself, speaking rarely, yet determined to hold her own.

The radio gave them their only news of outside events. They learned of Debray's capture a few days after it happened, but they received no clue to Che's whereabouts. Slowly Joaquín's band dwindled through desertions and deaths: one in May, two in June, three in July. And as the remaining members moved from place to place, the army became more adept at keeping track of them. Early in July a new regional commander, Colonel Luis Reque Terán, took over military activities in the zone south of Río Grande. "Operation Cynthia," as his strategy was called, aimed at the encirclement and destruction of Joaquín's column. As the noose tightened, the guerrillas found themselves backed against a mountain, all exits blocked by soldiers.

Early one morning, toward the end of July, the exhausted, poorly nourished remnants of the rear guard buried their remaining gear and, carrying ten or twelve pounds of corn on their backs, started off up the mountain, the only way out. Braulio led the way, cutting through the undergrowth with his machete. That day and for five days following, the band climbed and walked until they were beyond the reach of Colonel Reque's carefully laid trap. Their incredible exertions earned them a single night's rest, for the next morning they awoke to the sounds of ambush. Troops lay just above the encampment, and as bullets splatted into their campfire, Joaquín called a rapid retreat to the southern flank of the highest mountain in the region. Within two days they were trapped again. Troops fired on them, and only by accidentally splitting into two groups did they manage to escape.

In that skirmish on August 9, Pedro, a Bolivian guerrilla, was killed as he strugged to carry the machinegun up a steep incline. Of all the guerrillas, he was the best loved for his compassion and optimism. Among his code names was Pan Divino, Divine Bread.

Tania's escape from these ambushes was nothing short of miraculous. The rough terrain and unrelenting anxiety taxed the energies of the strongest men in the group. Although she bore the weight of increasing mental instability, nervousness, and horrible, repetitive nightmares, her determination to survive, to keep up, carried her on. Several of the men sympathized with her plight; others turned against her as she edged toward complete collapse. One dark night, while camped on a remote mountainside, two of the guerrillas tormented her by performing an obscene dance by the campfire. Tania fled from the scene in tears. Later she pleaded with Joaquín to let her strike out alone, but he roundly refused to let her go. The next day Tania trudged on in her usual place near the end of the column as it made its way north toward Río Grande and, everyone hoped, reunion with Che Guevara's column.

On a rise above Río Grande sat a flea-infested, thatched hut, the home of a farmer named Honorato Rojas. Che had passed by Rojas's house half a year earlier while on the training march, and he had recorded his impressions of Rojas in his diary: "This peasant is typical: capable of helping us, but incapable of foreseeing the dangers involved and therefore potentially dangerous." Rojas, father of eight, collaborated with the guerrillas until the army became suspicious. On two occasions he was detained, questioned—some say tortured—and finally persuaded to notify the army should the guerrillas return.

On August 30, a pair of soldiers, one of them a military health officer named Faustino García, hiked to Rojas's house, some thirteen kilometers upstream from La Laja, where a part of their battalion was stationed. At about two o'clock, three guerrillas approached the hut. García quickly lay down on a cot, covered his rifle with a blanket, and became, as Rojas explained to the haggard, bearded guerrillas, a "sick peon." Joaquín's men arranged for Rojas to buy provisions in a nearby village and offered to send a doctor to look at the sick man. They would return later that night.

Paco, the sole survivor of Joaquín's column, recalled that it was Honorato Rojas who first suggested the Río Grande crossing. Joaquín had planned to camp on the south side of the river, sending small search parties out periodically to look for Che. Rojas, however, told them that he knew of an excellent campsite across the river, a site that was not only safe, but boasted a spring as well. Against Braulio's advice the group agreed to Rojas's proposal. On August 31 just at dusk Rojas would show them where to ford the river in order to reach the new camp.

As soon as the guerrillas left, Rojas sent his eight-year-old son to notify the army. Twenty-eight soldiers under Captain Mario Vargas Rojas traveled approximately a mile upstream, where they organized the ambush. All day long they lay in wait as the sun followed its course across the sky. As it dipped out of sight behind the hills Joaquín's men broke camp and went to Rojas's hut. The farmer greeted them cordially, offered them some corn soup, and then accompanied them upriver to the ford. Braulio and Rojas led the column. Several times Braulio halted to examine the trail for footprints, but each time he was persuaded that all was well. Twenty yards from the ford, Honorato Rojas stopped. "I'll stay back here," he said. "Keep going until you come to the crossing. I don't want anyone to see me." Braulio asked him a few questions about the trail, and then Rojas bid everyone goodbye and quickly withdrew to higher ground just as the column reached the ford.

Braulio was the first to enter the water. At midstream he stooped to take a drink, then turned and signaled the others to follow quickly. As Joaquín, the last in line, stepped into the water, Braulio reached the opposite bank. At that moment the guerrillas were completely exposed, defenseless: the ambush could not help but succeed. All save Paco were swept off downstream or hunted down; their bodies, torn and bloated with water and decay, were carried to the highway on muleback. Except for Tania, they were buried unceremoniously in a common grave near Vallegrande.

Tania's death preceded Che's by only six weeks. Her years of training and idealism were spent on an impossible mission, one that suffered from serious misconceptions and miscalculations from the start. Yet Fidel Castro has enshrined her memory in Cuba, calling her "the unforgettable guerrilla." A "Tania Brigade" cuts sugar cane every year at harvest time; a boarding school near Havana bears her name; magazines regularly run stories on her and include her among illustrious women of Cuban history. Today her name is a source of inspiration for Cubans and the hunted, frustrated revolutionaries of the hemisphere. In Bolivia, the country she worked to revolutionize, Tania is remembered by only a few. No public building, no avenue pays tribute to her memory. But down on Río Grande a trace remains: the ford where she met her death has come to be called Tania's Crossing.

# Glossary

*almagristas* (ahl-mah-GREES-tahs). Followers of Diego de Almagro.

*arepas* (ah-RAY-pahs). Toasted patties of ground white corn.

*audiencia* (ow-dee-EN-see-ah). The highest court in colonial Spanish America.

*bozales* (boh-SAH-lehs). Newly arrived African slaves.

*cabecitas negras* (kah-bay-SEE-tahs NAY-grahs). Pejorative term for Argentine laborers meaning "little black-haired ones."

*cabildo* (kah-BEEL-doh). Municipal or town council in colonial Spanish America.

*cacique* (kah-SEE-kay). Indian chieftain.

*campesino* (kahm-pay-SEE-noh). Country person; farmer; agricultural worker.

*capataz* (kah-pah-TAHS). Foreman or overseer.

*che* (CHAY). Pal; buddy. Used to call attention of a close friend.

*cimarrones* (see-mah-ROH-nays). Runaway slaves.

*comadre* (koh-MAH-dray). A name by which the parents of a child and its godmother call each other.

*comandante* (koh-mahn-DAHN-tay). Commander; a respectful title used for high-ranking military officers in Castroite Cuba.

*cordillera* (kohr-dee-YEH-rah). Mountain range.

*Côrtes* (KOR-tehsh). Portuguese assembly with parliamentary function.

*criada* (kree-AH-dah). Housemaid.

*criollos, -llas* (kree-OH-yohs, -yahs). Spanish Americans of European descent.

*cruzados* (kroo-ZAH-doosh). Portuguese coins.

*descamisados* (dehs-kah-mee-SAH-dohs). Pejorative term for Argentine laborers meaning "shirtless ones."

*despedida* (dehs-pay-DEE-dah). Farewell celebration.

*encomenderos* (en-koh-men-DAY-rohs). Those holding *encomiendas*.

*encomiendas* (en-koh-MYEN-dahs). Grants of Indian labor awarded by the king to early settlers in America.

*fazendas* (fah-SHEN-dahsh). Large plantations in Brazil, usually producing sugar cane.

*fico* (FEE-koo). I stay.

*fincas* (FEEN-kahs). Farms.

*frailejón* (fry-lay-HOHN). Plant that grows above the timberline on Latin American mountain ranges.

*hidalgo* (ee-DAHL-goh). Aristocrat of Spain or Spanish America.

*junta* (HOON-tah). Assembly or council.

*ladrón* (lah-DROHN). Thief.

*liceo* (lee-SAY-oh). High school.

*llama* (YAH-mah). Peruvian beast of burden related to the camel.

*llanos* (YAH-nohs). Flat, grassy plains found in various parts of Latin America.

*machismo* (mah-CHEES-moh). Manliness, virility.

*macho* (MAH-choh). Male who is distinguished by *machismo*.

*machista* (mah-CHEES-tah). One who practices *machismo*.

*majagua* (mah-HAH-gwah). Fiber of the *majagua* tree, used in making rope.

*Mambí* (mahm-BEE). Cuban patriot or rebel during the wars for independence from Spain.

*marianismo* (mah-reeahn-EES-moh). Femininity, homeliness.

*marqués; marquesa* (mahr-KAYS; mahr-KAY-sah). Marquis; marquise or marchioness.

*mazombos* (mah-ZOHM-boosh). Whites born in Brazil.

*mestiza, -zo* (mehs-TEE-sah, -soh). Offspring of Indian and European parents.

*mestiza de vasca* (mehs-TEE-sah day VAHS-kah). Woman of Indian and Basque ancestry.

*palenque* (pah-LEN-kay). Name given to communities of runaway slaves in Spanish America.

*patiloca* (pah-tee-LOH-kah). Footloose.

*Patria Boba* (PAH-treeah BOH-bah). Foolish Fatherland.

*patrón* (pah-TROHN). Patron, boss, chief.

*peninsulares* (pay-neen-soo-LA-rehs). Spaniards living in America.

*peso* (PAY-soh). A unit of currency used widely in Spanish America.

*pícaro* (PEE-kah-roh). Roguish vagabond.

*porteño* (pohr-TAY-nyoh). Resident of a seaport; in Spanish America refers to residents of Buenos Aires and their characteristics.

*reinóis* (rahee-NO-ehsh). Brazilian whites born in Portugal.

*repartimiento* (ray-pahr-tee-MYEN-toh). Temporary grant of Indian workers and land made early in the Spanish colonial period.

*resacas* (ray-SAH-kahs). Dregs; useless or untrustworthy persons.

*ruana* (roo-AH-nah). Woolen cape, cut square with a slit in the center for the head.

*sabana* (sah-BAH-nah). Wide, treeless plain; savanna.

*señora* (say-NYOH-rah). Mrs. or Ma'am.

*soldaderas* (sohl-dah-DAY-rahs). Women soldiers.

*tapadas* (tah-PAH-dahs). Women of colonial Lima who covered their faces with shawls.

*tiple* (TEE-play). Treble guitar having twelve strings in groups of three.

*tuna* (TOO-nah). Prickly pear.

*unidades básicas* (oo-nee-DAH-days BAH-see-kahs). Small women's clubs organized by the Peróns.

*viva* (VEE-vah). Hurrah.

*yanaconas* (yah-nah-KOH-nahs). Indians placed at the personal service of Spaniards living in the viceroyalty of Peru.

*yerba mate* (YAIR-bah MAH-tay). A tea used widely in southeastern South America.

# Selected Bibliography

*Introduction*

Arciniegas, Germán. *América mágica, II: Las mujeres y las horas.* Buenos Aires: Editorial Sudamericana, 1961.

Arrom, Silvia M. *La mujer mexicana ante el divorcio eclesiástico, 1800-1857.* Mexico City: SepSetentas, 1976.

Burkett, Elinor. "Early Colonial Peru: The Urban Female Experience." Unpublished Ph.D. thesis. University of Pittsburgh, 1974.

Carvajal, Gaspar de. "Carvajal's Account." *The Discovery of the Amazon.* Ed. José T. Medina, trans. B. T. Lee. New York: American Geographical Society, 1934.

Diner, Helen. *Mothers and Amazons: The First Feminine History of Culture.* Ed. and trans. John Philip Lundin. New York: The Julian Press, 1965.

Hahner, June E., ed. *Women in Latin American History.* Los Angeles: U.C.L.A. Latin American Center, 1976.

Lavrin, Asunción. "Historia y mujeres en América Latina." *Boletín documental sobre las mujeres.* Vol. 4, pp. 9-18.

Massare de Kostianovsky, Olinda. *La mujer paraguaya: Su participación en la Guerra Grande.* Asunción: Talleres Gráficos de la Escuela Técnica Salesiana, 1970.

Mexico, Secretaría de Educación Pública. *La mujer en América Latina.* 2 vols. Mexico City: SepSetentas, 1975.

Stevens, Evelyn. "*Marianismo,* the Other Face of *Machismo* in Latin America." *Female and Male in Latin America.* Ed. Ann Pescatello. Pittsburgh: University of Pittsburgh Press, 1973.

*Chapter I: Malinche*
Díaz del Castillo, Bernal. *The Bernal Díaz Chronicles.* Trans. and ed. Albert Idell. Garden City, New York: Doubleday and Company, 1956.
Prescott, William H. *History of the Conquest of Mexico and History of the Conquest of Peru.* New York: Random House, Inc., 1952.
Rodríguez, Gustavo A. *Doña Marina, monografía histórica.* Mexico: Imprenta de la Secretaría de Relaciones Exteriores, 1935.
Shedd, Margaret. *Malinche and Cortés.* New York: Doubleday and Company, 1971.
Somonte, Mariano G. *Doña Marina, "La Malinche."* Monterrey, 1969.
Vaillant, George C. *Aztecs of Mexico: Origin, Rise and Fall of the Aztec Nation.* Baltimore: Penguin Books, 1966.
Wagner, Henry R. *The Rise of Fernando Cortés.* Los Angeles: The Cortés Society, 1944.


*Chapter II: Inés de Suárez*
Burkett, Elinor. "Early Colonial Peru: The Urban Female Experience." Unpublished Ph.D. thesis. University of Pittsburgh, 1976.
Errazuriz, Crescente. *Historia de Chile. Pedro de Valdivia.* 2 vols. Santiago: Imprenta Cervantes, 1911, 1912.
May, Stella Burke. *The Conqueror's Lady.* New York: Farrar and Rinehart, 1930.
Medina, José Toribio, ed. *Cartas de Pedro de Valdivia que tratan del descubrimiento y conquista de Chile.* Sevilla: Establecimiento Tipografía de M. Carmona, 1929.
Pocock, H. R. S. *The Conquest of Chile.* New York: Stein and Day, 1967.
Vernon, Ida Stevenson Weldon. *Pedro de Valdivia, Conquistador of Chile.* Austin: University of Texas Press, 1946.
Vicuña, Alejandro. *Inés de Suárez.* Santiago: Editorial Nascimiento, 1941.


*Chapter III: The Nun Ensign*
Ferfer, Joaquín Maria de, ed. *Historia de la Monja Alférez, Doña Catalina de Erauzo, por ella misma.* Paris: Imprenta de Julio Didot, 1829.
Heredia, José María de. *La monja alférez.* Santiago de Chile, 1906.
León, Nicolás. *Aventuras de la Monja Alférez.* Mexico City: Colección Metropolitana, 1973.
Leonard, Irving A., ed. *Colonial Travelers in Latin America.* New York: Alfred A. Knopf, 1972.

Madariaga, Salvador de. *The Fall of the Spanish American Empire.* New York: Collier Books, 1963.

Morales-Alvarez, Raúl. *La monja alférez: Crónica de una vida que tuvo perfil de romance.* Chile: Editorial Nuñoa, 1936.

Palma, Ricardo. "¡A iglesia me llamo!" *Tradiciones peruanas: primera selección.* Buenos Aires: Espasa-Calpe Argentina, S.A., 1956.


*Chapter IV: Sor Juana Inés de la Cruz*

Anderson Imbert, Enrique, and Eugenio Florit. *Literatura hispanoamericana: Antología e introducción histórica.* New York: Holt, Rinehart and Winston, Inc., 1960.

Cruz, Sor Juana Inés de la. *Obras completas.* Ed. Alfonso Méndez Plancarte. Mexico: Fondo de Cultura Económica, 1951.

Leonard, Irving A. *Baroque Times in Old Mexico.* Ann Arbor: University of Michigan Press, 1966.

Nervo, Amado. *Obras completas, Vol. VIII: Juana de Asbaje.* Madrid: Biblioteca Nueva, 1920. Contains Calleja, S.J., Diego de, "Vida de la Madre Juana Inés de la Cruz" (Lisbon, 1701), manuscript found in Real Biblioteca de Madrid.

Wallace, Elizabeth. *Sor Juana Inés de la Cruz: Poesía de corte y convento.* Mexico: Ediciones Xochitl, 1944.


*Chapter V: La Pola*

Caballero, José María. *Particularidades de Santafé.* Bogotá: Biblioteca Popular de Cultura Colombiana, 1946.

Cordovez Moure, José María. *Reminiscencias de Santafé y Bogotá.* Madrid: Aguilar S.A. de Ediciones, 1957.

Díaz Díaz, Oswaldo. *Los Almeydas. Episodios de la resistencia patriota contra el ejército pacificador de Tierra Firme.* Bogotá: Editorial A.B.C., 1962.

Henao, Jesús María, and Gerardo Arrubla. *Historia de Colombia.* 8th ed. Bogotá: Editorial de la Librería Voluntad, 1967.

Jaramillo Uribe, Jaime. *Mestisaje y diferenciación social en el Nuevo Reino de Granada en la segunda mitad del siglo XVIII.* Bogotá: Imprenta Nacional, 1967.

Monsalve, José Dolores. *Mujeres de la Independencia.* Bogotá: Imprenta Nacional, 1926.

Montoya de Umaña, Enriqueta. *La criolla Policarpa Salavarrieta.* Bogotá: Ediciones Tercer Mundo, 1969.

Posada, Eduardo. *Apuntes sobre la Pola*. Tunja, Boyacá: Imprenta del Departamento, 1917.

*Chapter VI: Leopoldina*
Bezerra, Alcides. *Conferencias*. "A Vida Domestica da Imperatriz Leopoldina." Rio de Janeiro, 1929.
Cintra, Assis. *O Favorito da Imperatriz*. Rio de Janeiro, 1930.
Corrêa da Costa, Sérgio. *Every Inch a King*. Trans. Samuel Putnam. New York: The MacMillan Company, 1950.
Harding, Bertita. *Amazon Throne: The Story of the Braganzas of Brazil*. New York: Bobbs-Merrill Co., 1941.
Norton, Luiz. *A Côrte de Portugal no Brasil*. São Paulo, 1930.
Oberacker, Carlos H., Jr. *A Imperatriz Leopoldina: Sua Vida e Sua Epoca. Ensaio de uma biografia*. Conselho Federal de Cultura, 1973.
*Publicações do Archivo Nacional*. (Collected letters of Empress Leopoldina on the centenary of her death.) Ed. Alcides Bezerra. Rio de Janeiro, 1927.
Smith, Robert Chester, and Gilberto Ferrez. *Franz Fruhbeck's Brazilian Journey*. Philadelphia, 1960.
Williams, Mary Wilhelmina. *Dom Pedro the Magnanimous*. New York: Octagon Books, 1966.
Worcester, Donald E. *Brazil: From Colony to World Power*. New York: Charles Scribner's Sons, 1973.

*Chapter VII: Mariana Grajales*
Bacardí y Moreau, Emilio, ed. *Crónicas de Santiago de Cuba*. 10 vols. Madrid: Breogán, 1973.
Castellanos, José G. *La casa donde nació Antonio Maceo*. Santiago de Cuba: Talleres Poligráfica, 1957.
Franco, José Luciano. *Antonio Maceo, apuntes para una historia de su vida*. Vol. 1, Havana, 1951.
Le Roig y Gálvez, Luis F. "Las heridas de Maceo en la Guerra de 1868." *Revista de la Biblioteca Nacional José Martí*. Vol. 10. September-December 1968, pp. 63-77.
Maceo, Antonio. *Papeles de Maceo*. 2 vols. Havana: Academia de la Historia de Cuba, 1948.
Martí, José. *Obras completas*. Vol. 1. Havana: Editorial Lex, 1946.
Martínez Alier, Verena. "El honor de la mujer en Cuba en el siglo XIX." *Revista de la Biblioteca Nacional José Martí*. January-April 1971, pp. 29-61.
O'Kelly, James. *The Mambi-Land*. Philadelphia: J. B. Lippincott, 1874.

Santovenia, Emeterio S. *Huellas de gloria. Frases históricas cubanas.* 2nd ed. Havana: Editorial Trópico, 1944.

Torres Hernández, Lázaro. "Mariana Grajales: una madre sublime." *Bohemia,* January 28, 1972, pp. 100-104.

*Chapter VIII: Gabriela Mistral*

Alone. *Los cuatro grandes de la literatura chilena durante el siglo XX.* Santiago de Chile: Editorial Zig-Zag, 1962.

Arciniegas, Germán. *América Mágica II: Las mujeres y las horas.* Buenos Aires: Editorial Sudamericana, 1971.

Comité de Homenaje a Gabriela Mistral, ed. *Antología general de Gabriela Mistral.* Santiago: Editorial Roble de Chile, 1970.

Gabriela Mistral. *Poesías completas.* Ed. Margaret Bates. 3rd ed. Madrid: Aguilar, 1966.

——————. *Selected Poems of Gabriela Mistral.* Trans. and ed. Doris Dana. Intro. Margaret Bates. Baltimore: Johns Hopkins Press, 1971.

——————. *Epistolario. Cartas a Eugenio Labarca (1915-1916).* Intro. Raúl Silva Castro. Santiago: Ediciones de los ANALES de la Universidad de Chile, 1957.

——————. *Los versos sencillos de José Martí.* Havana: Publicaciones de la Secretaría de Educación, 1939.

Iglesias, Augusto. *Gabriela Mistral y el modernismo en Chile.* Santiago de Chile: Editorial Universitaria, 1949.

Ladrón de Guevara, Matilde. *Gabriela Mistral, rebelde magnífica.* 3rd ed. Santiago de Chile, 1957.

Silva Castro, Raúl. *Estudios sobre Gabriela Mistral.* Santiago de Chile: Editorial Zig-Zag, 1935.

*Chapter IX: Eva Perón*

Bourne, Richard. *Political Leaders of Latin America.* New York: Knopf, 1970.

Cowles, Fleur. *Bloody Precedent.* New York: Random House, Inc., 1952.

Flores, María. *The Woman with the Whip: Eva Perón.* Garden City, New York: Doubleday and Company, 1952.

Hollander, Nancy Caro. "Women: The Forgotten Half of Argentine History." *History of Latin American Civilization.* Ed. Lewis Hanke. Boston: Little, Brown and Company, 1973.

*Latin American Perspectives. Argentina: Peronism and Crisis.* Vol. 1, fall 1974.

Liberal, José R. *Estudio literario y valorización sociológica de "La razón de mi vida."* Buenos Aires: Ediciones Argentinas, 1953.

Perón, Eva Duarte. *My Mission in Life.* Trans. Ethel Cherry. New York: Vantage Press, 1953.

*Chapter X: Tania*

González, Luis J., and Gustavo Sánchez Salazar. *The Great Rebel: Che Guevara in Bolivia.* Trans. Helen R. Lane. New York: Grove Press, 1969.

González Bermejo, Ernesto. "La columna de Joaquín. Odisea en la selva." *Cuba Internacional,* September 1971, pp. 28-33.

Gott, Richard. *Guerrilla Movements in Latin America.* Garden City, New York: Doubleday and Company, 1972.

James, Daniel, ed. *The Complete Bolivian Diaries of Che Guevara and Other Captured Documents.* New York: Stein and Day, 1968.

Janet, pseud. "Recuerdos de Tania: Entrevista a sus padres." *Bohemia,* September 18, 1970, pp. 10-13.

Rojas, Marta, and Mirta Rodríguez Calderón. *Tania la guerrillera inolvidable.* Havana: Instituto Cubano del Libro, 1974.

Rojo, Ricardo. *My Friend Che.* Trans. Julián Casart. New York: The Dial Press, 1968.

Sauvage, Léo. *Che Guevara. The Failure of a Revolutionary.* Trans. Raoul Fremont. Englewood Cliffs, New Jersey: Prentice-Hall, 1971.

"Vado de la traición: La muerte río abajo." *Cuba Internacional,* September 1971, pp. 34-45.

Welles, Benjamin. "Blunders by Woman Spy for Soviet Trapped Che Guevara." *New York Times,* July 15, 1968, 14:2.

# Index

Aconcagua Valley, 38
Aguilar (Cortés's translator), 7, 9, 10
Aguilera, Vicente, 155
Aguirre, Francisco de, 34, 39
Aguirre Cerda, Pedro, 176, 178, 188
Alcayaga, Emelina, 172, 174
Alcayaga, Petronila, 172
Alderete, Jerónimo de, 43, 44
Almagro, Diego de, 27, 31, 33; *almagristas*, 33
Almeyda, Ambrosio, 113-18
Almeyda, Vicente, 113-14, 116-18
Alto Peru, 33, 49, 58, 69. *See also* Bolivia
Alvarado, Captain Pedro de, 17
Amazons, xiii, xv, xvii-xviii
Amar y Borbón, Antonio, 103, 105-6
Ambalema (Nueva Granada), 107
Andalusians, 68
Apurimac Chasm, 59
Araucanian Indians, 31, 43, 47, 58, 60-62
Arcos, José María, 112, 116-17
Arellano (Nueva Granadan patriot), 116, 117
Arellano, Carlos de, 54
Argentina: Eva Perón and, 193-94, 198, 202-3, 211; Tania and, 216, 222, 231
Asbaje, Juana Inés de. *See* Cruz, Sor

Juana Inés de la
Asencio, Ascencio de, 153, 155, 157, 161
Asturias, Miguel Angel, 169
Atacama Desert, 33, 35-36
Atlantic crossing, 25-26
Austria, 121, 123, 125, 138
Ayacucho. *See* Huamanga
Aztec: architecture, 5; artists, 9; communications system, 8; empire, 1, 3; fall of empire, 19-20; priests, 5-6, 7; religion, 5-6, 10

Baroque poetry, 77-78, 82-84
Barrientos, Moisés, 225
Barrientos, René (Bolivian president), 225, 233
Basques, 49, 51, 71, 173; characteristics of, 53; conflict, 68-69; in New World, 55, 60, 62; provinces of Spain, 52
Bates, Margaret, 190
Bay of Pigs, 220
Bello, Andrés, 171
Black women (and mulatto), xxii
Bogotá. *See* Santafé de Bogotá
Bolívar, Simón, 108, 120, 152
Bolivia, 213, 223, 225, 228-30, 233, 240. *See also* Alto Peru
Bonaparte, José, 102

251